I0793053

IMAGES
of America

AROUND DEWEY-HUMBOLDT

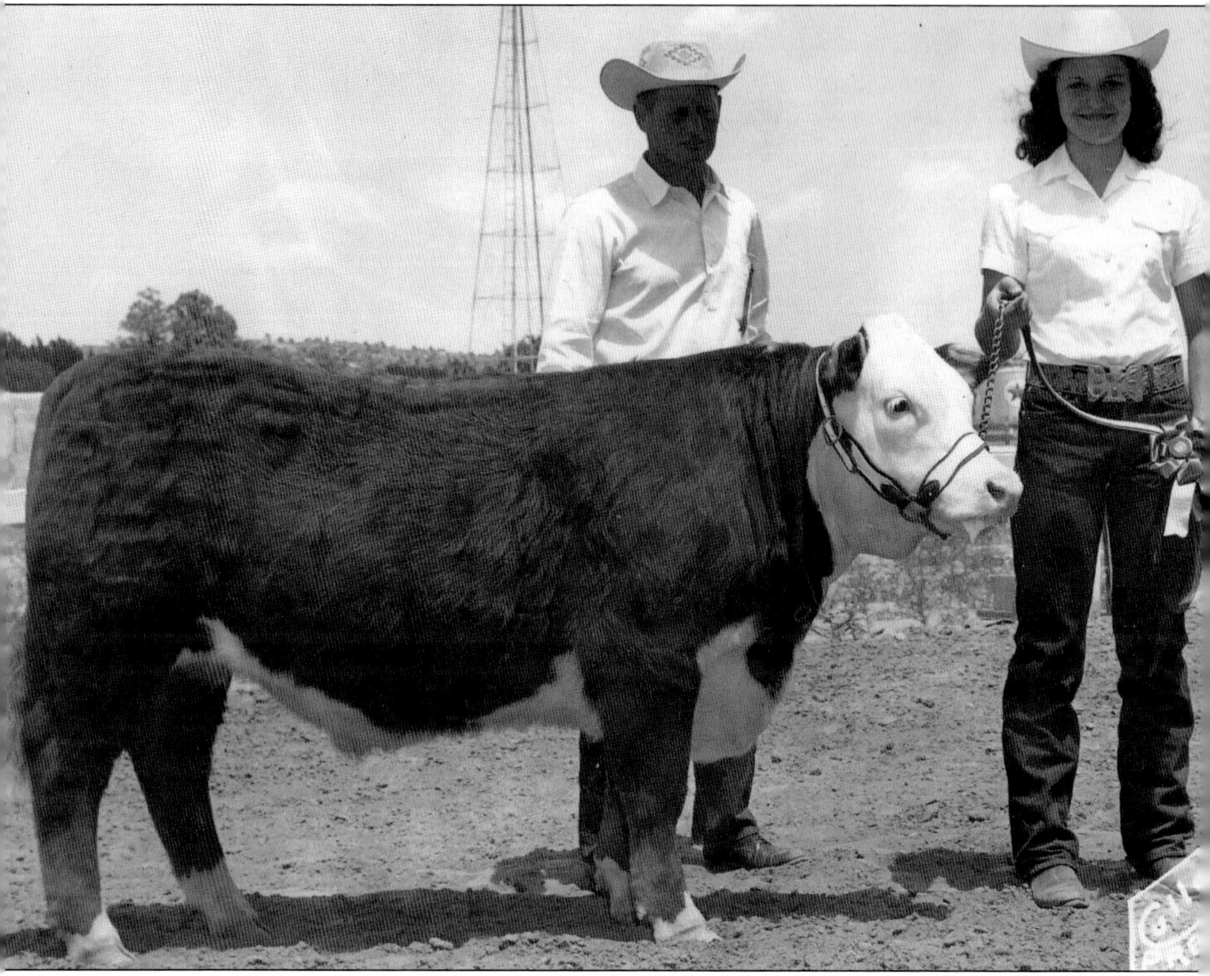

Pictured here are Dewey 4-H leader Elmer Young with Martha Henderson and her winning steer at the Country Fair in Prescott. This was 1958, when Martha was winning her third Grand Champion in a row, a record that still stands today.

On the Cover: Posing in front of the Henderson house in the fall of 1937 are, from left to right, Jane Henderson (holding Helen Henderson Cain), Ester Cherry Henderson, Mary Lou Jones, Edd Jones, Bill Jones, Marjorie Jones (with doll), Norma Jones, George Jones, Belva Jones, and Perry Henderson.

IMAGES
of America

AROUND DEWEY-HUMBOLDT

J.P. Gorham

ARCADIA
PUBLISHING

ISBN 978-1-4671-3112-4

Published by Arcadia Publishing
Charleston, South Carolina

Printed in the United States of America

Library of Congress Control Number: 2013944807

For all general information, please contact Arcadia Publishing:
Telephone 843-853-2070
Fax 843-853-0044
E-mail sales@arcadiapublishing.com
For customer service and orders:
Toll-Free 1-888-313-2665

Visit us on the Internet at www.arcadiapublishing.com

This book is dedicated to Audrey Brooks, Helen Henderson Cain, and John Charles Young, without whom this book would surely have never been completed.

Contents

Acknowledgments

First and foremost I'd like to thank Helen Henderson Cain for her invaluable help and countless meetings with me sorting through her extensive, impressive, and mostly never-before-seen family collection. Also special thanks to John Charles Young for his constant support and allowing me access to both the John and Gina Young Collection and the Dewey-Humboldt Historical Museum collection. To Sonja, George, and Harold Chemas for allowing me full access to the Chemas family collection and to Helen D. Swenson for compiling and editing the booklet "We Remember Humboldt and Dewey, Arizona," which was an important tool in the making of this book.

To the residents of Dewey-Humboldt, this is my gift to you to ensure that your hard work preserving the history of this wonderful area has as much documentation as possible for future generations.

The three photographs that are labeled as taken recently are by the author. Unless otherwise noted, all other photographs are from the Dewey-Humboldt Historical Society collection.

INTRODUCTION

This is a book about two vastly different yet completely intrinsic worlds nestled next to each other in the Arizona mountains. After thousands of years of sparse and migratory native habitation, it all changed suddenly with the appearance of one King Woolsey, the first white settler in the area. Until then, a handful of prospectors courageous enough to risk Indian attacks had worked hard to try to strike gold in the untapped soil, rock, and creek beds. They certainly welcomed Woolsey when he arrived and hired them to build his two-room homestead. The workers used stones from the long-abandoned Sinaque Village ruins of the Anasazi Indian tribe in the area next to the current Mortimer Farms (originally Young Farms). In 1863, King Woolsey was with the Walker party when they discovered gold along Lynx Creek after reports of paying quantities found by prospectors on the Hassayampa, Antelope, Indian, Agua Fria, Big Bug, and Lynx Creeks shortly prior to that. He enjoyed the mild climate and decided to stay to raise cattle and hay. The Union army was encamped nearby and desperately needed both.

The ranch was immediately under constant attack by the local Apache Indians. While returning with a wagonload of hay soon after his arrival, Woolsey and two ranch hands were attacked by about 20 members from that tribe. With only one shotgun, his ranch hands escaped with the mules, and Woolsey defended himself, killing the chief of the tribe. The chief's body was hung from a nearby tree, a warning to others to leave the area alone. There was a long-lasting friendship with members of the Yuma, Pima, and Maricopa tribes, some even employed to work there. But the Apaches were hostile to the other tribes as well as any white travelers who dared to enter the region.

Throughout the summer of 1864, Woolsey led 150 men on constant hunting parties to eradicate the Apache tribe, and was certainly successful. Appointed lieutenant colonel of the Indian fighting volunteers and an aide to territorial governor Goodwin, Woolsey headed out on three expeditions to finally annihilate the tribe. The large group of white civilians and Maricopa and Pima Indians set out to find the Apaches, discovering them at nearby Fish Creek Canyon. An interpreter was sent to invite the leaders to a parley, and the tribal members arrived to the sight of a large feast of Pinole (a mixture of corn and sugar) and Tiswin (a strong fermented drink made from corn). The Pinole, however, was laced with strychnine, and the chief himself was shot on the spot. The others scattered, but were all shot as they tried to escape. Known as "The Pinole Treaty," this incident forever changed the landscape of the area.

During this encounter, a young Yaqui girl of about 10 years old wandered into Woolsey's camp after escaping from the Apaches. She was brought back to the Woolsey ranch to be an attendant to Mary, Woolsey's companion, and learned household skills and the ways of the white man. A few years later, Lucy, as she was now known, was given a small house of her own after Mary realized there was more going on between her and King Woolsey than originally thought. Lucy bore two daughters with Woolsey, who, having no children with Mary, named them Clara and Johanna. They were included in his will, but Mary never acknowledged them, and the courts sided with her. Later, the Catholic Church intervened, and the daughters received support from the estate, which reverted back to the church upon their passing as part of the agreement.

The ranch house also became a place of refuge for many passing through the area, having a well within its walls. The first territorial legislature meetings were held there. At these meetings, Prescott was decided upon as the territorial capitol over Wickenberg by a mere two votes.

In 1871, Woolsey sold the ranch to Nathan Bowers, and the house became known as the halfway house, because of its central location between Camp Verde and Prescott. King and Mary Woolsey married and moved to Phoenix, where King passed away on June 29, 1879. He was considered by many early settlers as the most influential citizen of the Arizona Territory.

With the area secured from hostile attack, the mining industry soon established a strong presence. By 1880, there were over 7,000 mines in Yavapai County, and the need to feed the miners quickly became a concern. Ranches and homesteads sprang up in the Dewey (Cherry Creek Station) area to supply the mines in Humboldt (Val Verde) and surrounding areas. Among these mines were the following (listed under their current names): Cherry, Poland Junction, Mayer, Cordes Junction, Cleator, Crown King, and Bumble Bee. Other areas simply vanished as the mines were depleted and the residents left suddenly to find work elsewhere. These other areas are briefly covered in this book, to stress the fact that many workers and their families moved between them, following available jobs. The historical fates of these places were forever tied together.

The area in and around Dewey-Humboldt, Arizona, is an extraordinary place, with far too many details and nuances to fully cover here. In a book like this, it is best to try to convey a broad overview of the history, as opposed to a dense account. It is simply impossible to sum up over 150 years of history in so few pages. But, in a proverbial nutshell: Dewey essentially consisted of ranching families who bought or homesteaded their properties, intending to settle down and raise their families. Humboldt was the mining boomtown where most people rented their houses, ready to move on when opportunities suddenly dissolved. Looking back from a current perspective, the two towns were dependent upon each other and will always be linked together, no matter on which "side of the tracks" they lie. It is truly fitting that they are now incorporated as one small city separated only by a hyphen, which symbolizes the close proximity and vast differences between them. I sincerely hope you enjoy the journey.

One

Dewey
Agua Fria, Cherry Siding

If only one word could be used to describe Dewey, it would be "ranching." For lack of a better description, Dewey initially grew because of the ever-growing needs of area miners. As, next door, Humboldt boomed from its mines and support services, Dewey quietly continued to expand the size and efficiency of its cattle and farming operations. From the time King Woolsey moved to the area, clearing it of hostile natives and starting an irrigation system from the Agua Fria River to farm the fertile soil, cattle and produce were its main commodities.

One by one, families began moving in with the intention of staying. Sharlot Hall, the famous writer and first woman elected to public office in Arizona, lived here at the Orchard ranch for many years beginning in 1882. The Human family homesteaded here in the late 1890s and married into the Henderson family, who would have a huge impact on the area for decades to come. Perry Henderson started the Dewey Rodeo in 1926 at the age of 19, building it into "The Biggest Little Rodeo in the World," renowned in rodeo circles in its day. When a new homesteader would move into the area, it was often Perry who showed up first and offered assistance in plowing, seeding, fence building, or anything else that would help them be successful. It was neighbors like this and many others who developed the helpful and friendly character of the community.

Nowadays, while the area maintains a rural atmosphere, most residents go to jobs that let them earn the money for their basic needs. For a long time, however, the residents needed to be as self-sufficient as possible to survive the constant pendulum swings of the volatile mining industry on which their goods and services depended.

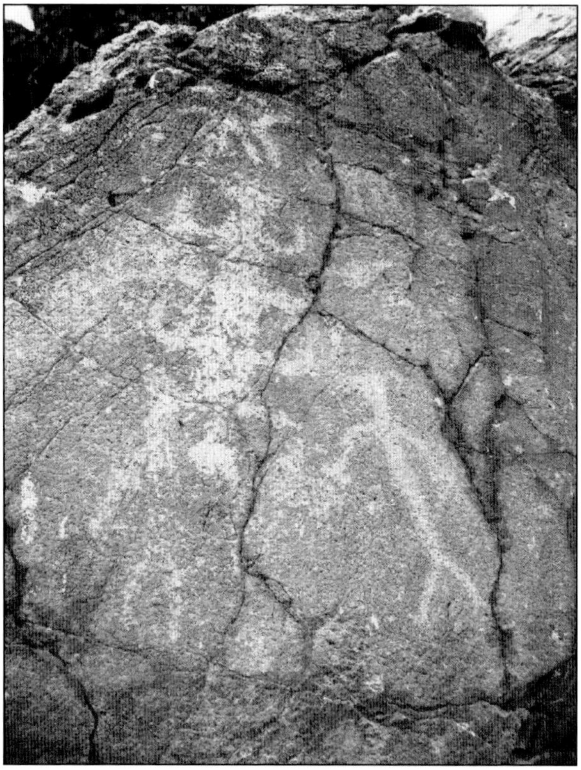

Petroglyphs can still be found in and around the area, but were most likely created before the Yavapai tribe arrived. The Yavapai did not write on walls in general. Hohokam and Anasazi tribes were prevalent from about 900 A.D. to 1300 A.D., when they mysteriously disappeared. Evidence shows a buildup of Hohokam people much farther south in the latter part of this period, suggesting that drought drove them out of the area, never to return. The other tribes in the area referred to the local natives as "The tribe with the white dogs," but were never very abundant here. This photograph was taken on the steep banks of the Agua Fria River.

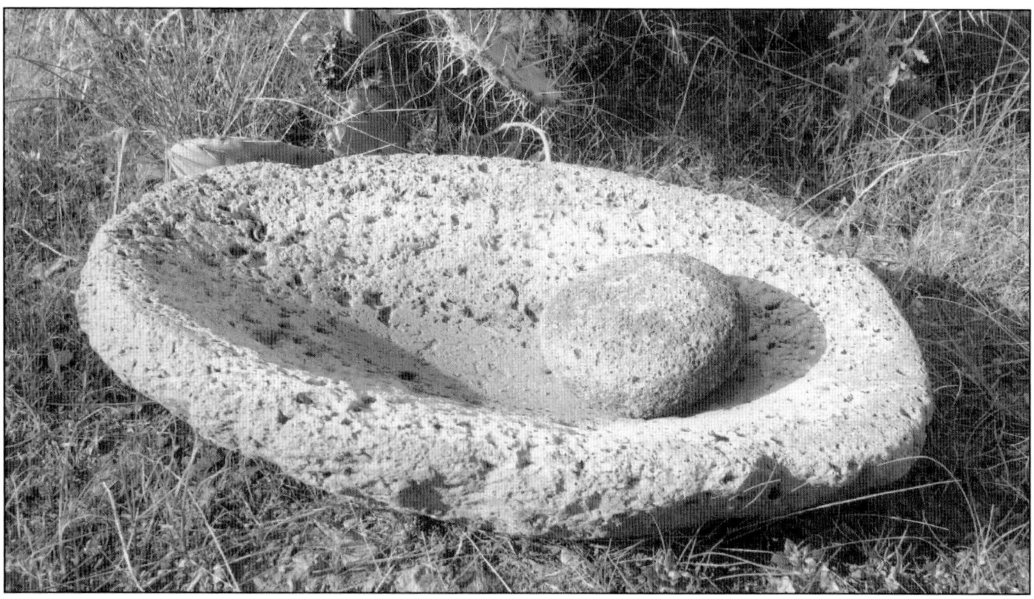

This mortar and pestle, found along the Agua Fria River, is now housed at the Dewey-Humboldt Historical Museum. The Hohokam were hunters and gatherers, and some evidence of farming has been found. The population, never very large, is estimated to have been about one person per 13 miles on average. Ruins on the Henderson Ranch were excavated in 1969 to make way for Highway 169, but very little evidence is left today. In 1875, the remaining native peoples were rounded up and marched on a "trail of tears" to the San Carlos Reservation.

King Woolsey, the first white settler in the area, arrived in 1863. He was considered by many early residents to be the most influential person in the Arizona territory. He is certainly controversial today because of his pivotal role in eradicating the hostile Apache tribe, clearing the way for mining and ranching industries. Woolsey's house was often referred to as a fort. While not technically true, the home certainly fulfilled all the requirements of a fort, including a well within its walls. Woolsey passed away on June 29, 1879, in Phoenix.

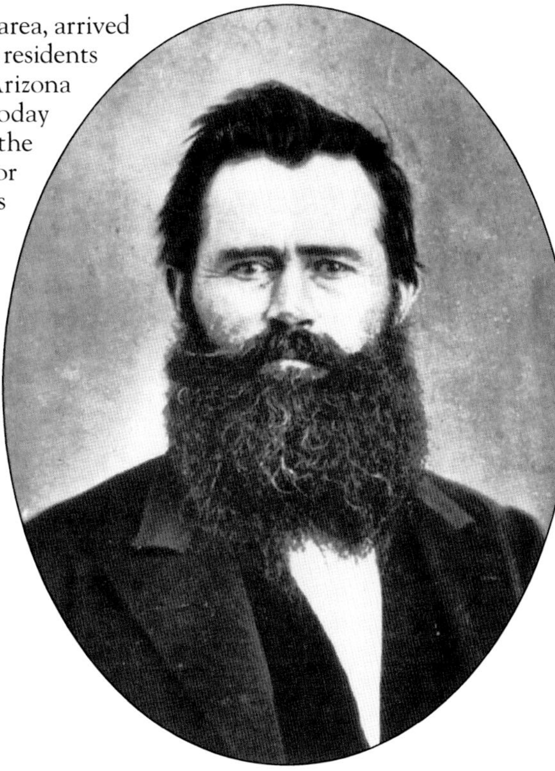

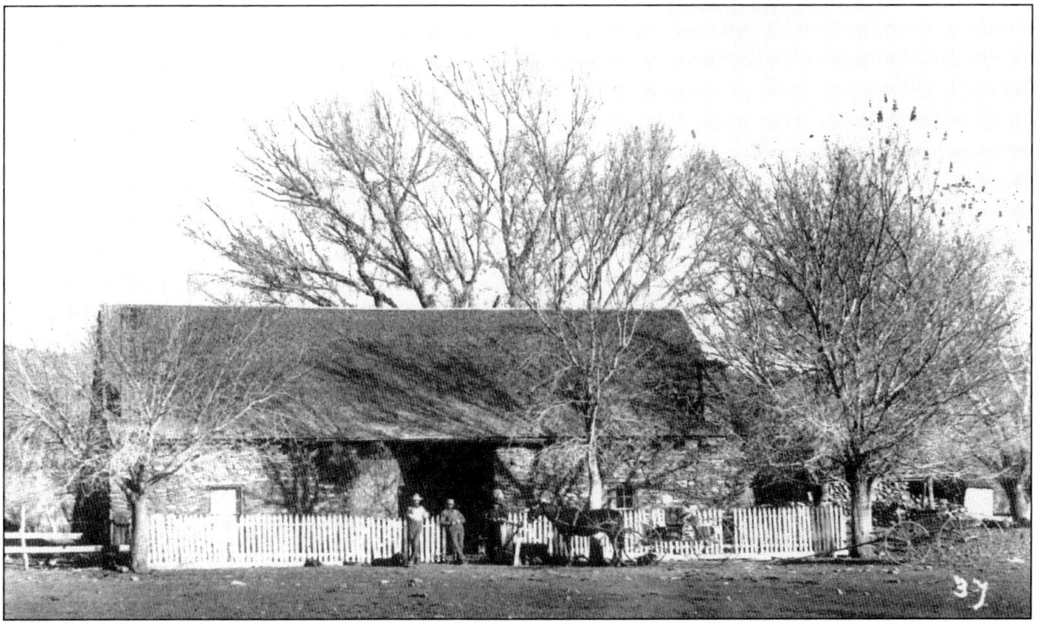

The Bower house, shown here, was halfway between Camp Verde and Prescott, earning it the nickname "halfway house." The Bower brothers made improvements to the original Woolsey dwelling. They grew hay and produce for the expanding mining market. While making a contribution to the local economy, the Bowers never approached the influence Woolsey had on the area. It is fitting that only the Woolsey ruins remain today.

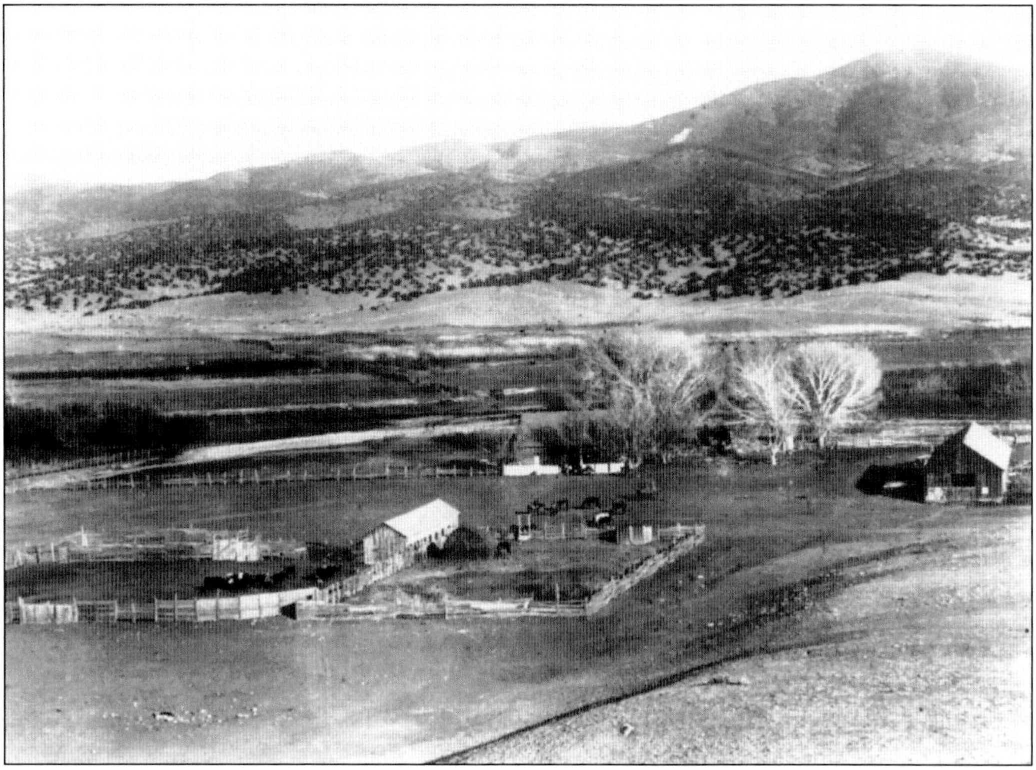

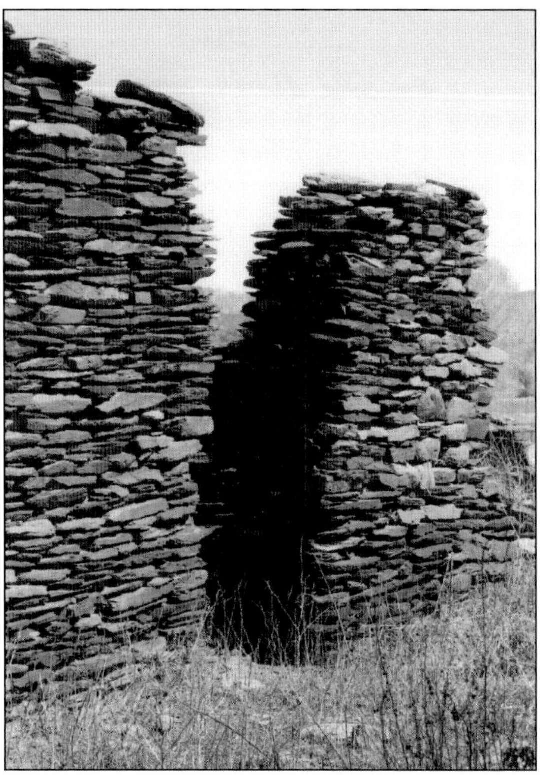

This is an aerial photograph of the Bower ranch, bought from King Woolsey in 1871 and run by the Bower brothers for many years. The fertile land produced many crops, and still does to this day. Corn, barley, and other agricultural products were grown here originally, enhanced by the irrigation system built by King Woolsey from the nearby Agua Fria River. The Bowers had been sutlers (civilian merchants who provided goods to the army) at Fort Whipple in Prescott prior to acquiring the property.

The Woolsey ruins are still visible along the Old Black Canyon Highway. Although the Woolsey house was expanded upon by the Bowers, only the ruins of the original house remain. It was built by hired hands with stones from long-abandoned native dwellings. For years, arrowheads and other remnants were found around the property, telling of its storied history.

James and Mary Human first homesteaded the area before the turn of the 20th century. They came from the Verde Valley, which they helped settle after arriving on the original Bristow train in the mid-1860s. They remained in the Dewey area for the rest of their lives. This image is believed to have been produced in the late 1860s.

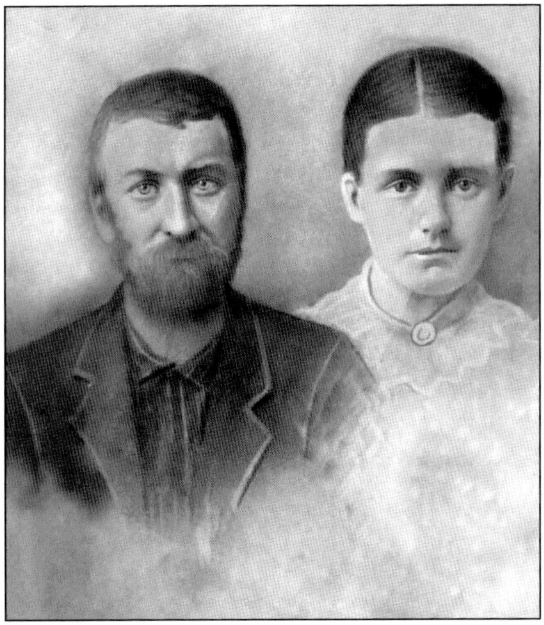

Pictured here are James and Mary Human with their children, George (left), Frank (on James's lap), Art (on Mary's lap), and Jane. This photograph was taken in nearby Prescott in 1880.

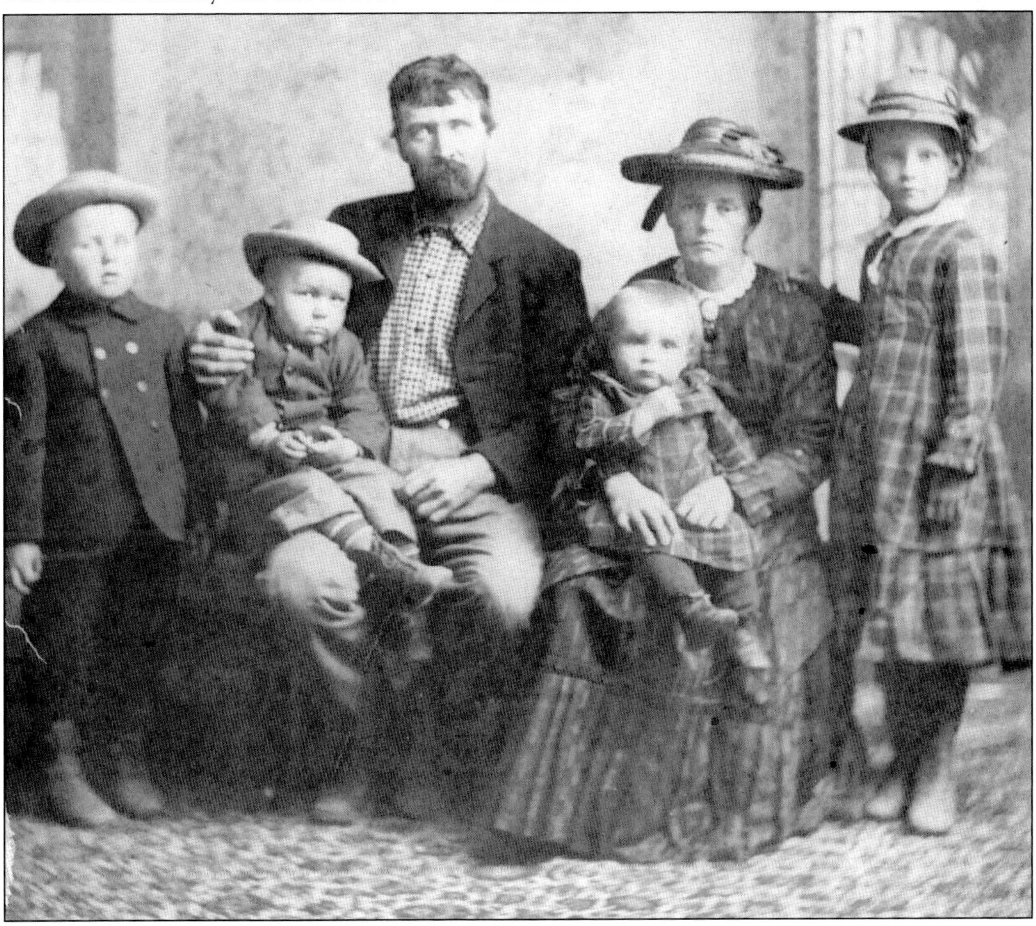

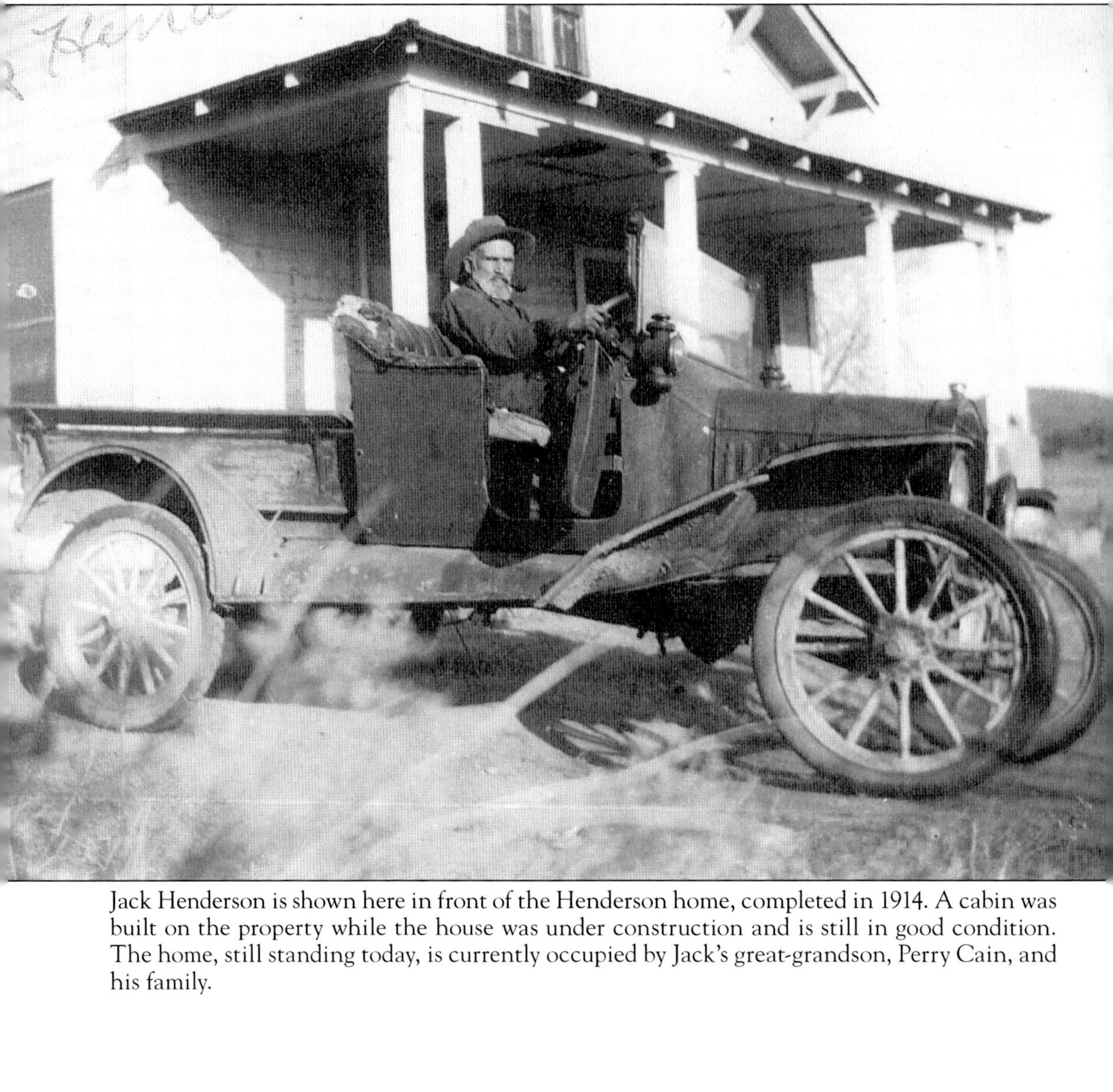

Jack Henderson is shown here in front of the Henderson home, completed in 1914. A cabin was built on the property while the house was under construction and is still in good condition. The home, still standing today, is currently occupied by Jack's great-grandson, Perry Cain, and his family.

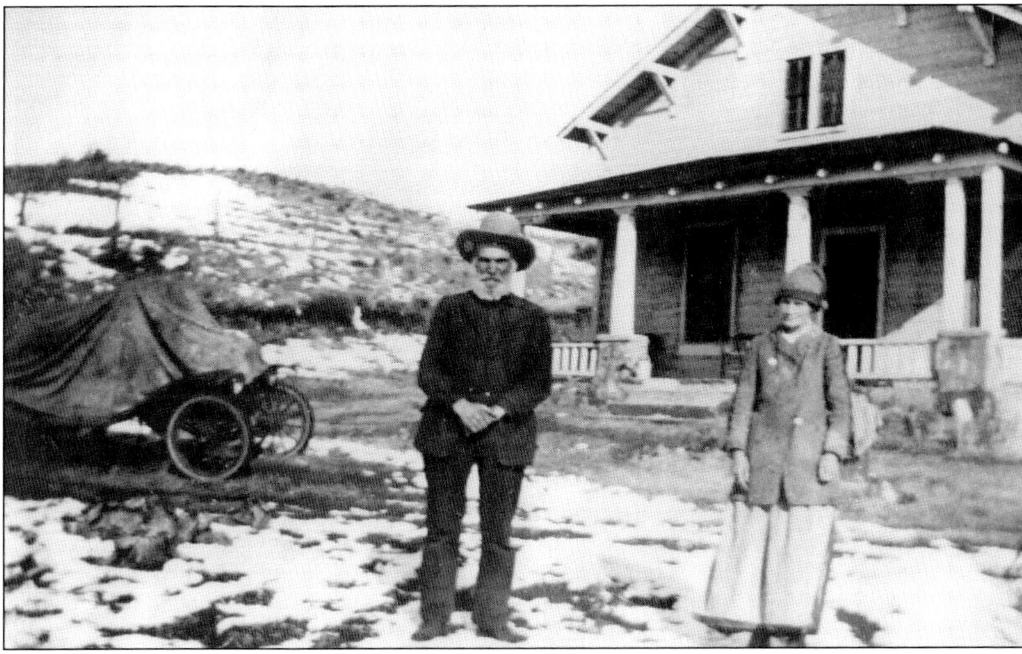

The Hendersons were one of the most influential families in the history of Dewey. The Henderson property eventually comprised over 26,000 acres. Perry Henderson was well known for helping out newcomers and neighbors alike and offering a helping hand when families moved in. He eventually bought out 15 local homesteads when they were up for sale, adding to the Henderson holdings.

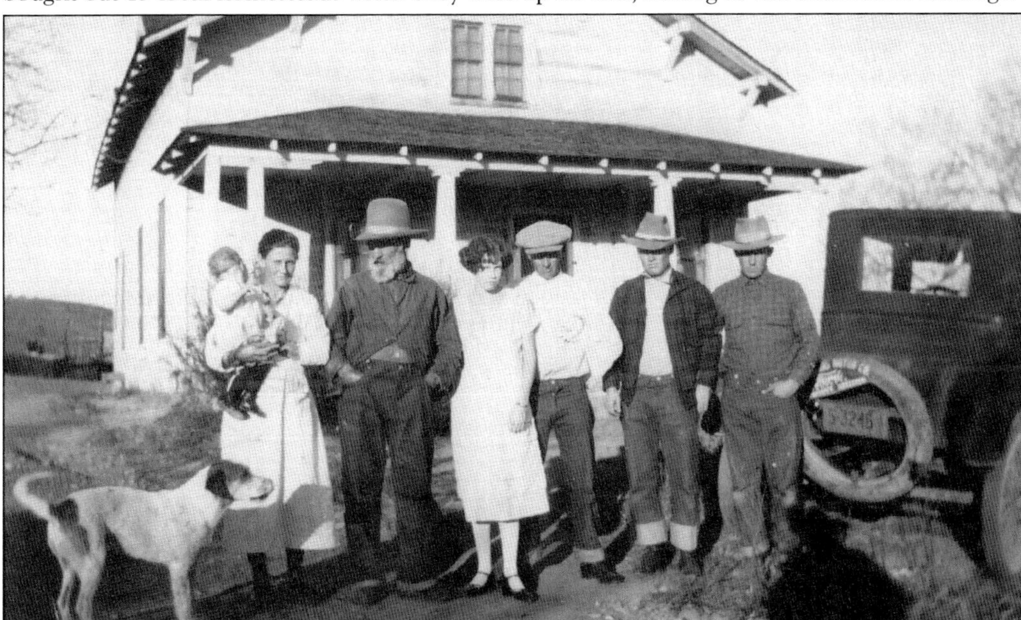

The growing Henderson family and friends are seen here in 1928. Helen Henderson, Jack's granddaughter, still lives on the site. She works the remaining Henderson holdings, including cattle, although much of the property was sold off over the years to make up the current town of Dewey and part of Humboldt.

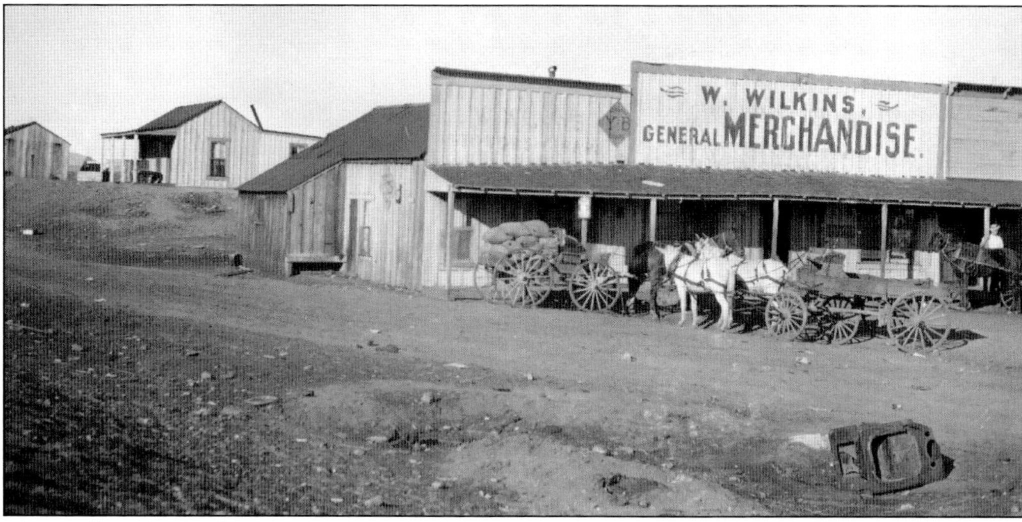

The Wilkins general store opened in Dewey in 1917 and alleviated the need to travel to nearby Humboldt to shop at Wingfield's store. The Wilkinses owned many cattle themselves, and local ranchers and farmers would be extended credit throughout the year until taking their own animals to market. They would then pay their bills and start charging all over again. Such a relationship was instrumental in the early part of Dewey's history.

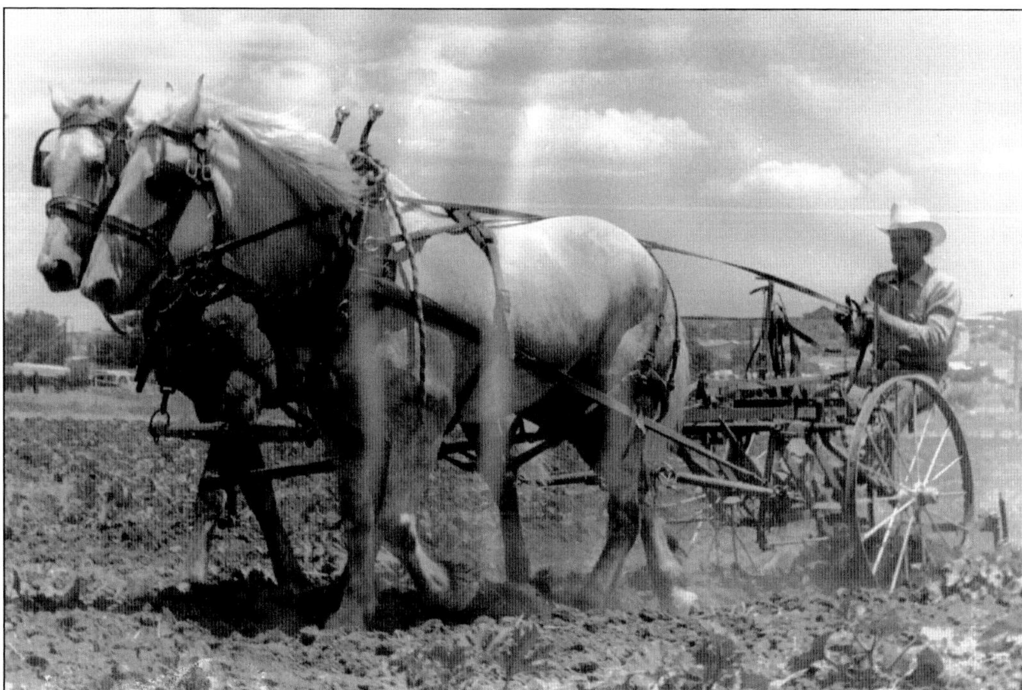

This is believed to be Stan Young tilling the ground for planting on Young's farm. The land was originally farmed by King Woolsey, then the Bower brothers. The Iron King mining company bought the land, then sold it to the Young family, who owned it for many years until new water restrictions forced them out of business. The Mortimer family eventually bought the property and currently run it as a farm and event site.

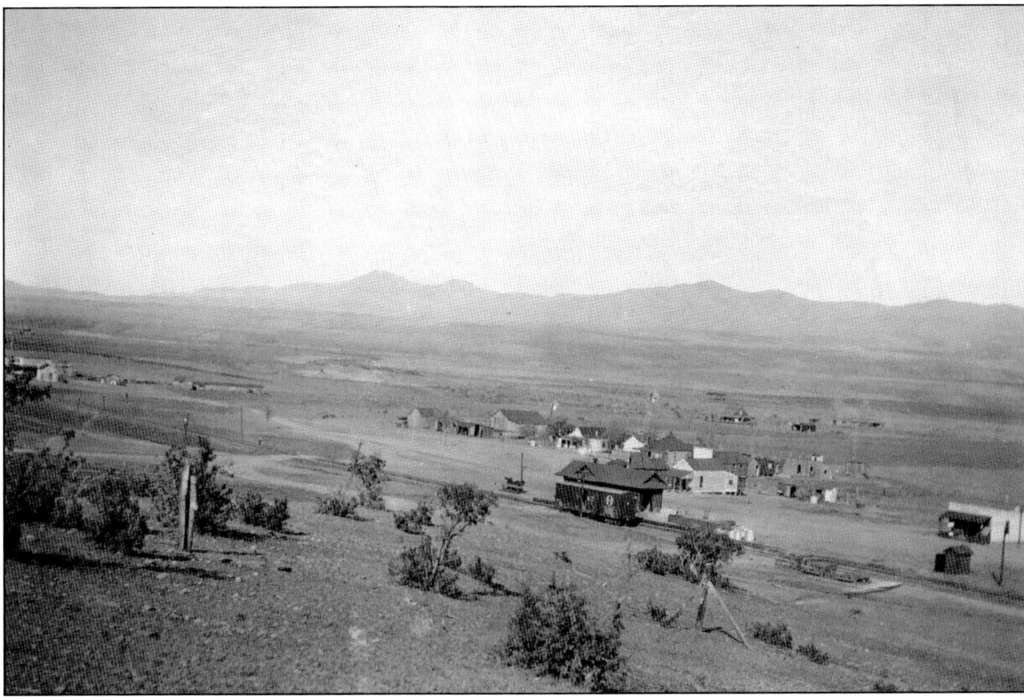

This is an aerial view of the Cherry Creek station house. The area was first known as Agua Fria, then Cherry Creek, Cherry Siding, and eventually, Dewey. The station house was eventually moved to the nearby Skull Valley area. Fully restored, it is part of the historical museum there.

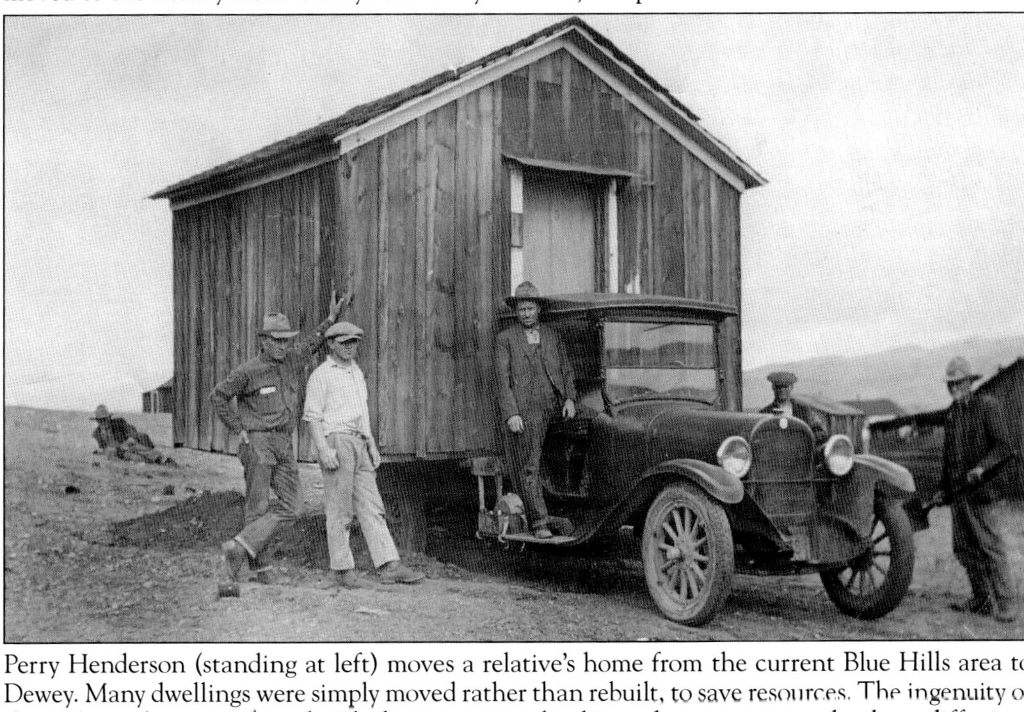

Perry Henderson (standing at left) moves a relative's home from the current Blue Hills area to Dewey. Many dwellings were simply moved rather than rebuilt, to save resources. The ingenuity of the early residents, combined with their strong work ethic and team spirit, made a huge difference in the turbulent economy of the area.

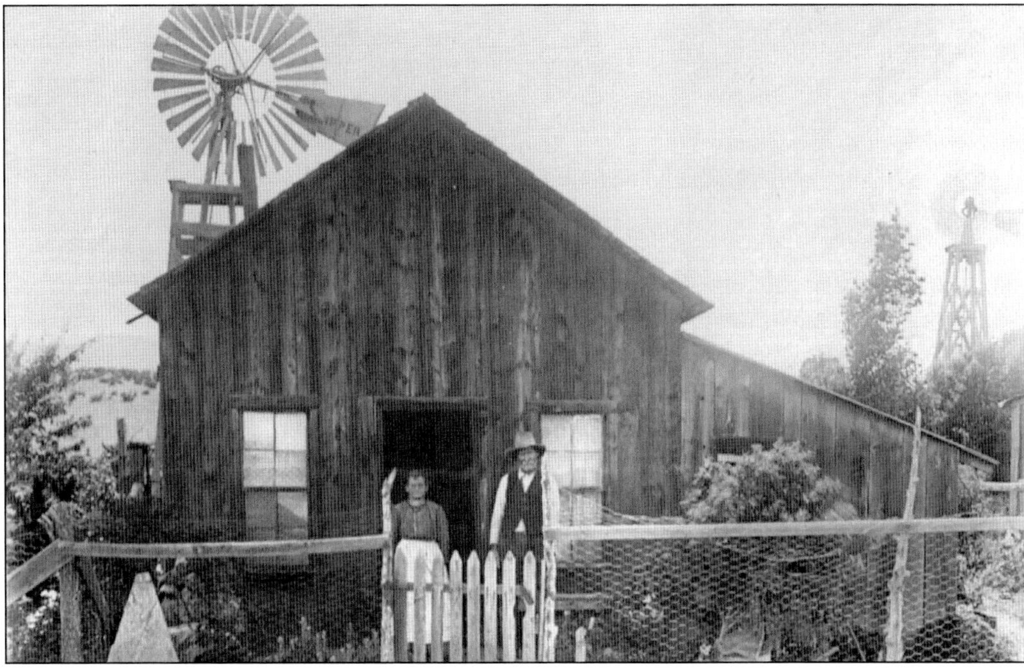

James and Mary Human pose in front of their original homestead house. Galpin Ford now occupies this site in Dewey. This photograph was taken on June 24, 1916. It was also run as a dairy, with locals coming by to pick up products, and it provided a local delivery service to residents. The Humans used a giant milk pail and a quart-sized pitcher to transfer the product to the consumer. Many early residents who are still around fondly remember coming here for dairy products.

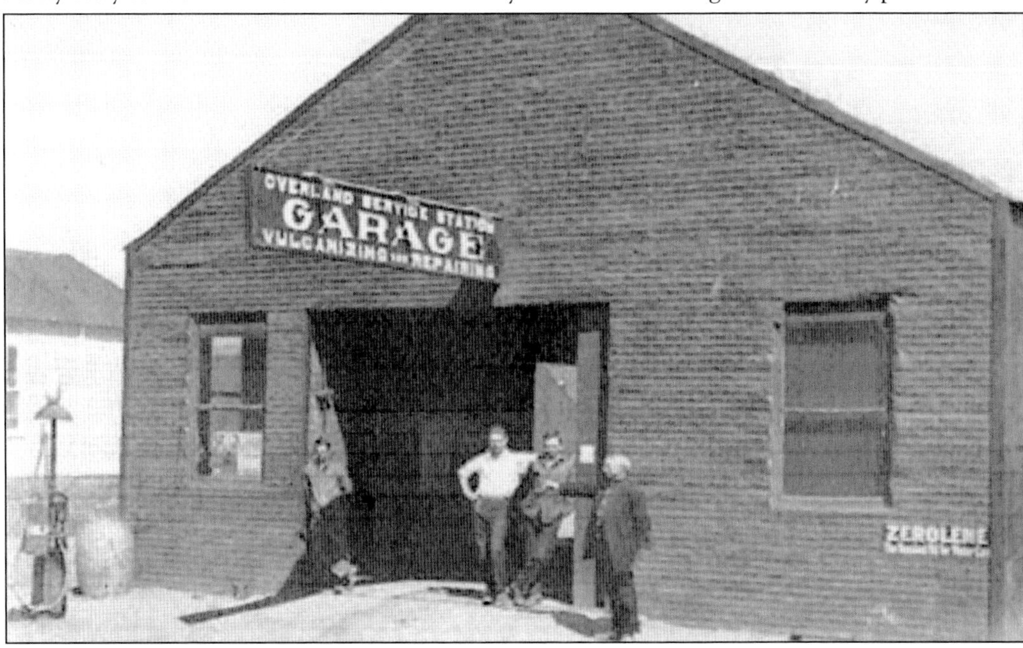

The Overland Service Station in Dewey is shown here around 1919. Albert Warren is leaning against the door at left. With the growing automobile market coming to the area, several service stations sprung up to meet the motorists' needs as miners and ranchers grew more prosperous.

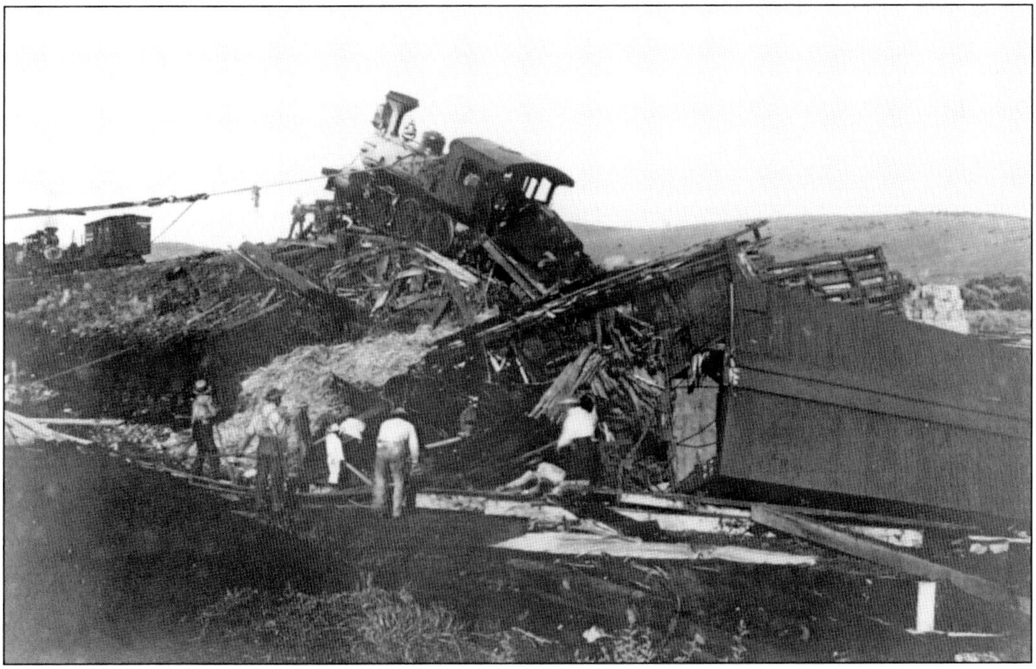

Shown here is a 1920 train pileup just outside the Cherry Creek (Dewey) station. While the railroad route opened up the area for further development, train travel was not without mishaps. This was one of the worst in the area's history. The rail lines were eventually removed in the early 1970s, but they had certainly served their purpose.

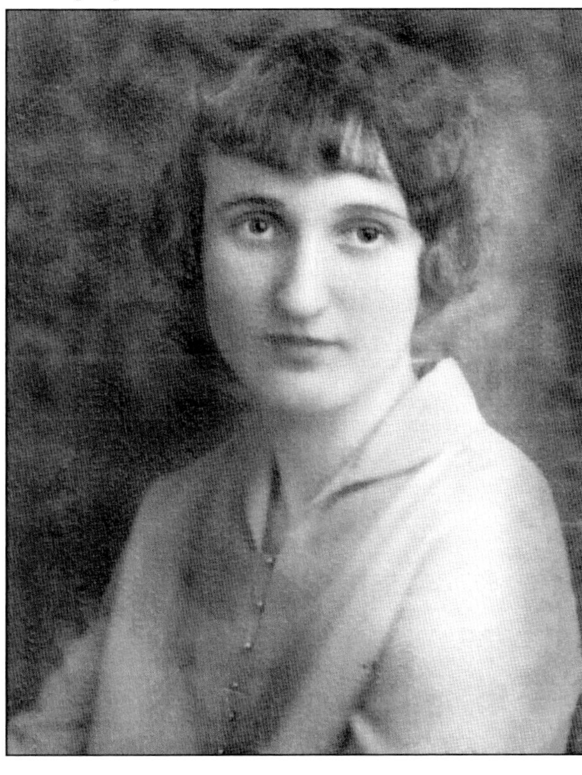

This is a young Esther Cherry Henderson, wife of Perry Henderson, founder of the Dewey Rodeo. Esther lived in the family home until her late 90s. She then moved to the nearby Arizona Pioneer home in Prescott, passing away just before turning 100.

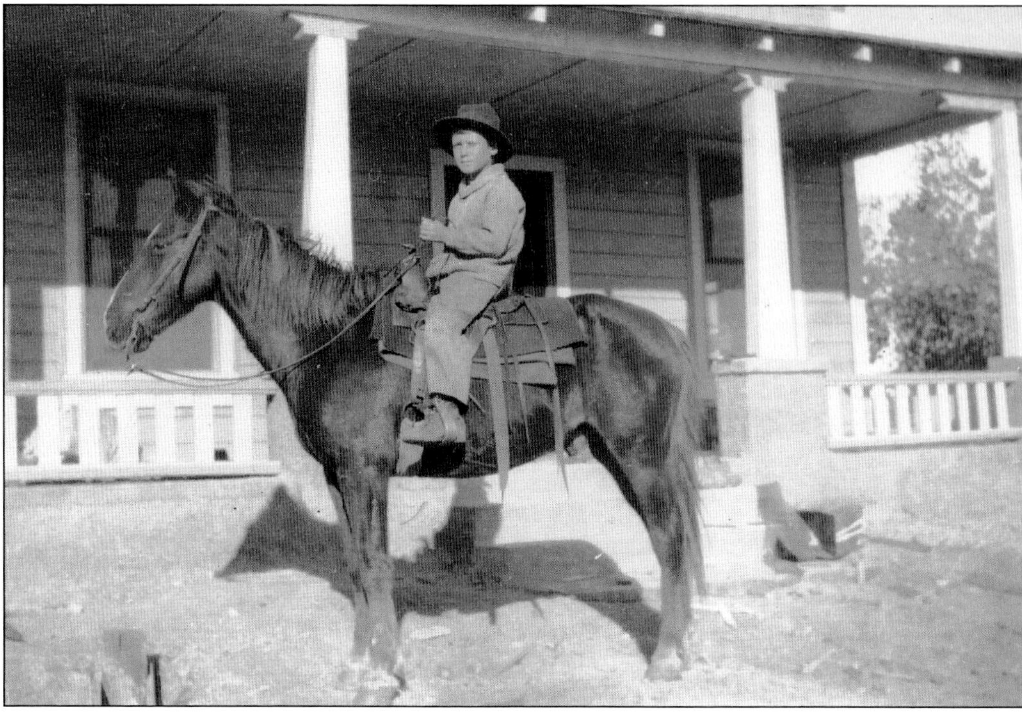

A young Perry Henderson is seen outside the Henderson home. He would later found the Dewey Rodeo at the age of 19 and run it for 34 years, until his death in early 1961 at the age of 56. Perry started taming wild horses, also known as breaking broncos, at the age of 12.

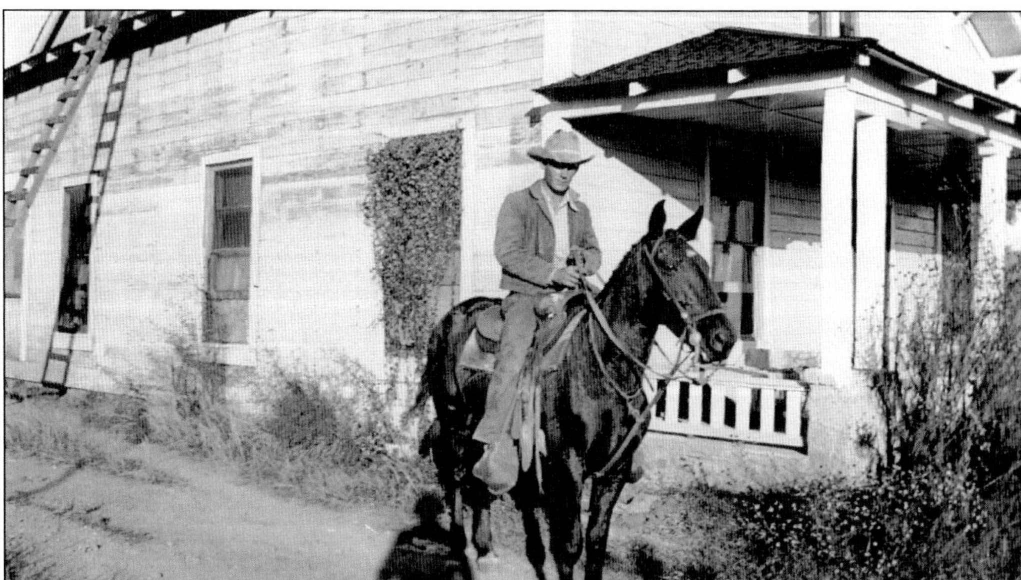

Perry Henderson, probably the most influential resident of Dewey, is seen here around 1928. He was widely respected in the area and also had an impact in Prescott, the territorial capitol of Arizona until it became a state in 1912.

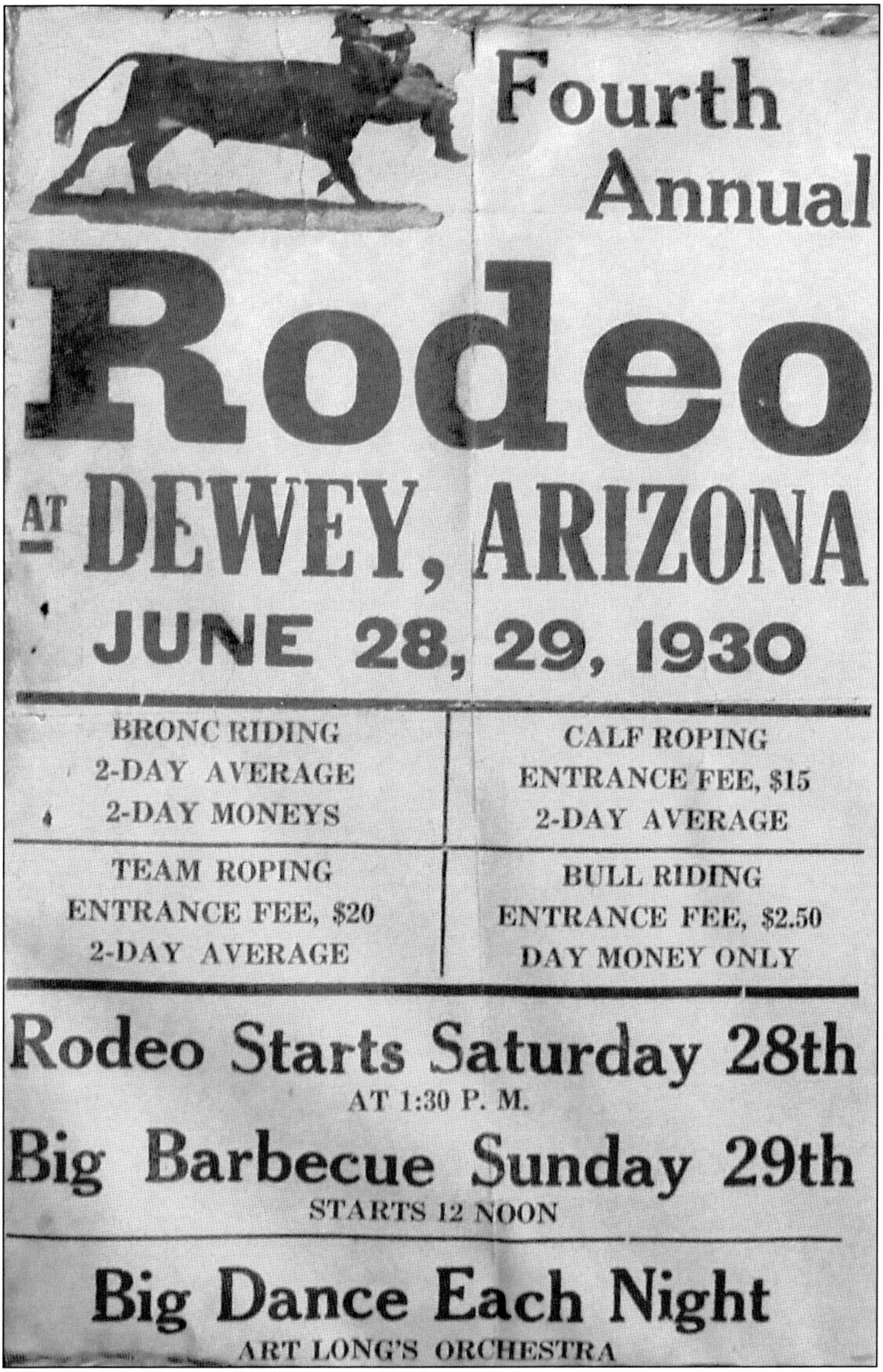

This is a poster from the fourth annual Dewey Rodeo. Many cowboys would earn their entrance fees to other rodeos for the rest of the year with their winnings at the Dewey Rodeo. For most of its existence, it was held the week before the world's oldest rodeo, in nearby Prescott.

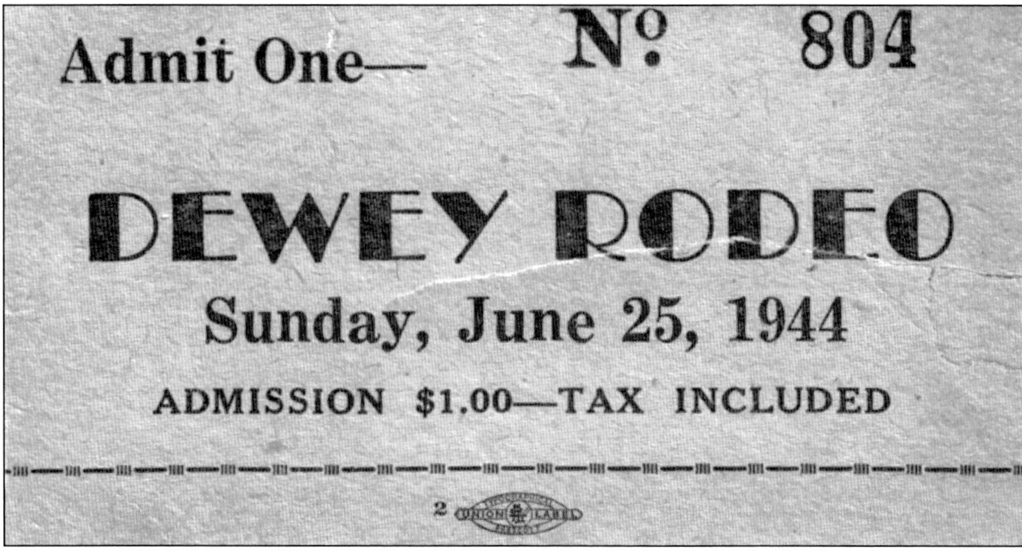

Admit One— No. 804

DEWEY RODEO

Sunday, June 25, 1944

ADMISSION $1.00—TAX INCLUDED

2

Shown here is an entrance ticket to the 1944 Dewey Rodeo. In 1943, the city of Prescott decided to cancel its rodeo for the first time since 1888. But Perry Henderson gathered together area businessmen to raise funds and drove all of his stock 20 miles to ensure the Prescott event's continuity. This was the only year the Dewey Rodeo was not held between 1926 and 1960.

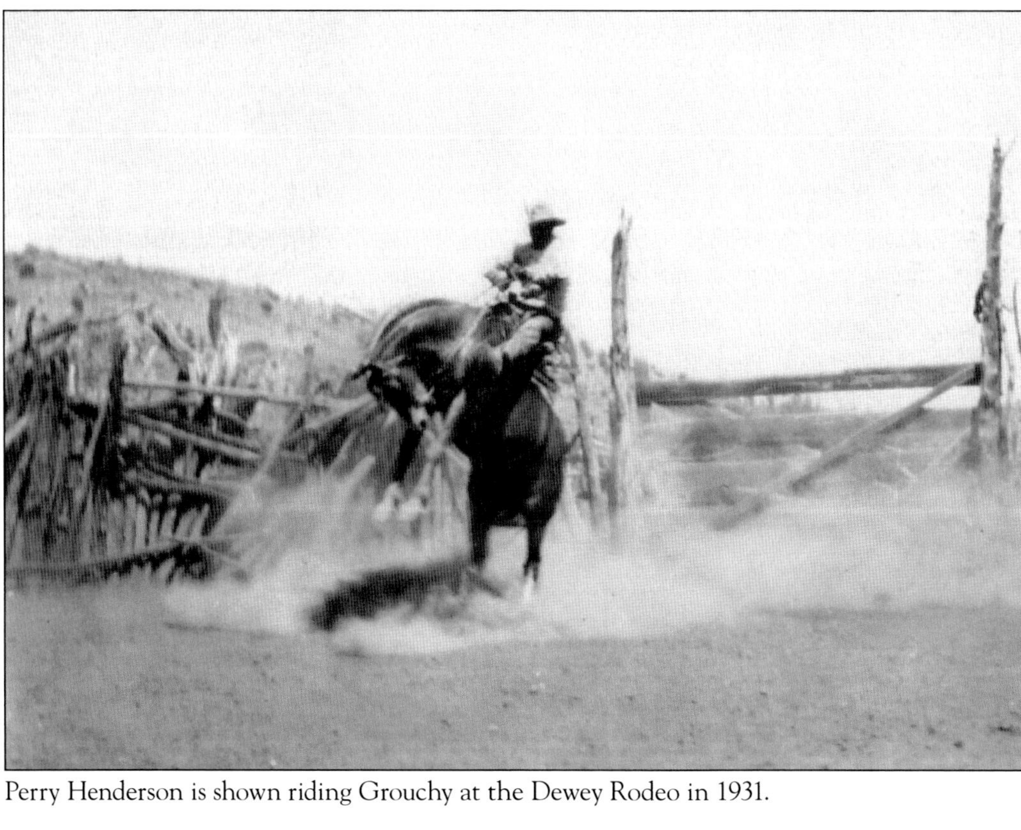

Perry Henderson is shown riding Grouchy at the Dewey Rodeo in 1931.

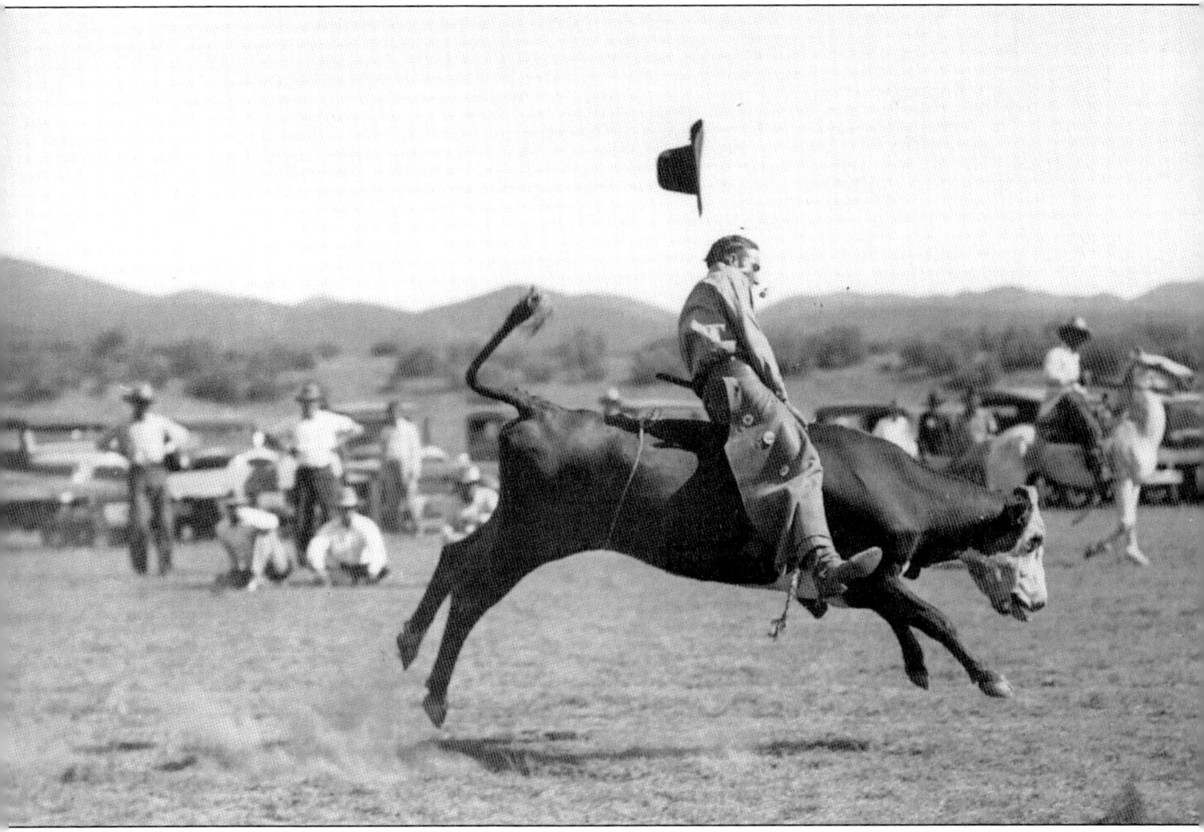

An arena fence was eventually erected over the years, but initially, the Dewey Rodeo's arena was established by parking cars around the riding area until the entire space was surrounded. This aspect of the rodeo's early days was long remembered fondly.

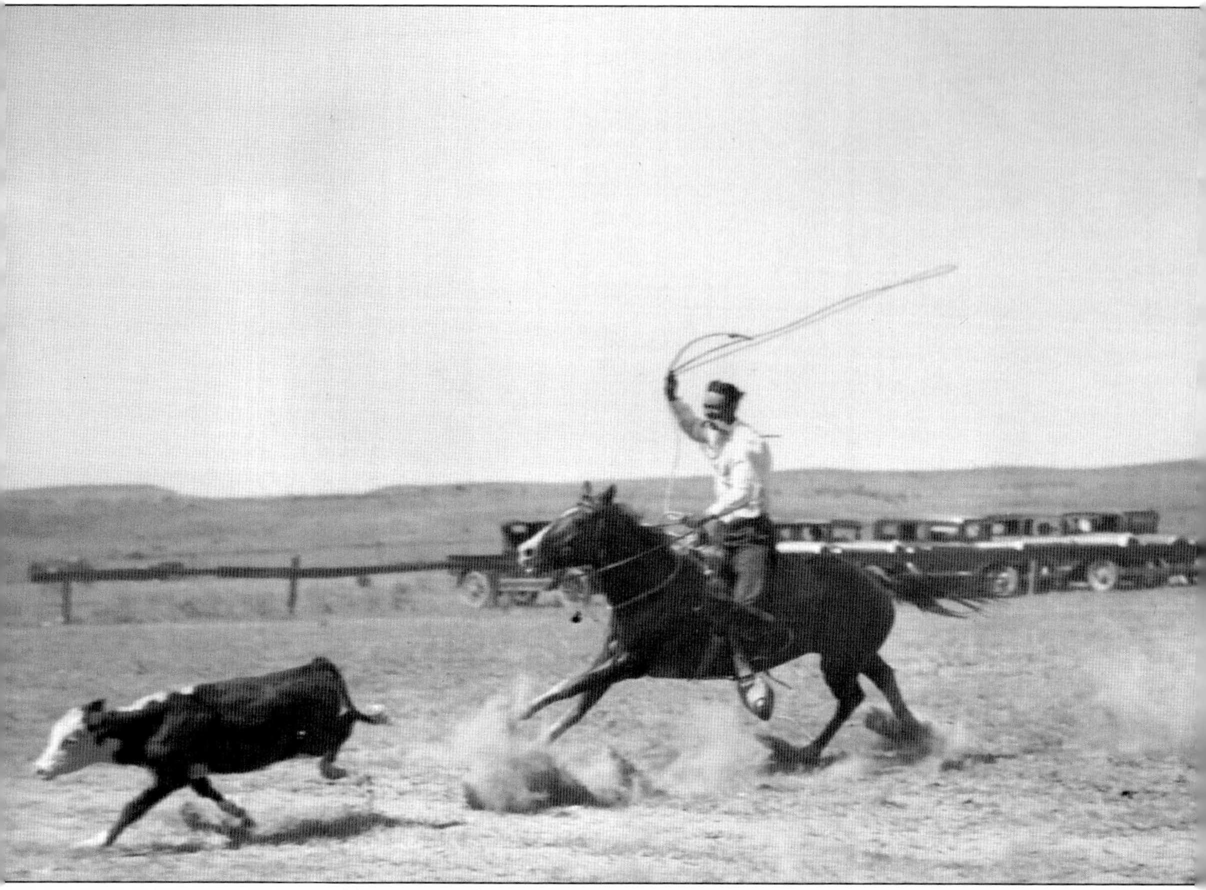

Les Jenkins is seen calf-roping at the Dewey Rodeo in 1930. The Dewey Rodeo was first held the same weekend as the Williams Reunion Rodeo, but its date was soon changed so that cowboys could attend both important events.

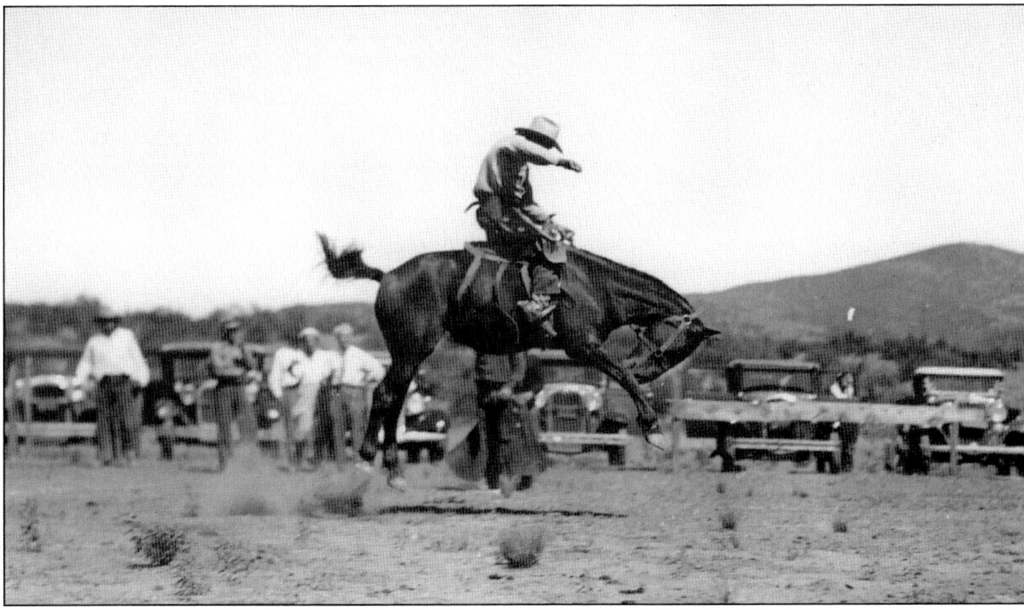

Perry Henderson rides Streak in 1930. He went on to become a three-time world champion, won the Prescott event twice, and later served as a judge in Prescott while running the Dewey Rodeo.

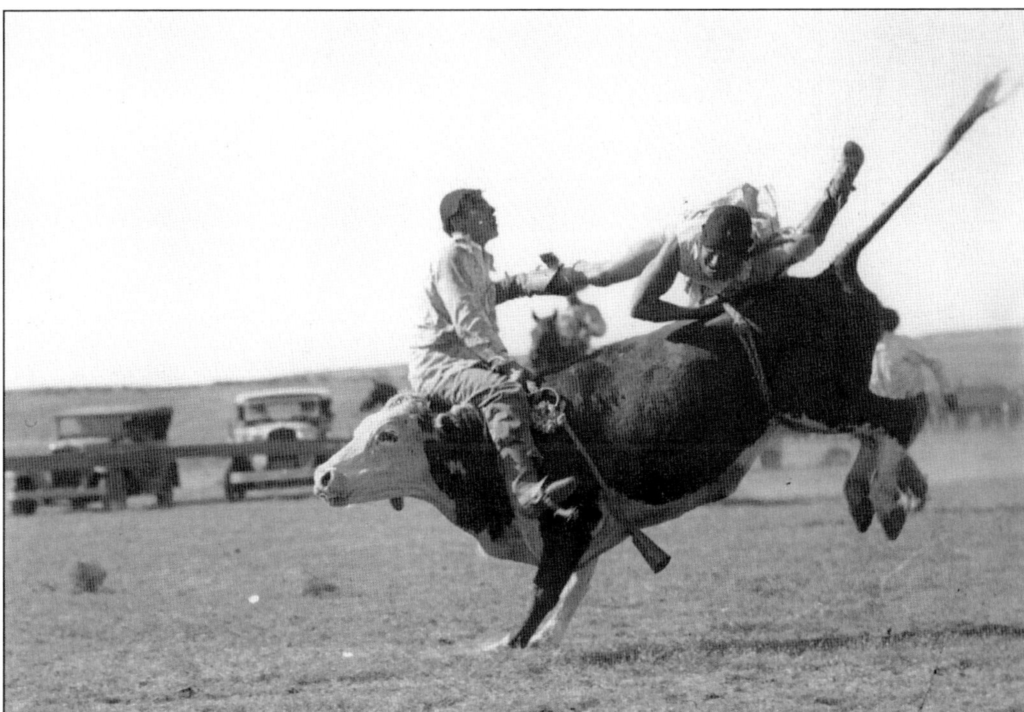

Here, rodeo clowns perform at the Dewey Rodeo. While providing entertainment, their primary purpose was to divert the attention of the bulls so the cowboy who was bucked off could reach safety. The world-famous clown Pinky, a regular at the Dewey Rodeo and at the Prescott rodeo the following weekend, became good friends with the Hendersons.

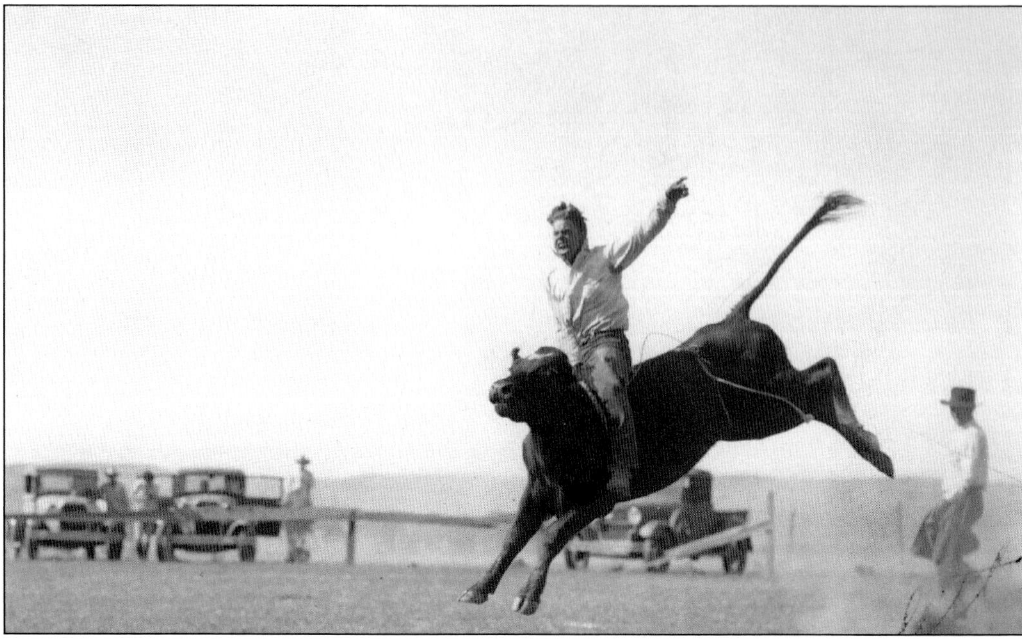

Howard Tripplett is pictured at the 1930 Dewey Rodeo. He was one of the best bull riders of the time and was well known in rodeo circles.

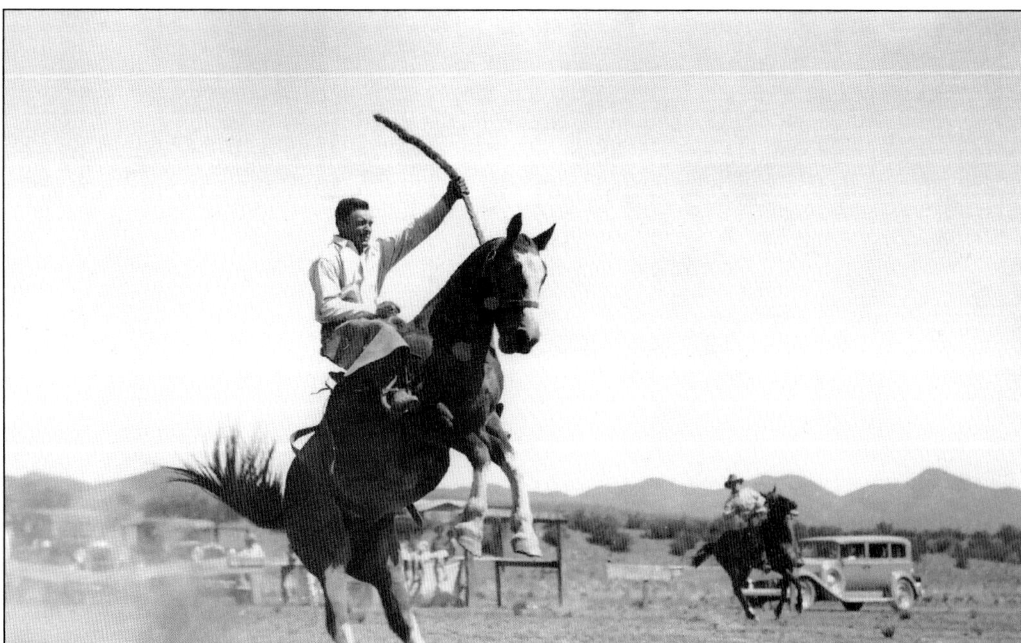

A bucking-horse-riding event commences at the Dewey Rodeo. It was well known at the time that if a rider did well at the Dewey Rodeo, he could be successful anywhere.

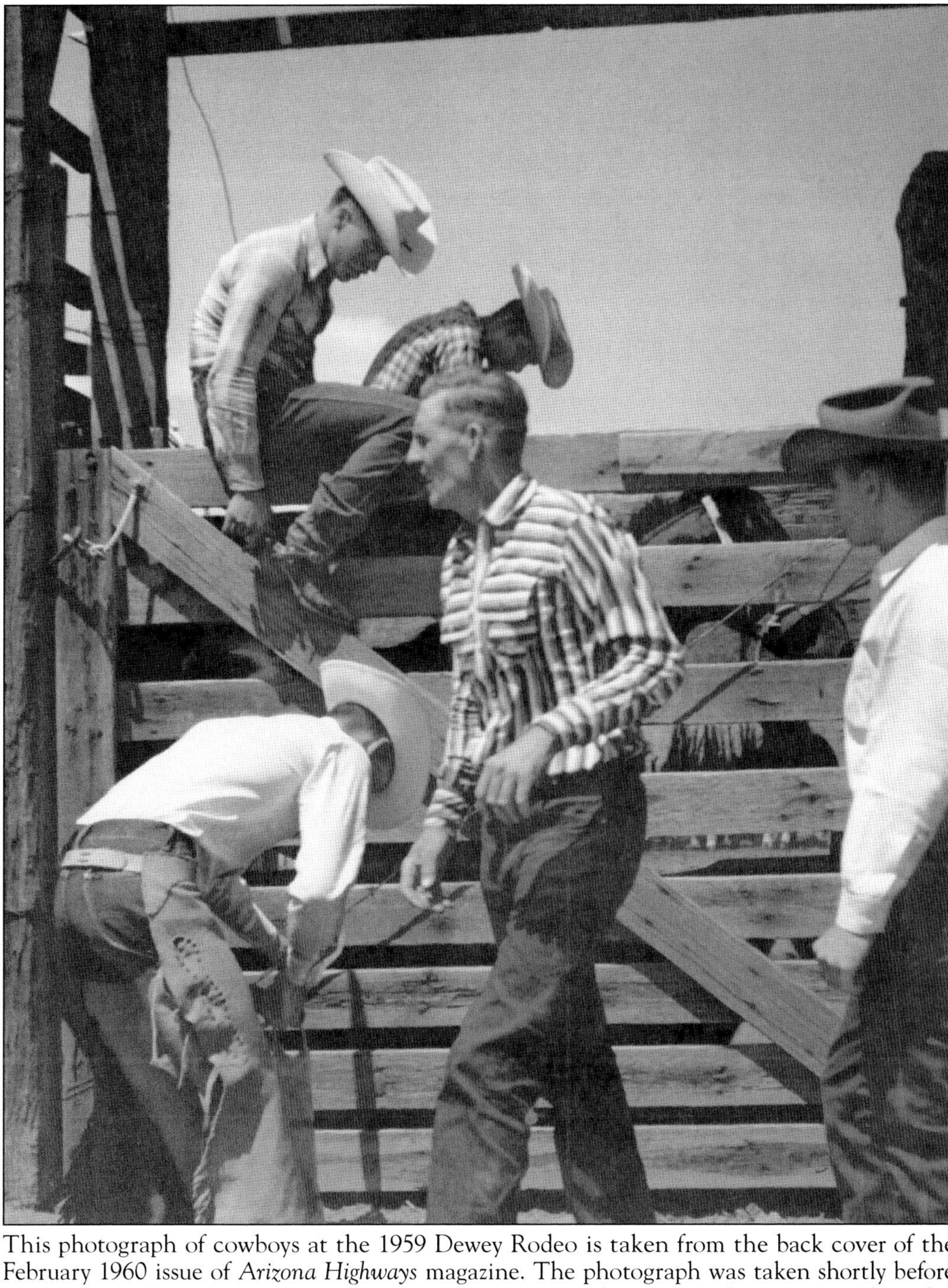

This photograph of cowboys at the 1959 Dewey Rodeo is taken from the back cover of the February 1960 issue of *Arizona Highways* magazine. The photograph was taken shortly before Perry Henderson (not pictured) passed away. The rodeo was known as "The Biggest Little Rodeo in the World."

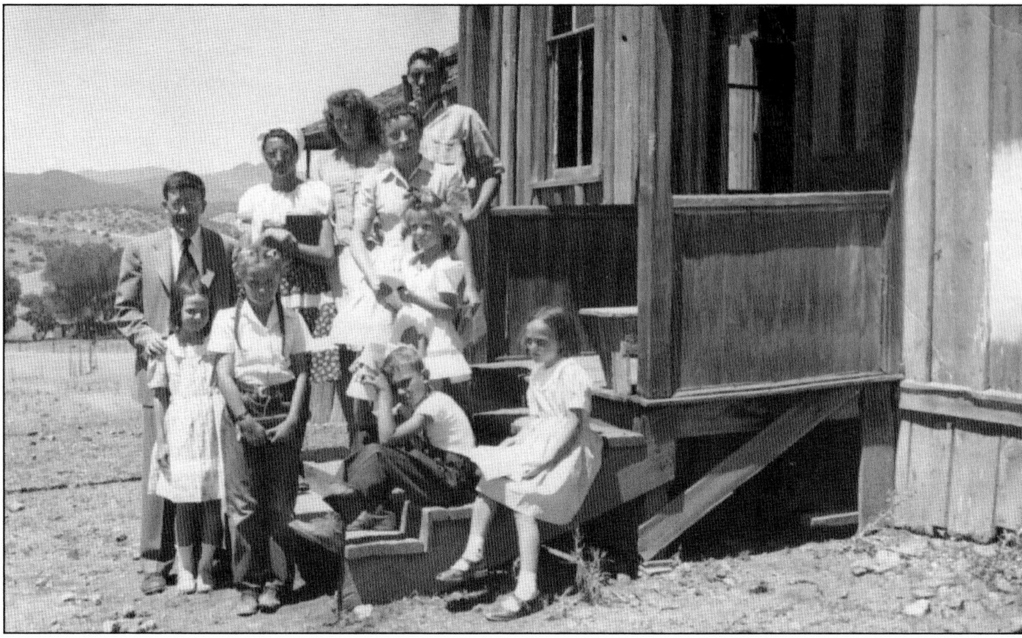

Humboldt children, including Helen Henderson from Dewey (first row, second from left with pigtails), gather outside the Agua Fria Community Church around 1945. Pastor Fox ran the church for many years.

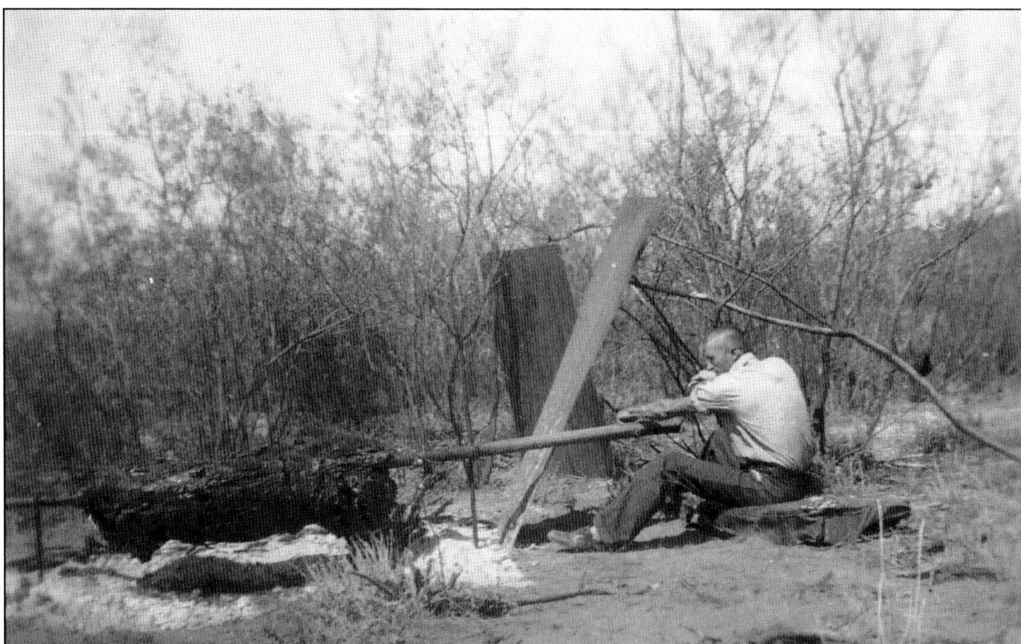

Here, Charlie Chemas is busy roasting a bear in Dewey. Chemas was a Humboldt resident, but the entire region was well known for hunting. A regular excursion meant going over a hill or two to seek out a targeted meal and returning home before nightfall to dress the trophy or eat it in the field with family and friends.

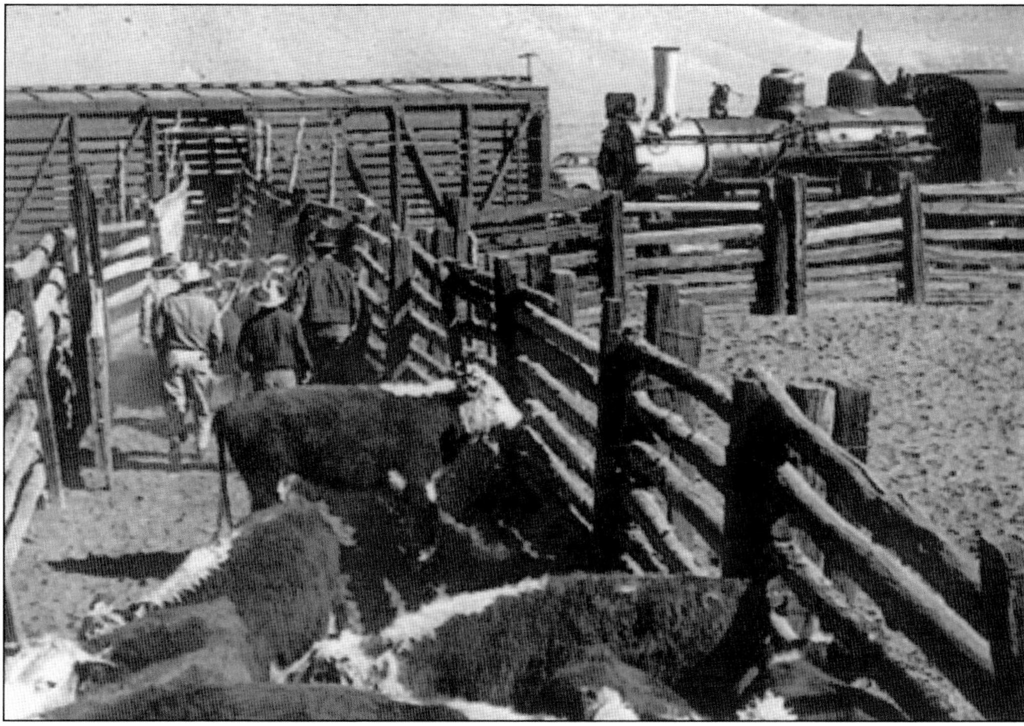

The Fain family loads their cattle at the Cherry Creek station in Dewey. The Wilkins family eventually entered the sheep market in the 1920s, joining with Dan Fain in this endeavor around 1922.

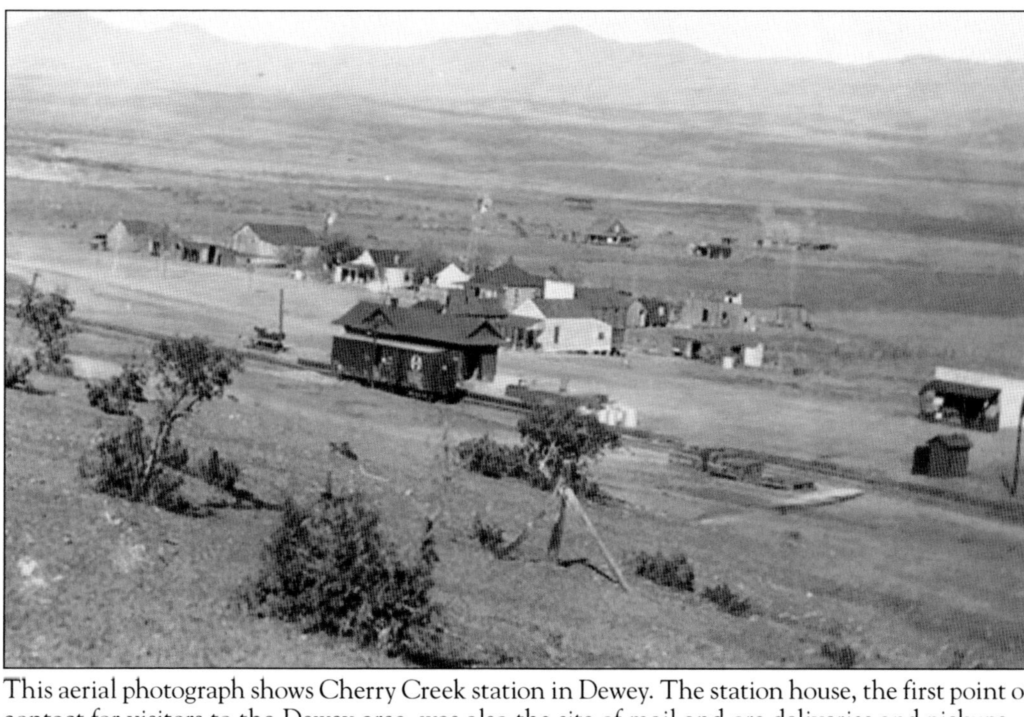

This aerial photograph shows Cherry Creek station in Dewey. The station house, the first point of contact for visitors to the Dewey area, was also the site of mail and ore deliveries and pickups.

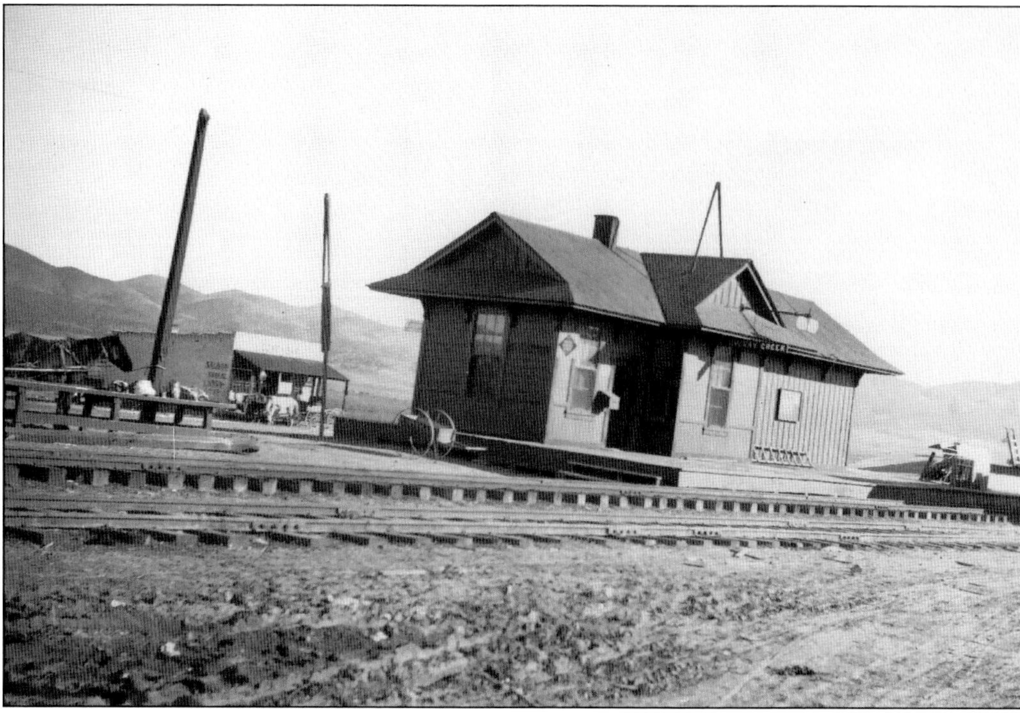

This is another photograph of the Cherry Creek station house in Dewey. Moved in 1926, the house is still intact in nearby Skull Valley. It is best remembered as a focal point of residents for many years as the area grew and shrank in size.

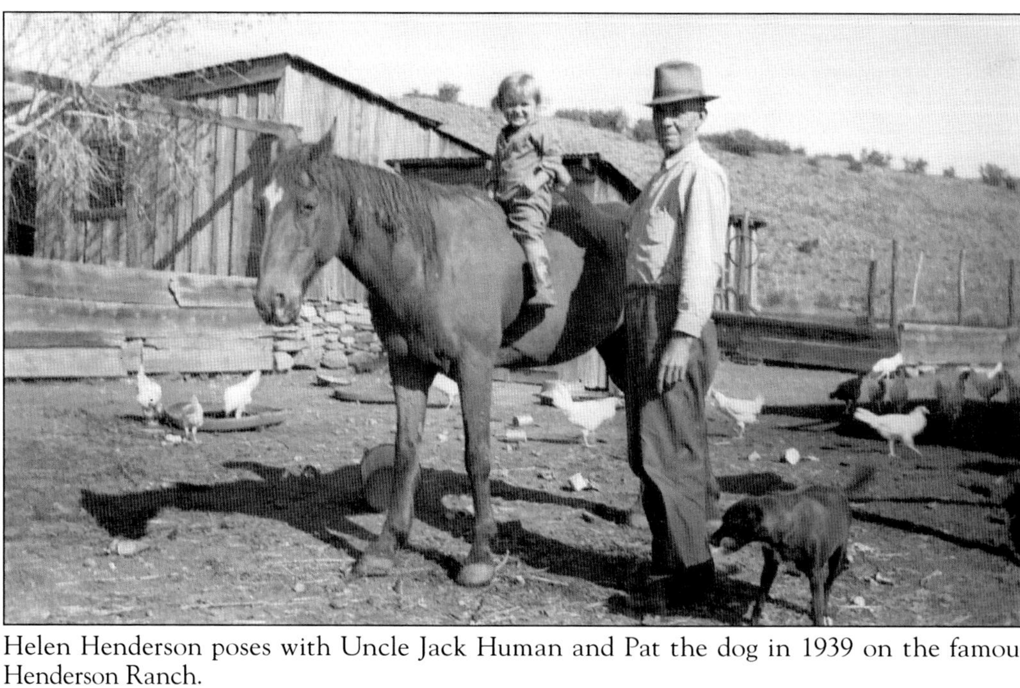

Helen Henderson poses with Uncle Jack Human and Pat the dog in 1939 on the famous Henderson Ranch.

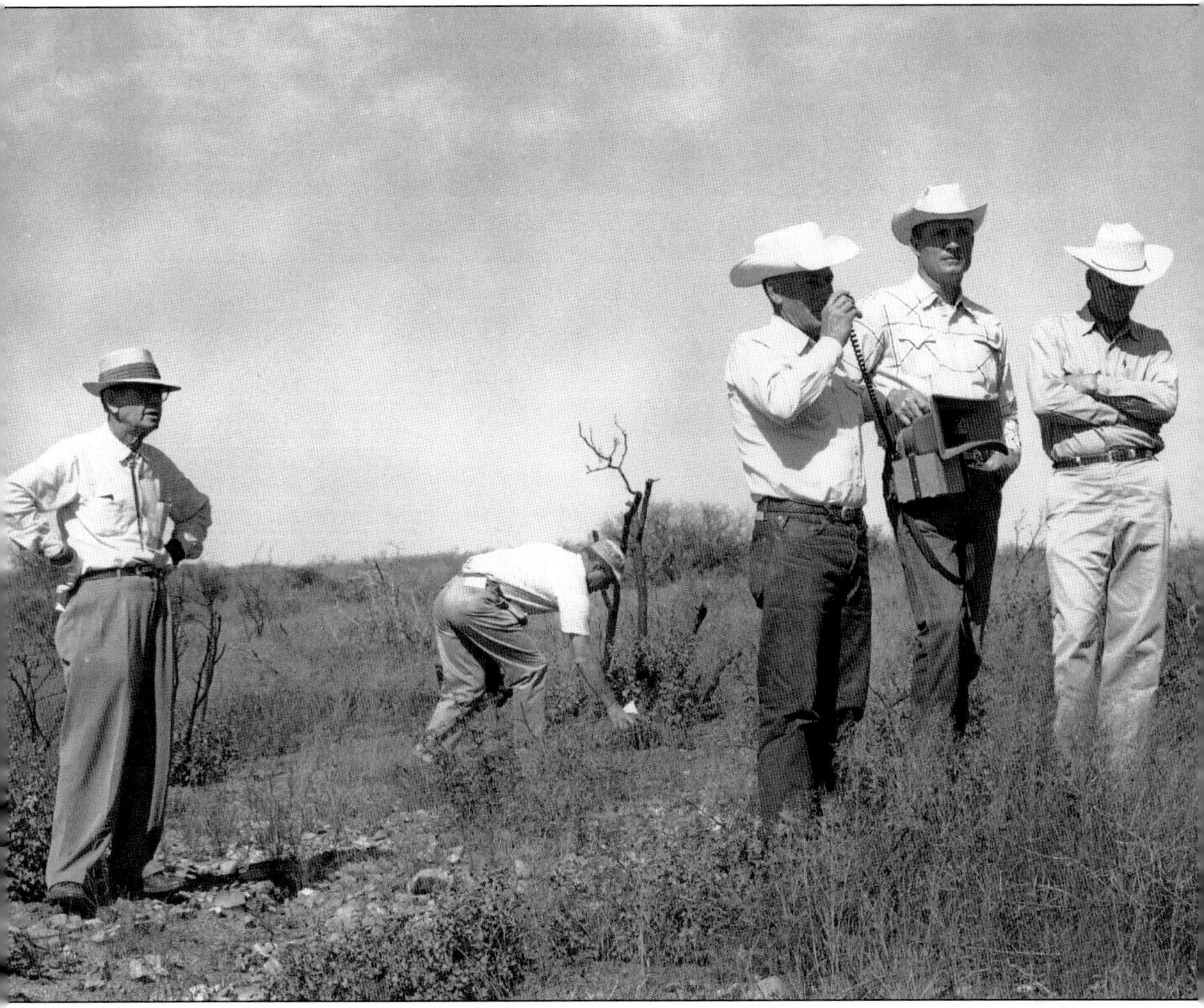

The Dewey ranchers conducted their own controlled burns in the area for many years until the government stepped in during the late 1950s, insisting that it had the expertise to operate the burns. The first year that the ranchers did not run the burn, officials lost control of the fire and it burned out of control. It was not the first time that local residents shook their heads at outside agencies coming in as local experts.

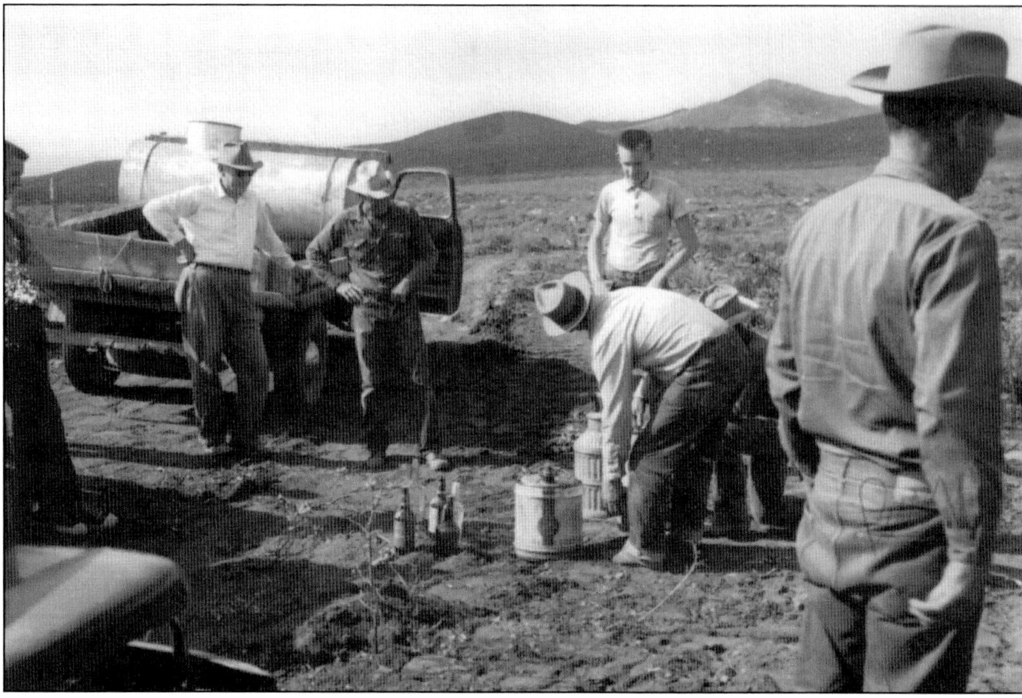

Dewey ranchers prepare for a controlled burn. These operations were well researched and organized and helped the area strike a balance, with the incorporation of human intervention. Ranchers at the time were good caretakers of the land and paid close attention to ensure future agricultural viability, while at the same time living off the land as well.

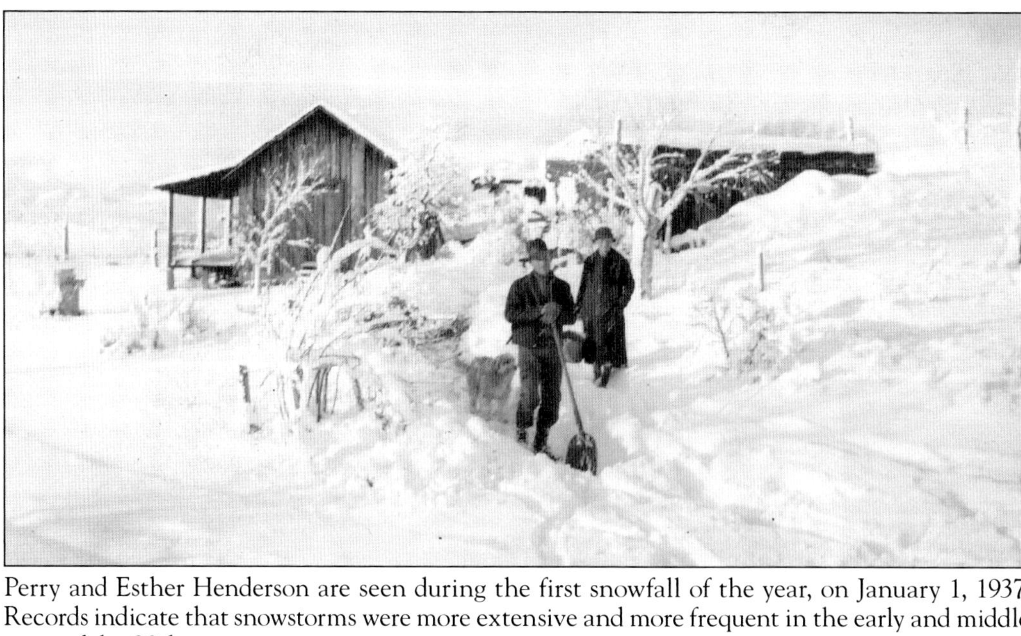

Perry and Esther Henderson are seen during the first snowfall of the year, on January 1, 1937. Records indicate that snowstorms were more extensive and more frequent in the early and middle parts of the 20th century.

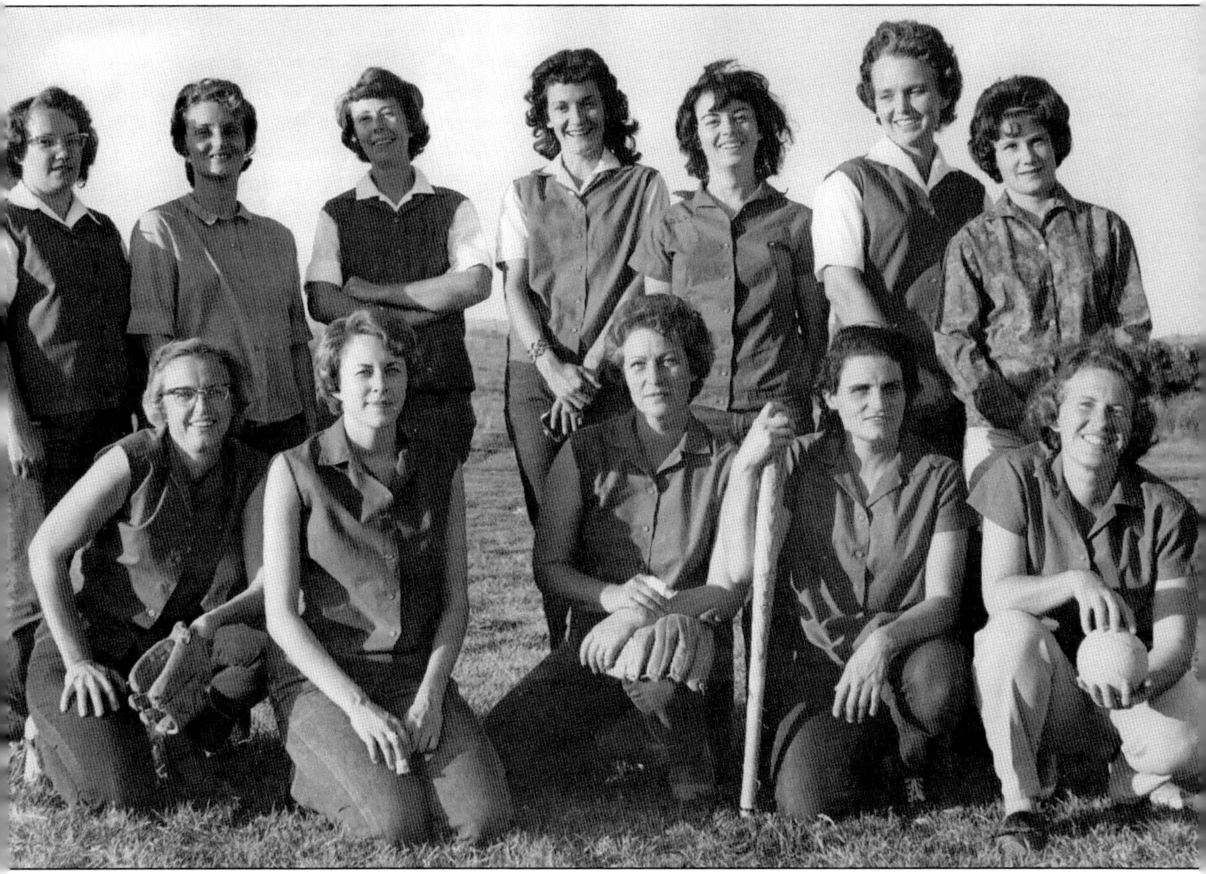

The Dewey women's baseball team poses in 1957. Helen Henderson is in the second row, center. This team successfully competed against other regional teams. The Little League teams started by the Iron King Mining Company in the early 1950s provided enjoyment for countless youth in the area.

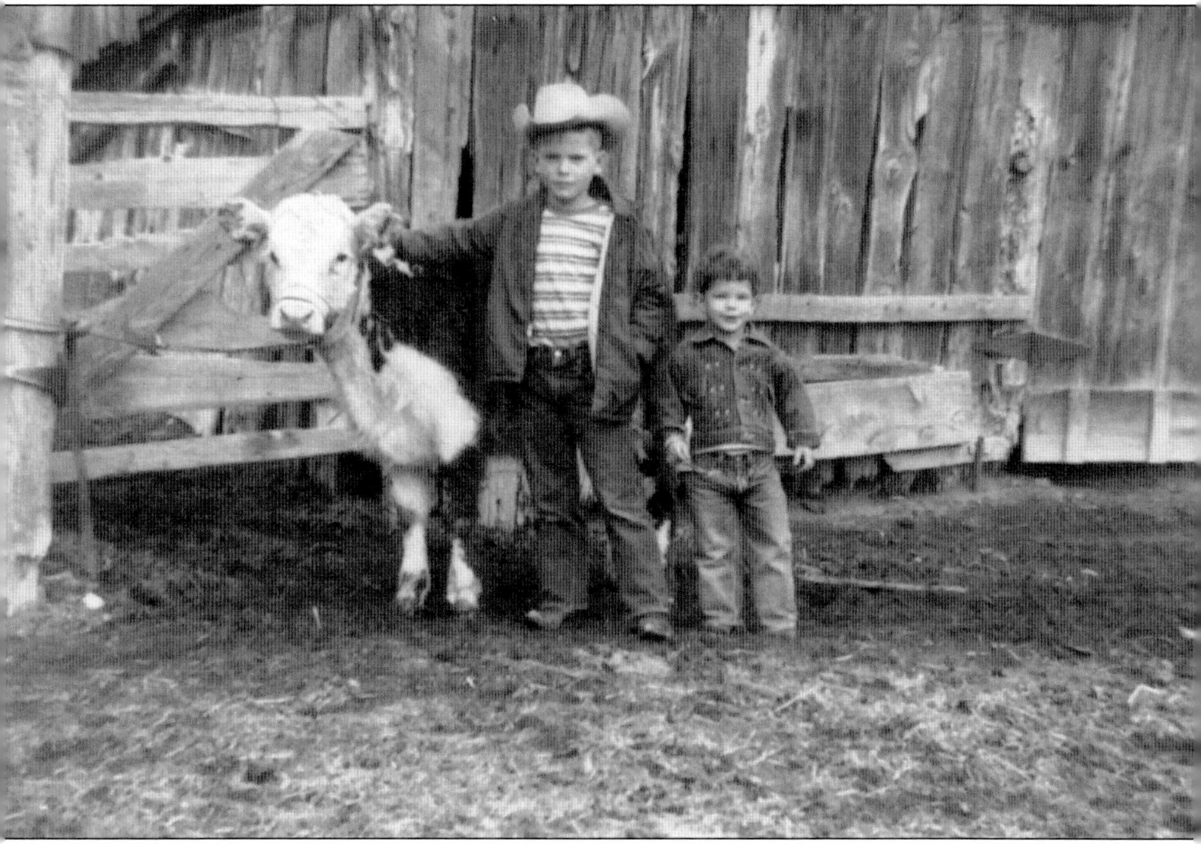

Helen Henderson's children, Perry and Lori Lee, are pictured here. Lori Lee still lives on a property that was part of the original Henderson ranch, and Perry is currently moving into the original Henderson homestead after retiring early from a job that often took him around the world. One certainty about the Henderson family is that their roots grow deep and strong here.

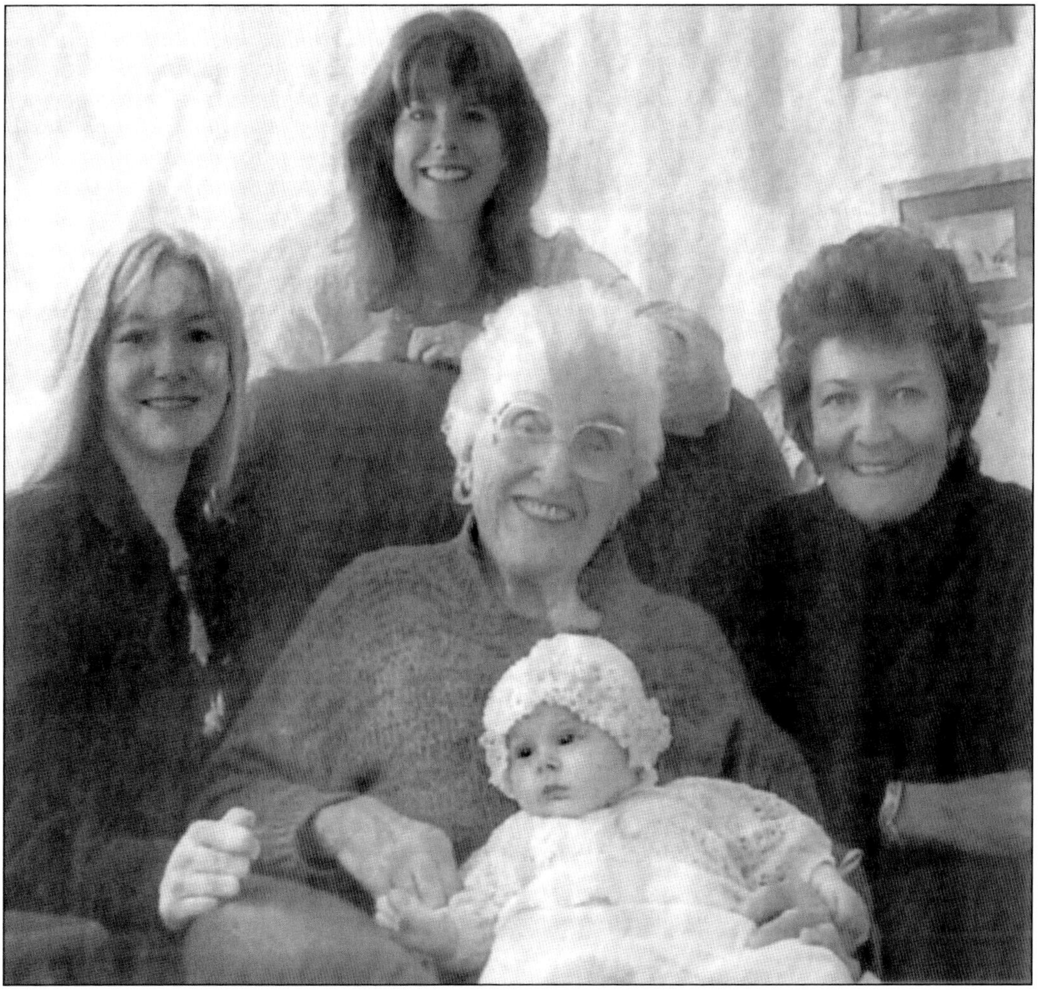

This photograph includes five generations of Henderson women. Esther (center) recently passed away, but everyone else is doing great and still remains in the area. On the right is Esther's daughter Helen Henderson Cain, at top is Helen's daughter Lori Lee Savage, and on the left is Lori Lee's daughter Deanna Tow. Deanna's Daughter Alicia Tow is sitting on Esther's lap, completing the circle.

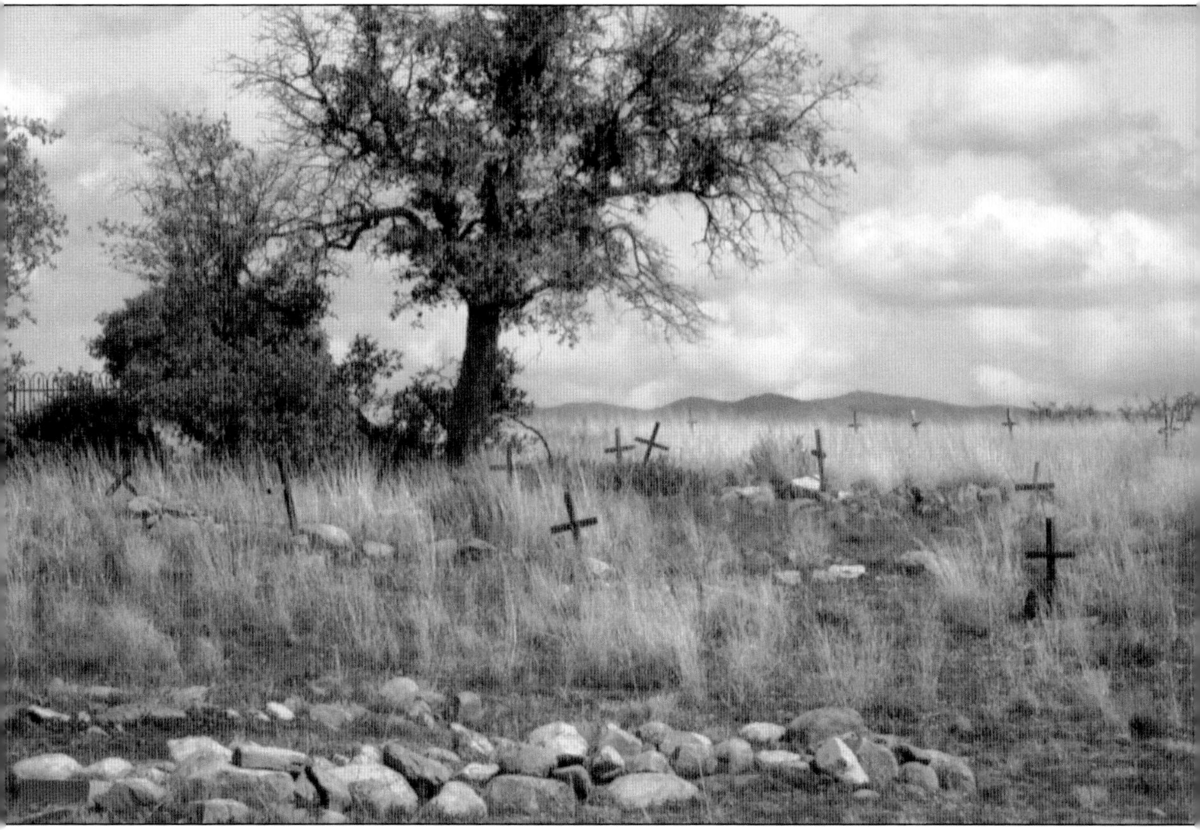

Services at the Dewey-Humboldt Cemetery, owned by Helen and Martha Henderson, are offered free to local residents. Kathy Jackson, a longtime resident and town hall employee, still cares for the property for the Henderson family. The history of the area's residents can be researched by wandering among the gravesites.

Two

HUMBOLDT
VAL VERDE

As "ranching" was for Dewey, the one word used to describe Humboldt would be "mining." While some families, including the Goswicks and Chemas, have stayed in the area, most residents moved on as soon as the work dried up, as it often did. Levi Bashford built the first mill here in 1876, opening the door to more prospecting and mining in the area. In 1899, when the Val Verde smelter was built, a town grew up around it, eventually changing its name to Humboldt in 1905. The smelter was later sold to the Bradshaw Mountain Company, which in turn sold it to the Arizona Smelting Company, which saw the smelter burn down days after buying it in 1904.

Immediately after the fire, construction began on a much larger smelter. Even with constant starts and stops in local mining operations, and the consequent sale of the smelter to consolidated mining company and others, the area's mining operations grew rapidly. The industry eventually supported hundreds of large and small mines in the area.

The smelter was soon employing more than 400 men. They both worked and played hard, spending much of their money at the 15 or so bars and bordellos in town. By 1907, there were also five restaurants, five general stores, three hotels, three churches, bakeries, meat markets, drugstores, a photography studio, billiard halls, livery stables, barbershops, and a jewelry store. In addition, banks and a hospital were established in the area to support the ever-expanding population. The railroad came to the area, and, eventually, 559 ore cars traveled in and out of Humboldt each day. At its peak, about two million pounds of pure copper left Humboldt a month.

The Humboldt smelter opened and closed several times, eventually closing for good in 1937. The Iron King mine closed for good in 1967, long after it had been sending its ore to smelters outside the area and the population dwindled to ghost-town levels. With its colorful history and mild mountain climate, however, residents have been slowly moving back, and it is now known as a quiet, peaceful place to live, within easy driving distance of busier, noisier areas of commerce.

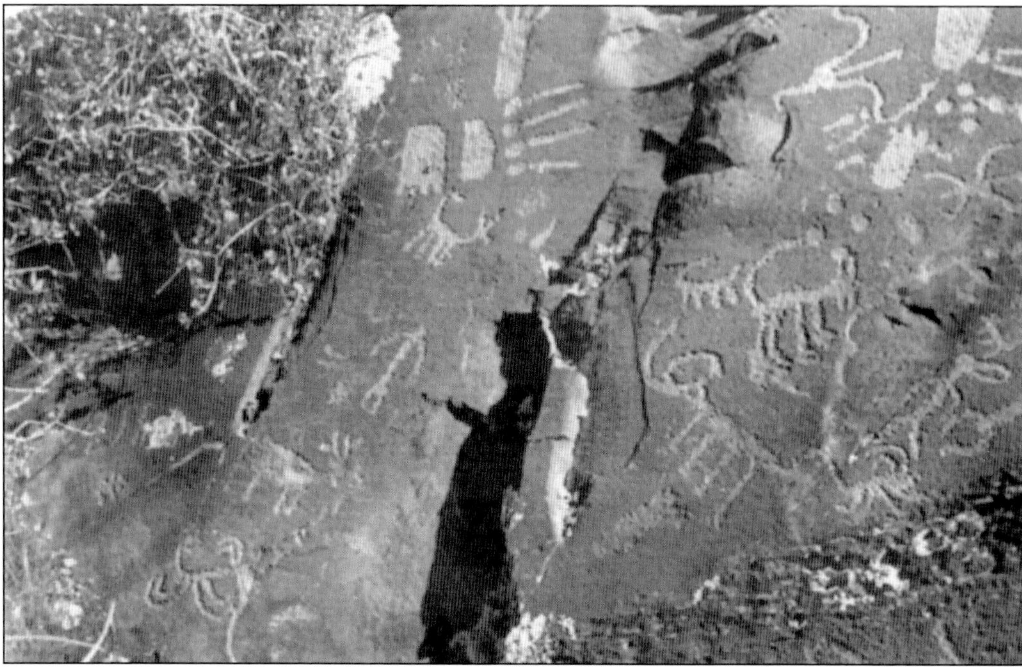

Petroglyphs are still found in the area, but they are few and far between. There was never a heavy concentration of Indians in Humboldt, and most were forced out of the area in 1875, but a few remained for many years after that. The petroglyphs shown here date back hundreds of years, long before the Yavapai tribe populated the area. The early tribes were mainly nomads, using the area as a home base and to plant crops. They traveled as far as Cave Creek to collect cactus fruit, Crown King to collect nuts, and Lonesome Valley to gather sunflower seeds.

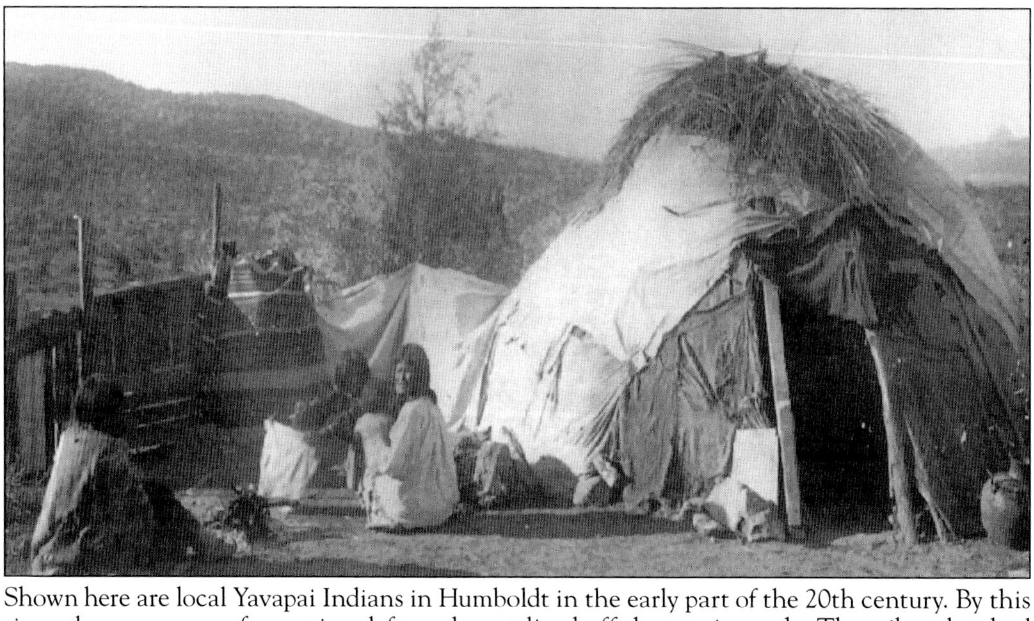

Shown here are local Yavapai Indians in Humboldt in the early part of the 20th century. By this time, there were very few natives left, and most lived off the tourist trade. The tribes that had lived here for thousands of years left little but rock art to document their presence. The ruins and pit houses found later were mostly Yavapai in origin.

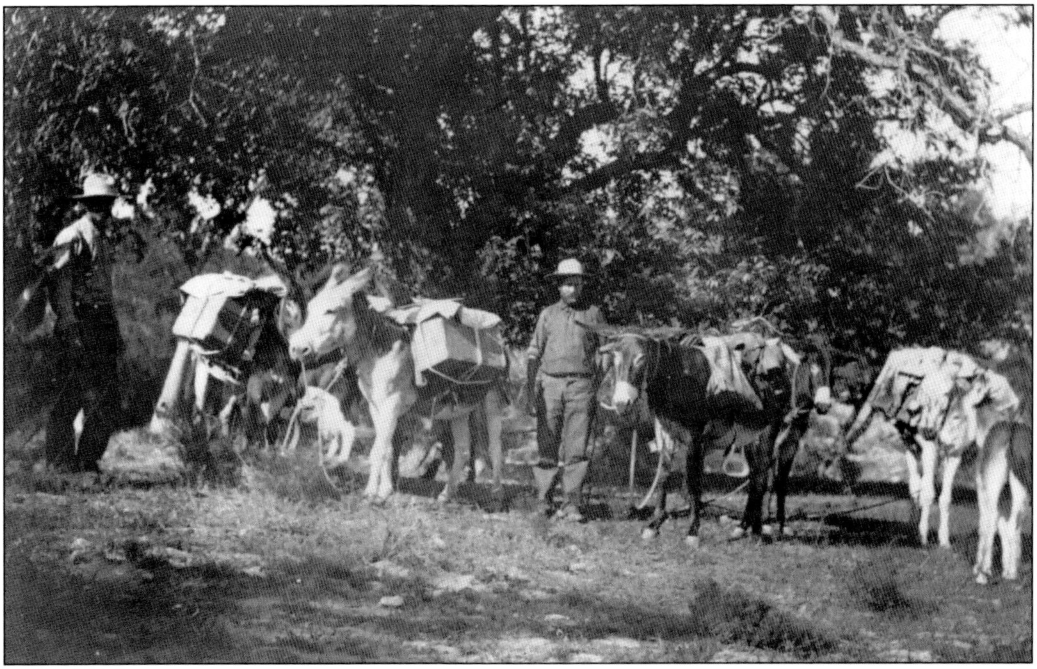

Early prospectors in Humboldt are seen here in 1900. Prospectors were the first white visitors to the area, and it was their findings and reports that originally drew attention to the region. Arriving when the native population was still strong, they risked their lives daily in their quest for riches. A different breed than most settlers, prospectors rarely stayed in an area for long, usually continuing to move, looking for the latest treasure.

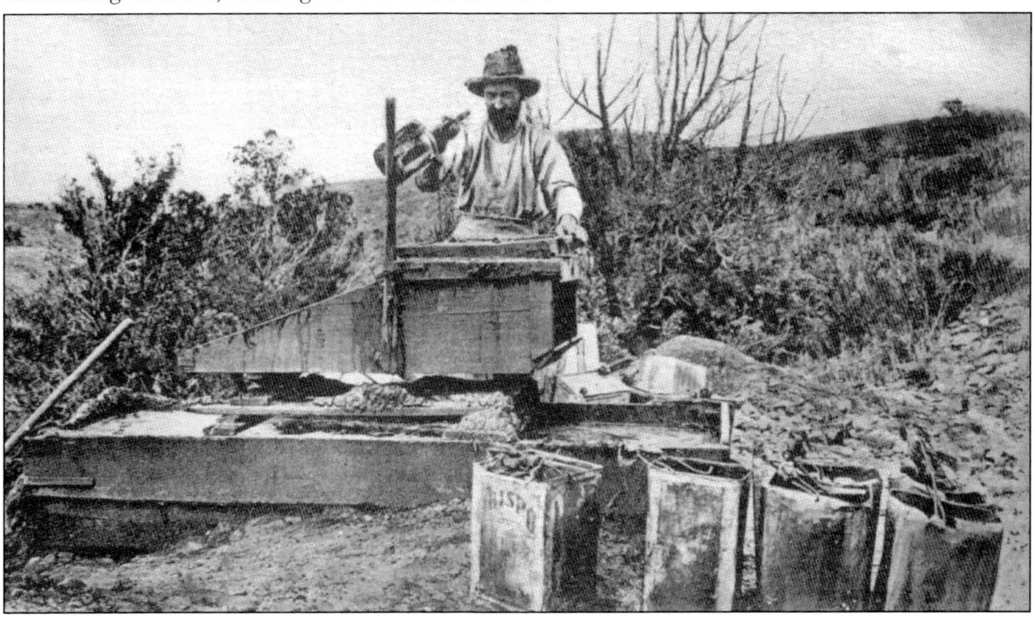

Placer mining involves the exploration of deposits in areas deemed too loose to tunnel into. While placer mining continued for many years, it was much more prevalent prior to the introduction of large mining companies and their equipment to the area. Some miners still use placer mining techniques today.

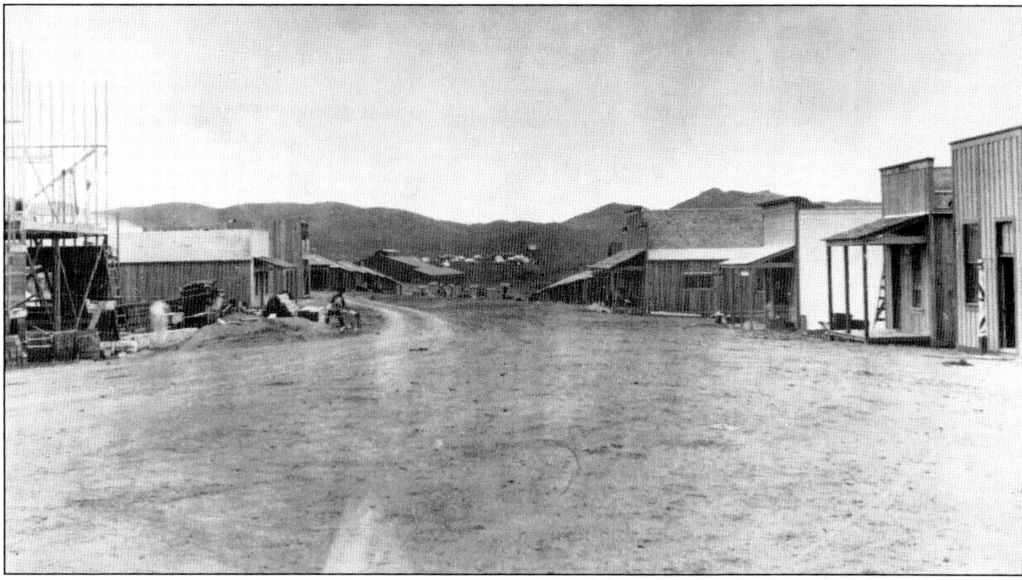

Main Street in Humboldt is seen here in the late 1870s, at the birth of this boomtown. Nob Hill is visible in the distance. Originally called Val Verde, the town was not officially named Humboldt until 1905, when the US Post Office opened. The town was named after Baron Von Humboldt, a noted naturalist and traveler, although it is not known if he ever visited the area.

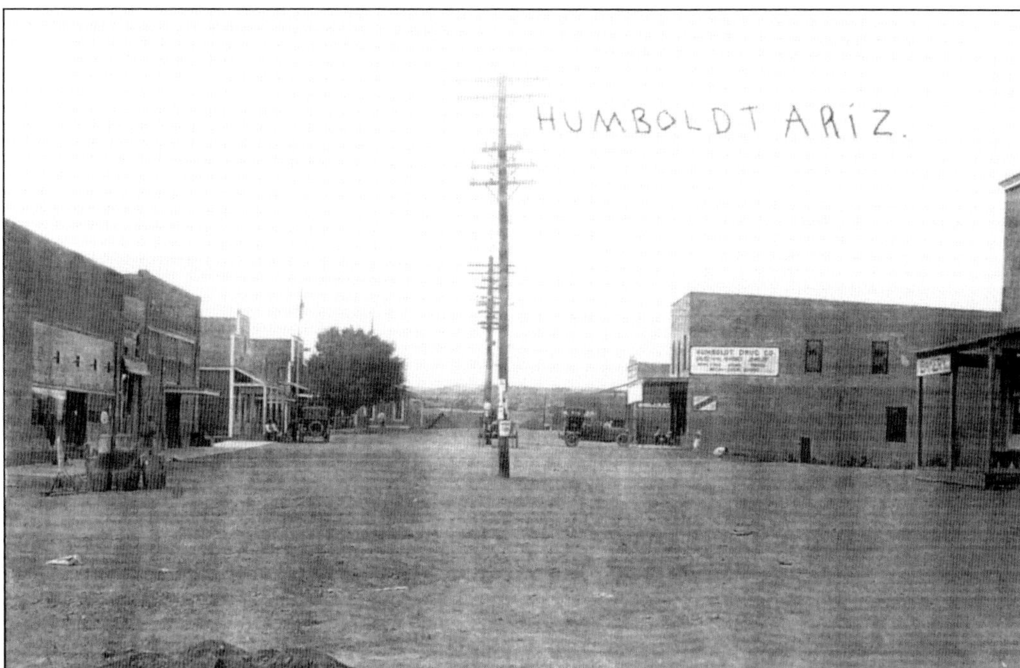

Humboldt's Main Street is seen here in the early 1900s. The town was well established by now, and businesses and services grew to meet the needs of the ever-growing population. No saloons or brothels were allowed on Main Street, lending a sense of security to the area. Prescott Street possessed a very different quality. Such establishments were firmly entrenched there. The street once boasted the best brothel in the Arizona territory.

Burros carry lumber for construction on Main Street in Humboldt in the early 1890s. Burros were an important part of early mining activity, providing hard labor not possible from humans. They were also instrumental in building the roads to the area, until motor vehicles supplied a more reliable method of transportation and hauling.

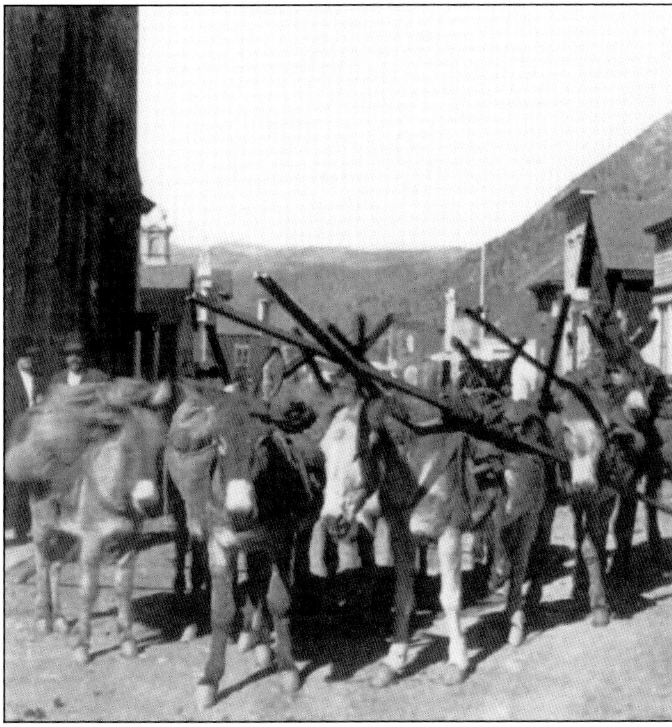

This is an early photograph of the Chemas family. Shown are, from left to right, Mary, Kate, Anna (holding August), Frank, Rudy, Mike (holding Pete), and George.

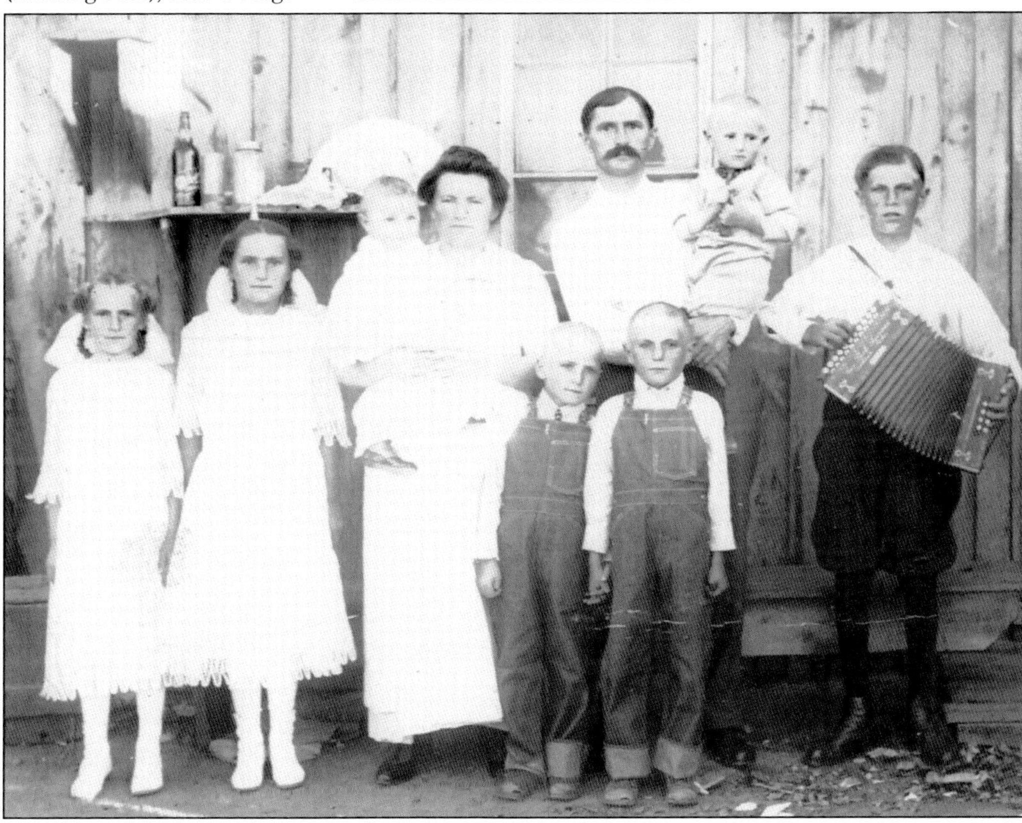

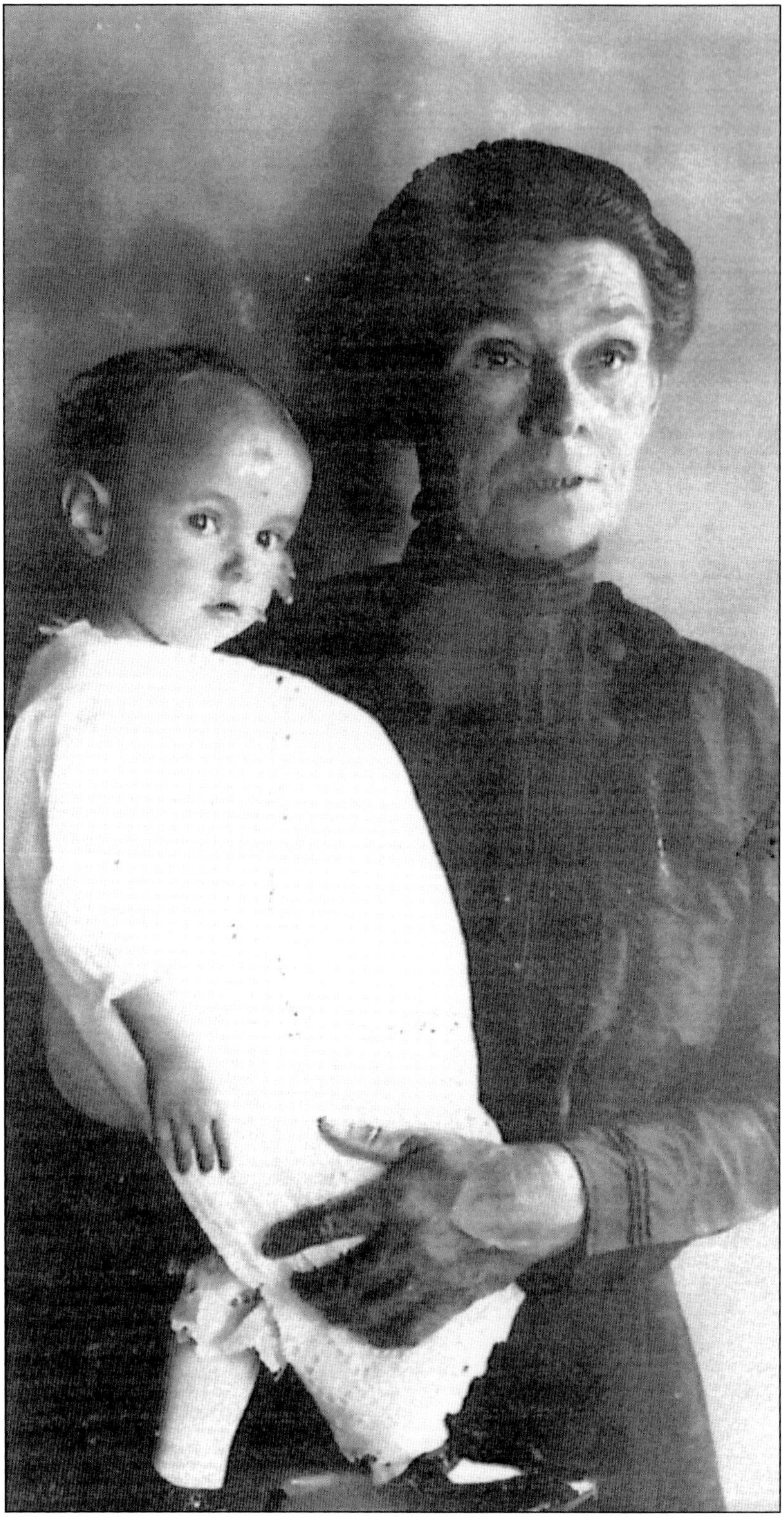

Quinnie Priscilla Larrimore came to Humboldt in a covered wagon. She is seen here with baby Joanna Bybee. The Bybee family lived for many years in Humboldt. Retired schoolteacher Phil Bybee still lives in Dewey with his wife.

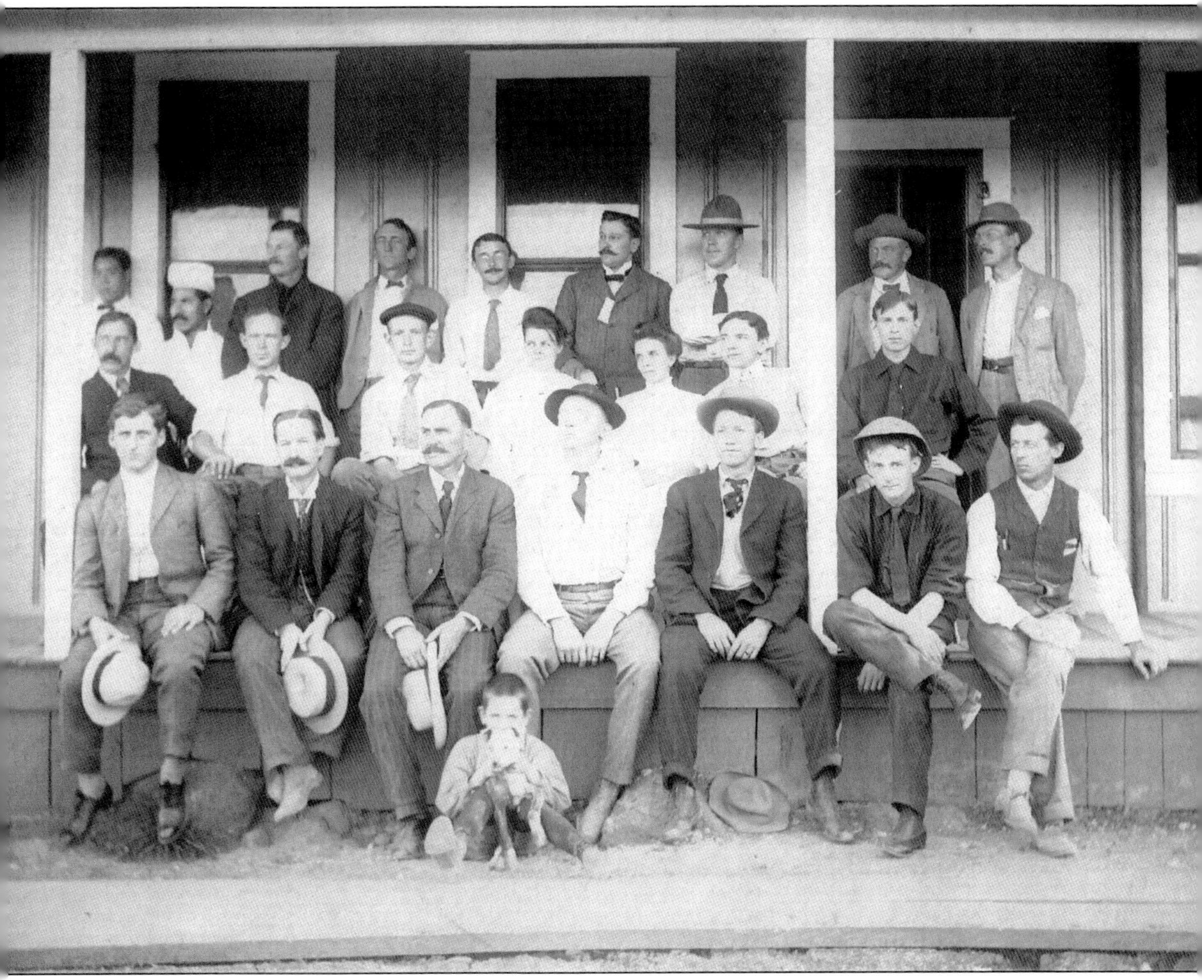

This is a photograph of early Humboldt businessmen. No other information is known about this interesting gathering.

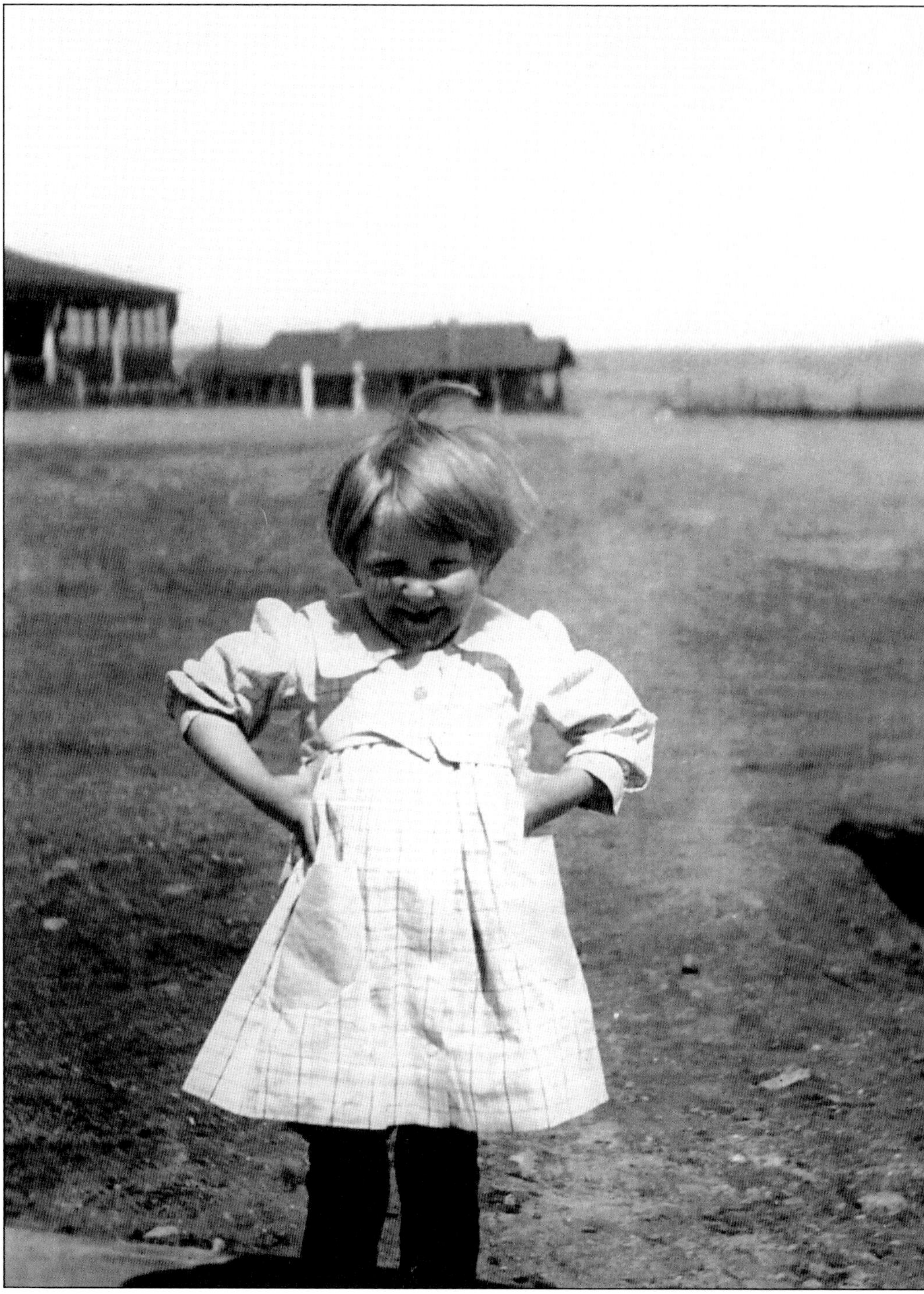

Vivian Riggs poses in Humboldt in 1917.

Vivian Riggs, seen here outside the Humboldt Pool Room and Hotel, is already prepared to start driving.

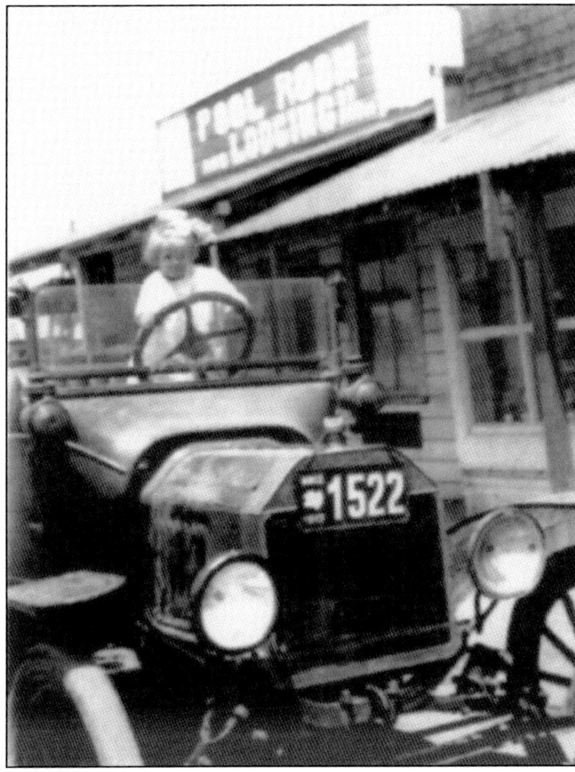

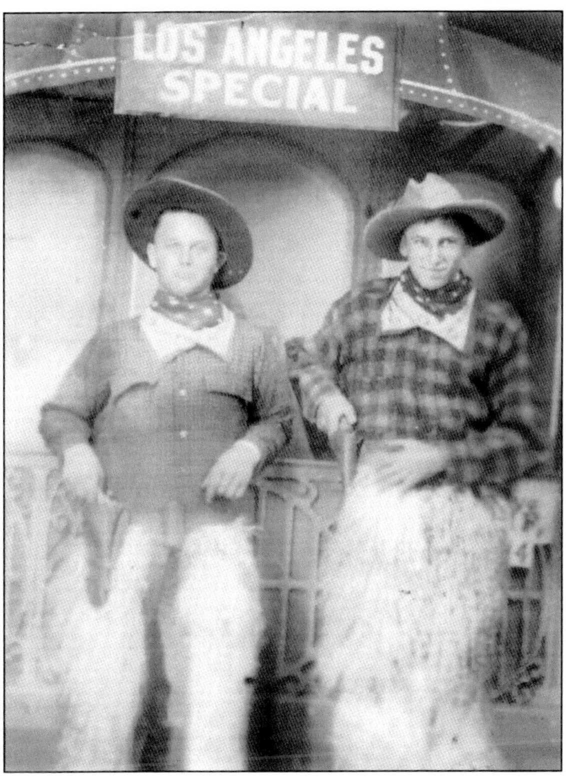

Local residents Joe Staranick (left) and Rudy Chemas ham it up in the 1920s on the Los Angeles Special at the San Fernando ranch of Verg Chemas's brother.

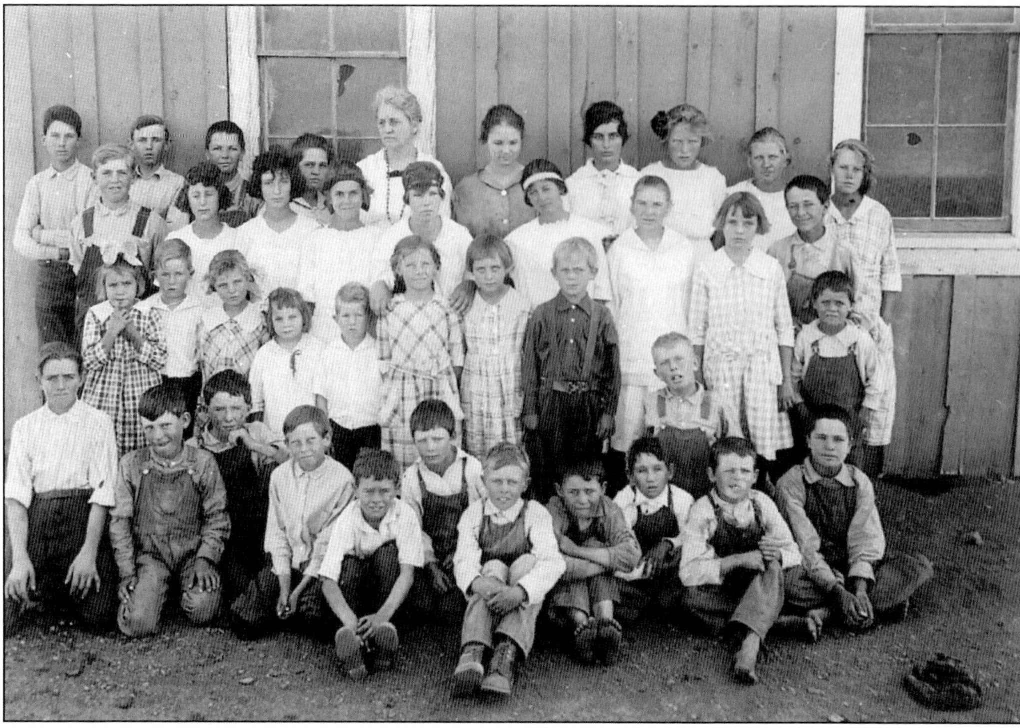

Humboldt School students are shown here in 1917. Perry Henderson is in the first row, second from left. Other notables in this photograph are Hank, Horace, Rose, and Gene Maders; Alfred and Vergie Human; and Ron Herdress.

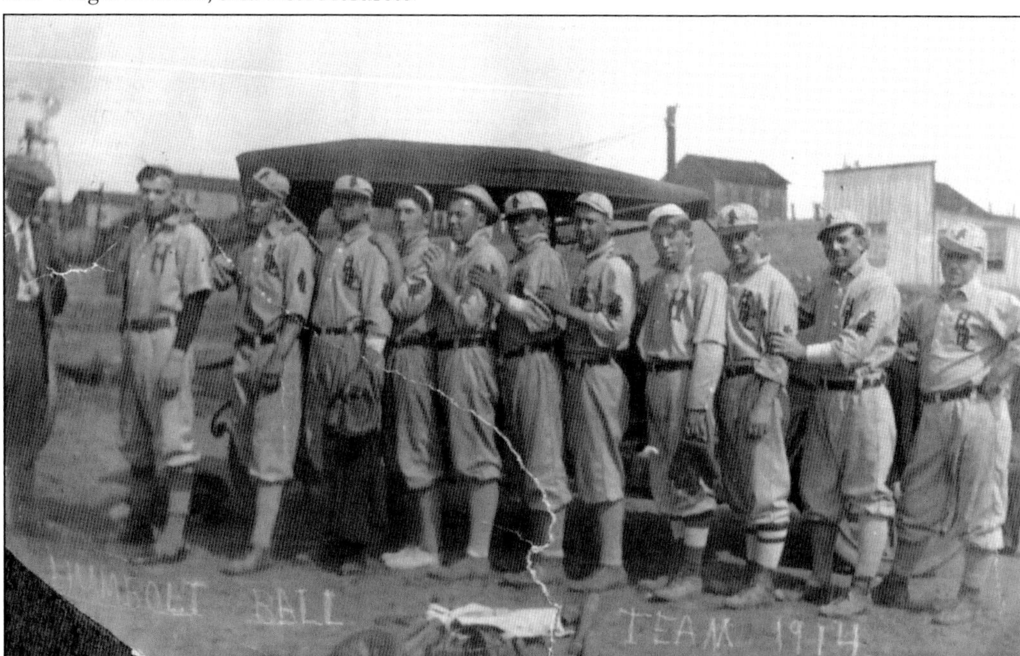

The Humboldt baseball team poses for a photograph in 1914. Baseball was always the favorite sport of locals, and teams from the area were usually very successful in regional competitions.

Charles Wingfield was the owner of the Wingfield stores in Prescott and Humboldt. The post office was located in the store itself. Wingfield's was the nicest store in town, attracting residents from all around the surrounding areas.

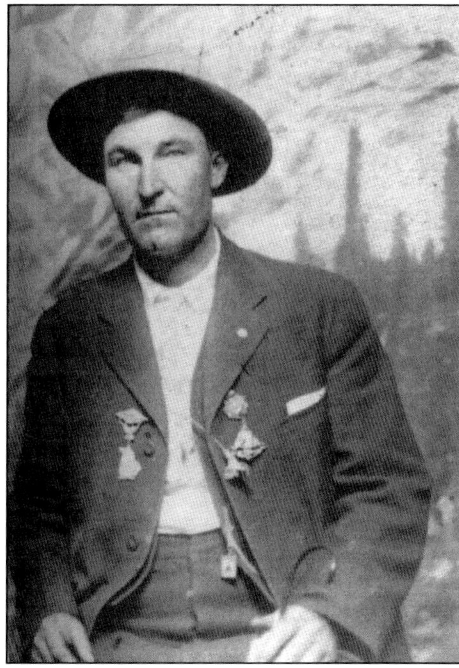

The Wingfield's store, located on Main Street in Humboldt, is pictured here in 1917. On one occasion, the Wingfield stores in Humboldt and Huron were robbed at the same time. The robbers used nitroglycerin, believed to have been obtained from a local mining operation, to open the safes.

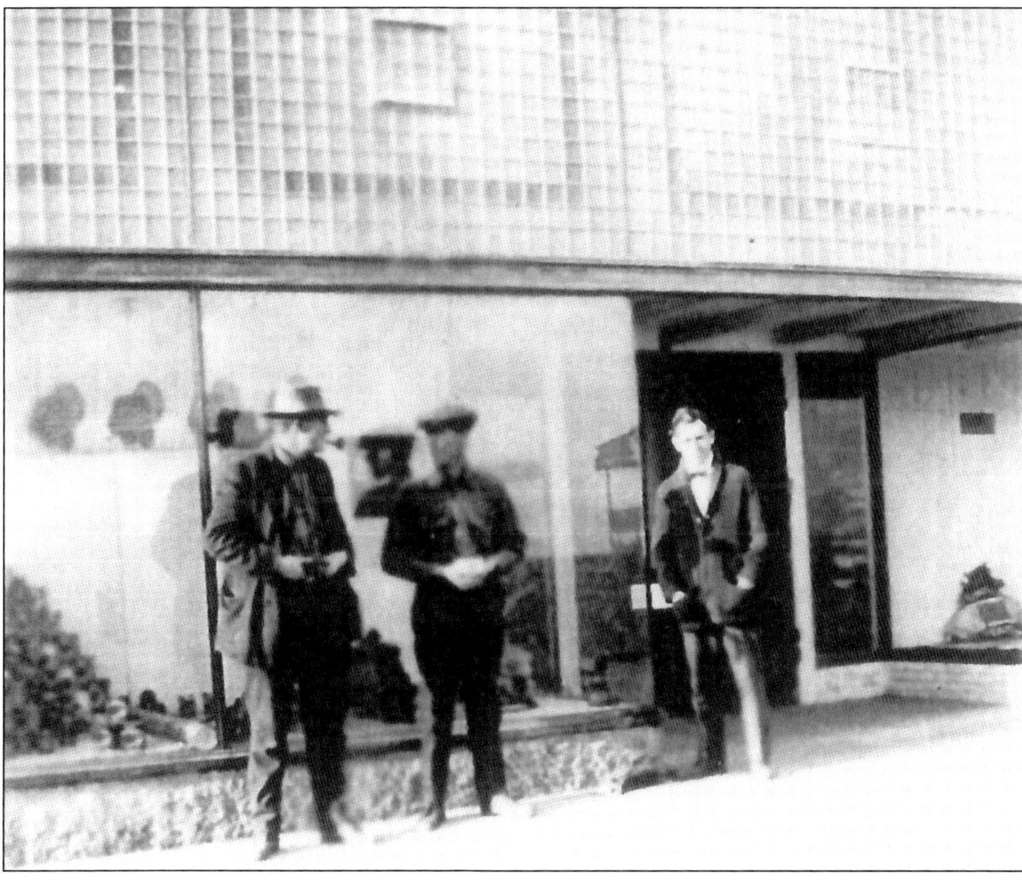

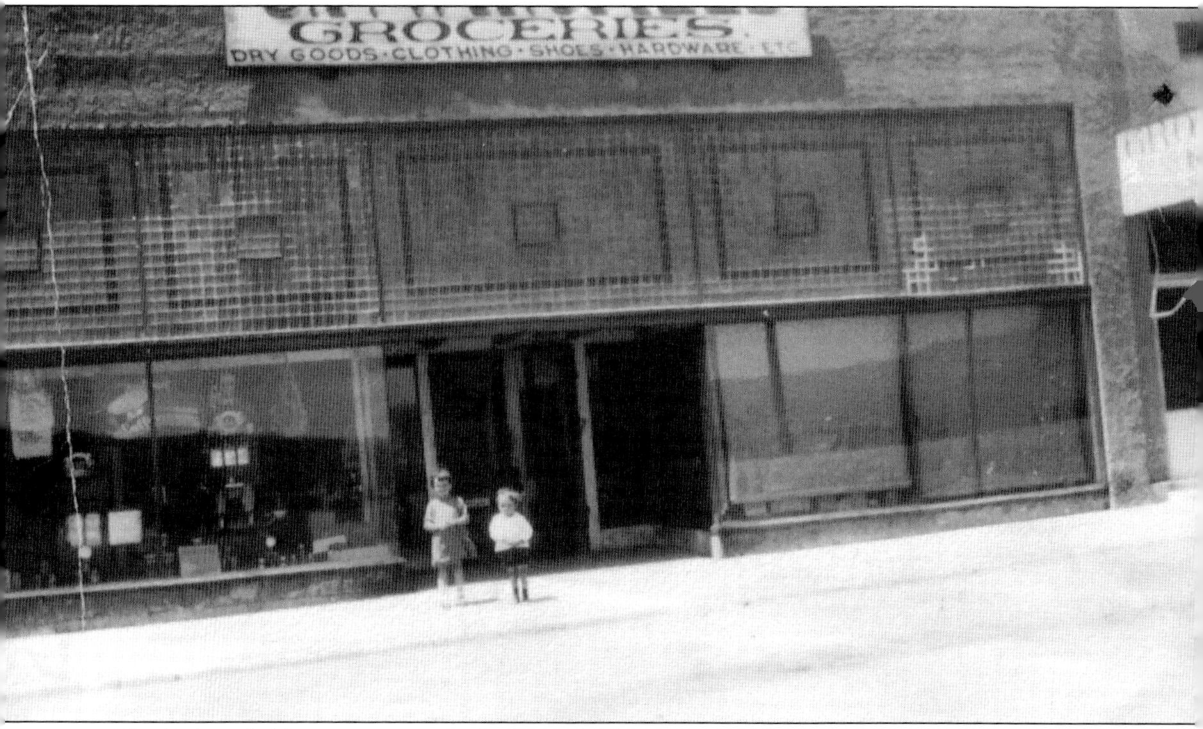

The Bybee children pose outside the Wingfield store.

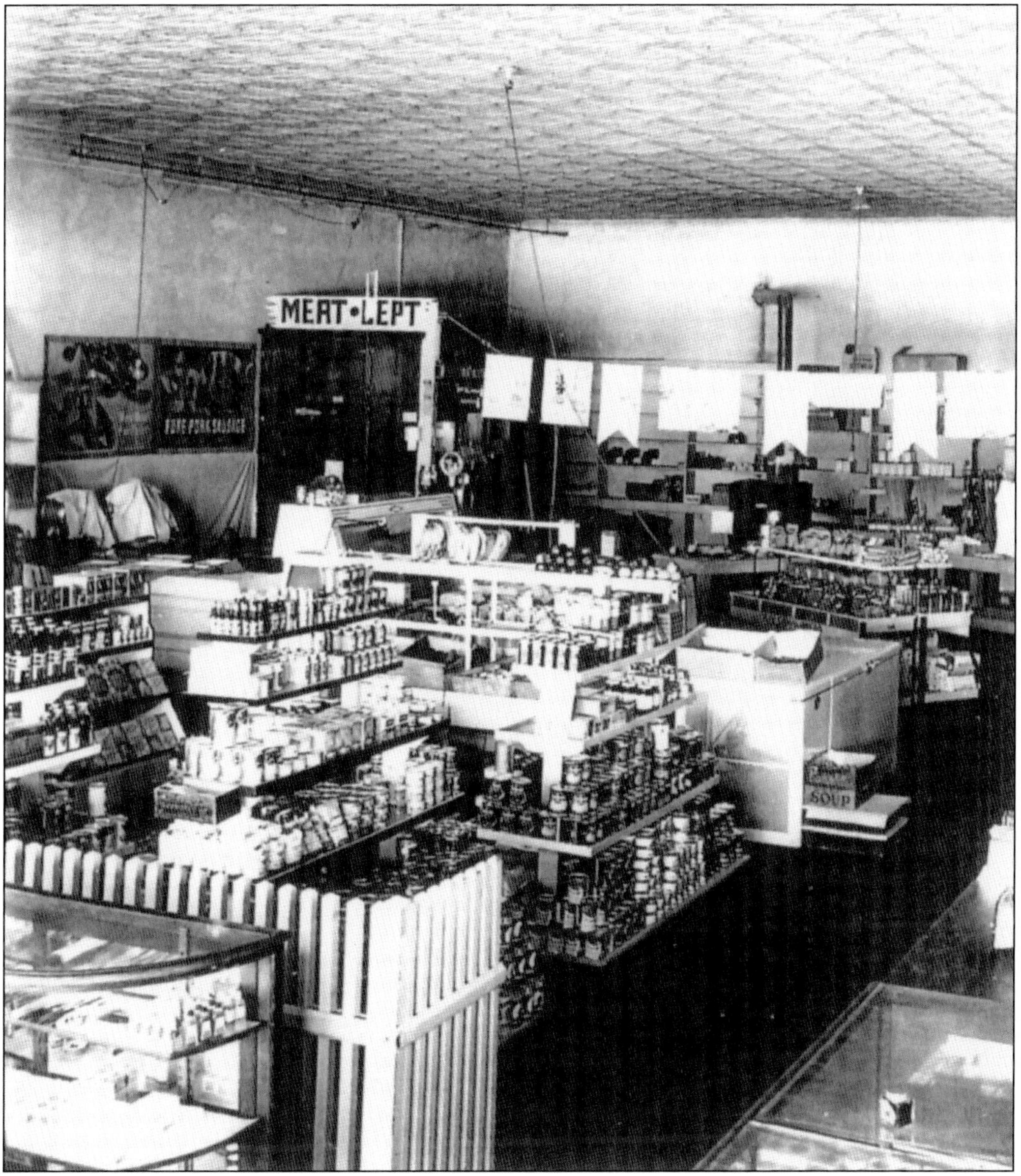

This is a photograph of the interior of Wingfield's store. Pristine organization and management are evident.

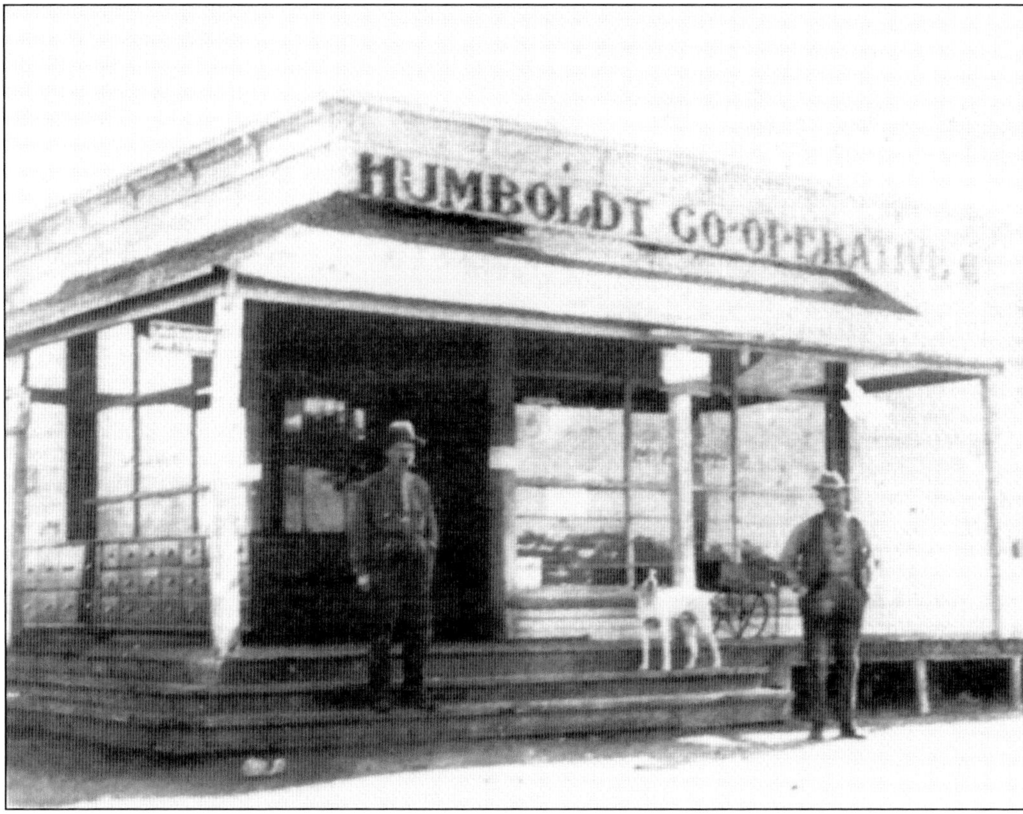

This is the Humboldt Co-Operative, seen at the turn of the century. It was begun by the Iron King mine as the smelter store, offering goods and services to local residents and employees.

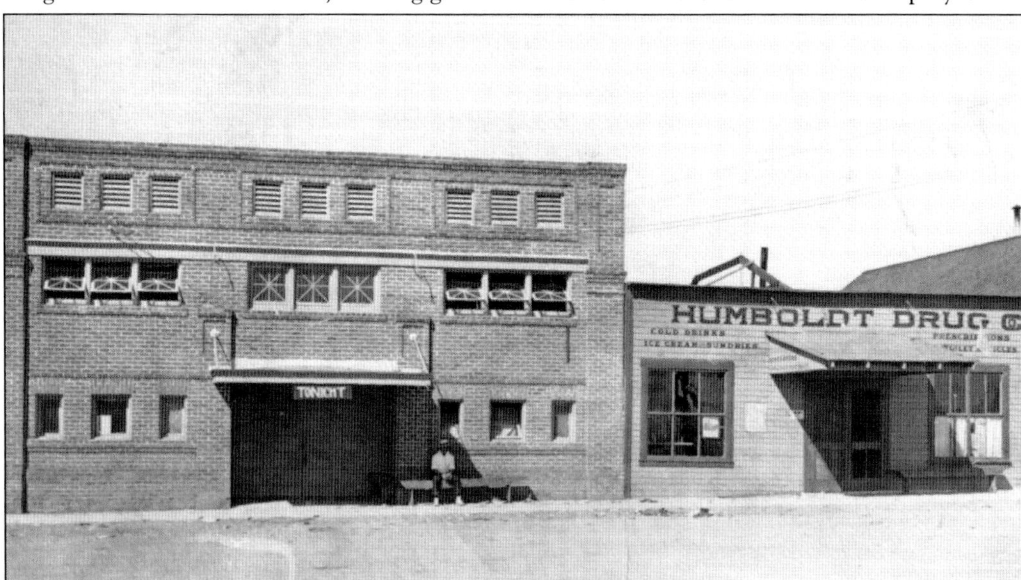

Pictured here are the Humboldt Theater and Humboldt Drug Store. Originally staging live plays, the theater showed silent films when they came into existence.

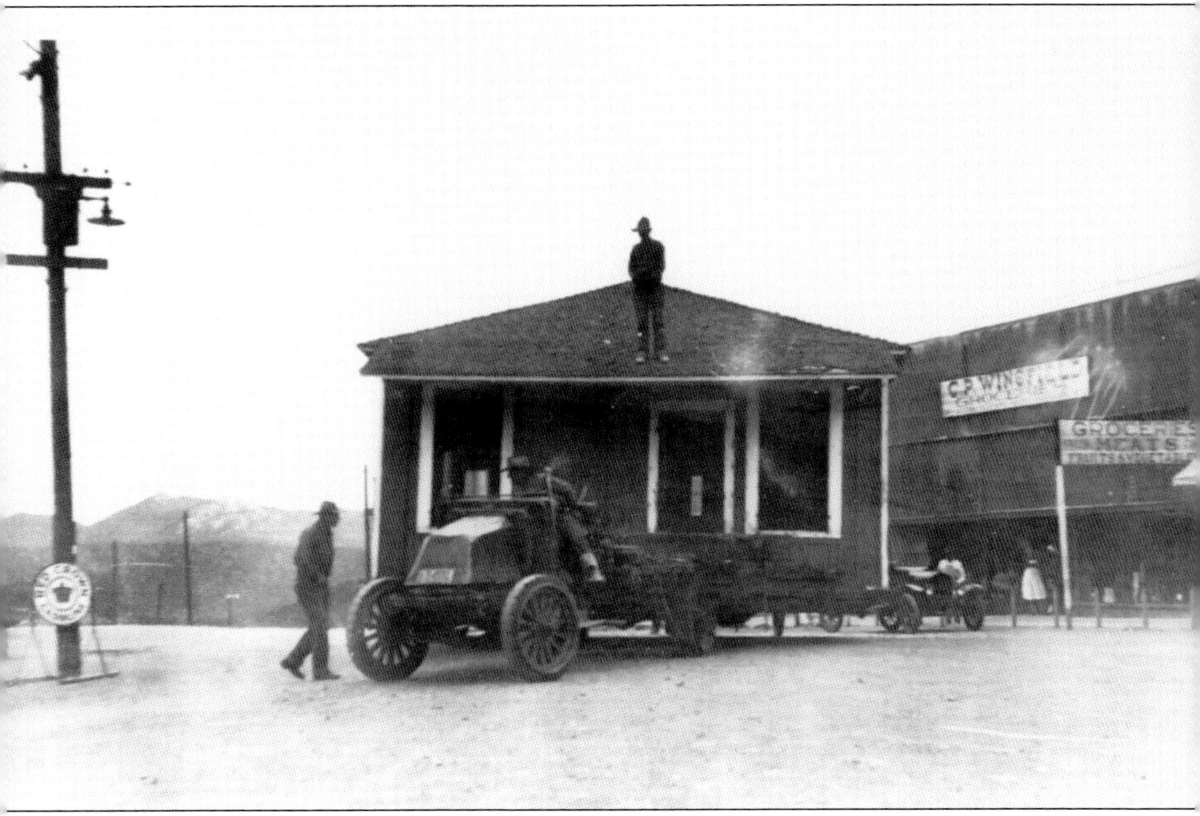

Pictured here are men moving a building into place on Main Street in Humboldt in the early 1900s. Most buildings were constructed on site, but if an existing building nearby was usable and available, early residents certainly seized the opportunity to do so.

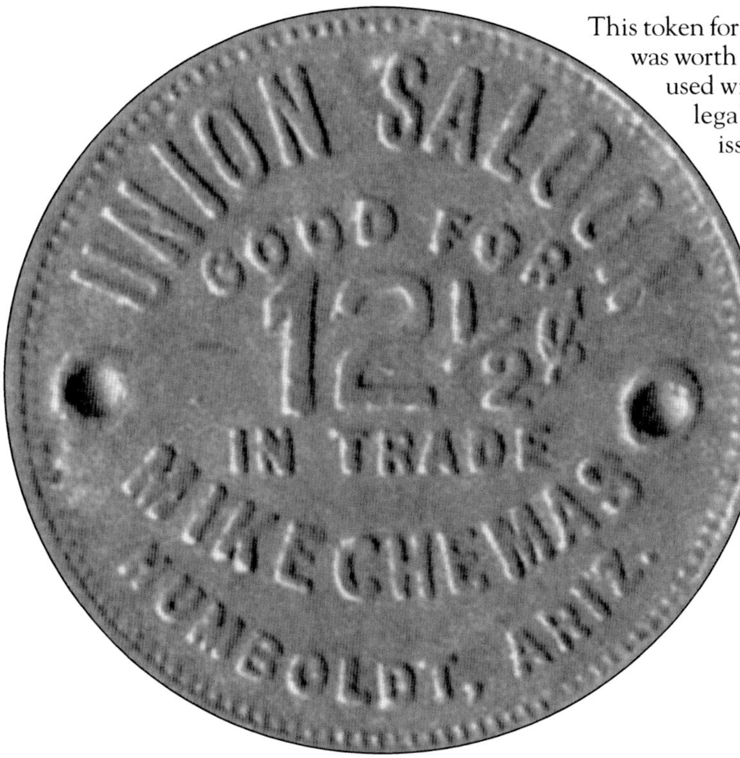

This token for the Chemas Union Saloon was worth 12.5¢ (one bit). Tokens were used widely in the area. They were legal tender only at the store issuing them.

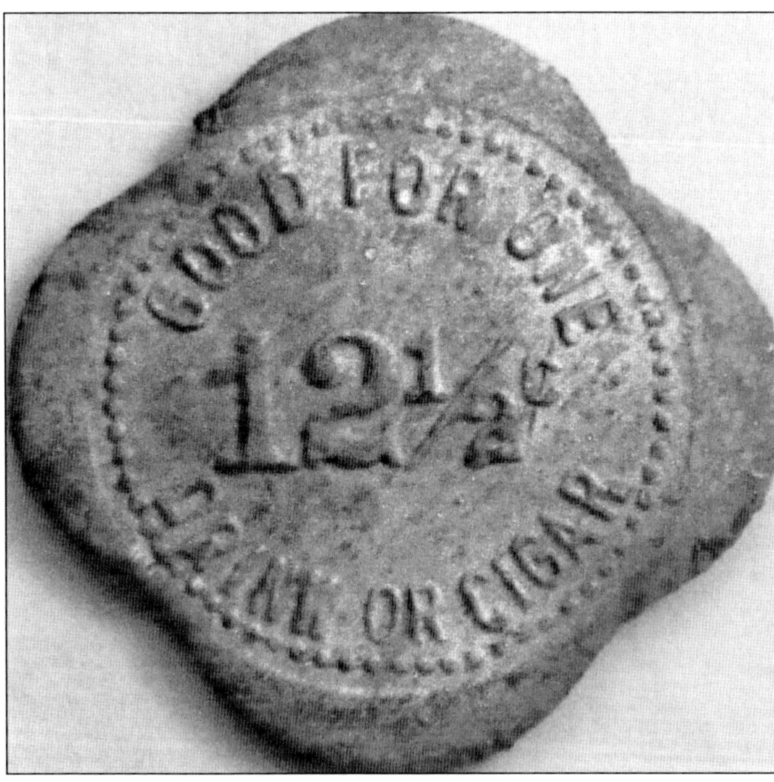

This Chemas token was good for one drink or a cigar. The term "two bits," the equivalent of a quarter, came from these widely distributed tokens.

This photograph shows a Shumate token. It is a piece from John Charles Young's private collection.

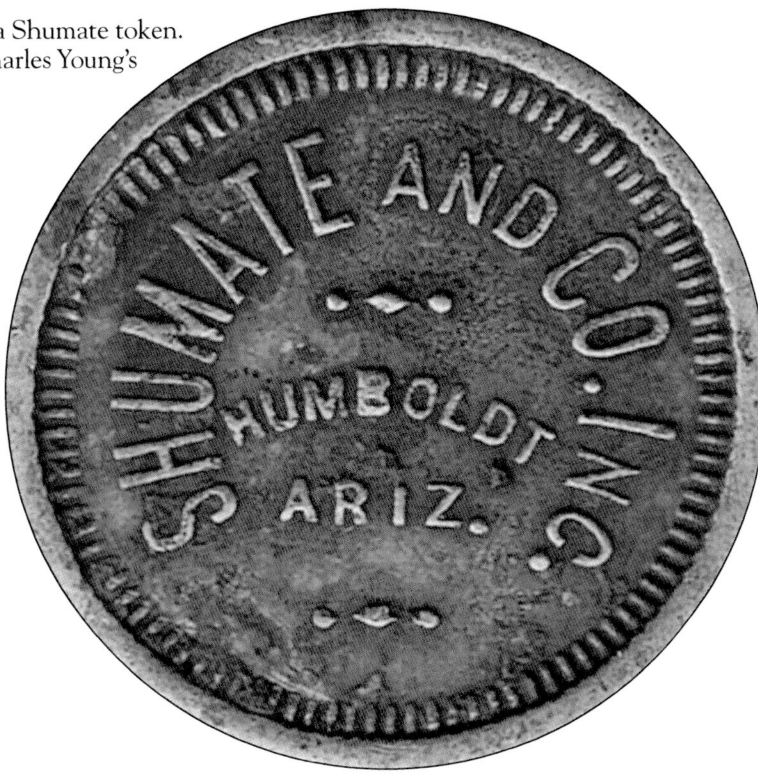

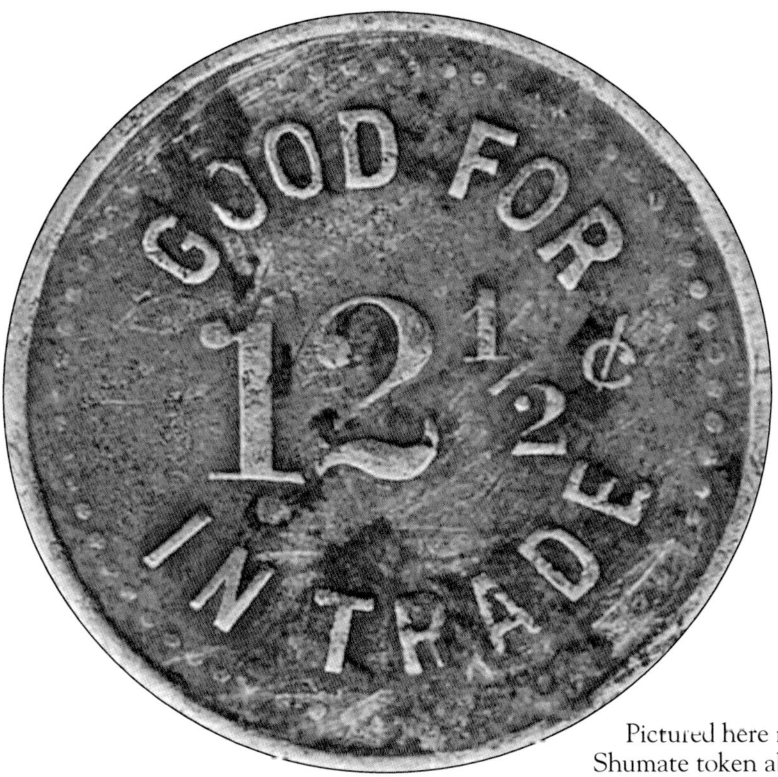

Pictured here is the reverse side of the Shumate token above.

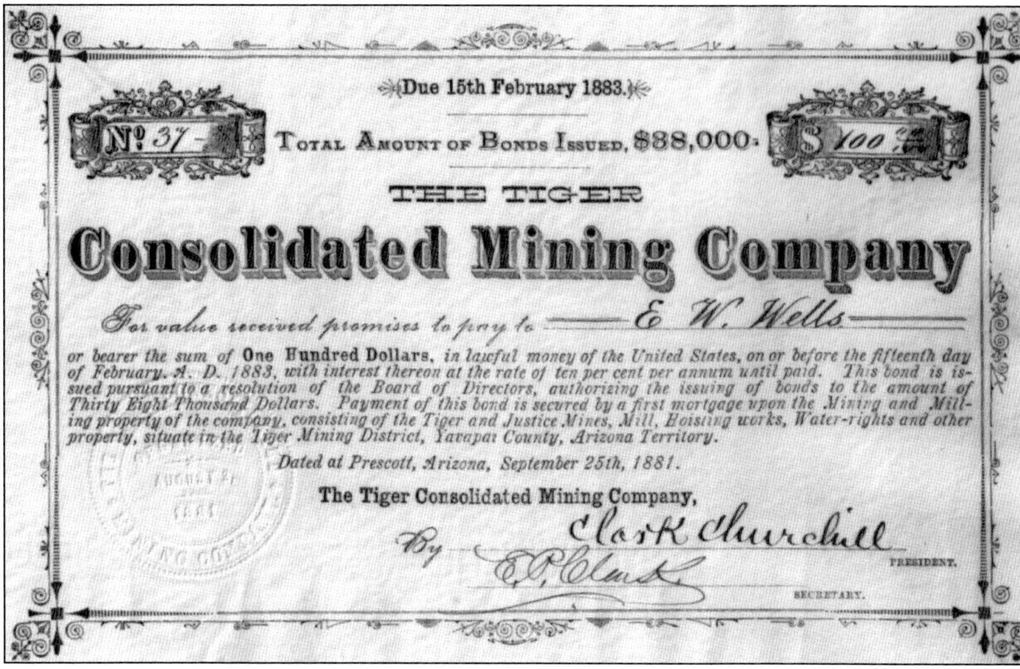

Due 15th February 1883.

Nº 37 — TOTAL AMOUNT OF BONDS ISSUED, $88,000. $ 100

THE TIGER

Consolidated Mining Company

For value received promises to pay to E. W. Wells or bearer the sum of One Hundred Dollars, in lawful money of the United States, on or before the fifteenth day of February. A. D. 1883, with interest thereon at the rate of ten per cent per annum until paid. This bond is issued pursuant to a resolution of the Board of Directors, authorizing the issuing of bonds to the amount of Thirty Eight Thousand Dollars. Payment of this bond is secured by a first mortgage upon the Mining and Milling property of the company, consisting of the Tiger and Justice Mines, Mill, Hoisting works, Water-rights and other property, situate in the Tiger Mining District, Yavapai County, Arizona Territory.

Dated at Prescott, Arizona, September 25th, 1881.

The Tiger Consolidated Mining Company,

By Clark Churchill PRESIDENT.

E. P. Clark SECRETARY.

This is an example of a Consolidated Mining Company bond from 1881. A widely used source of capital to start and run the mines, bonds were also very risky, due to the volatility of the mining business.

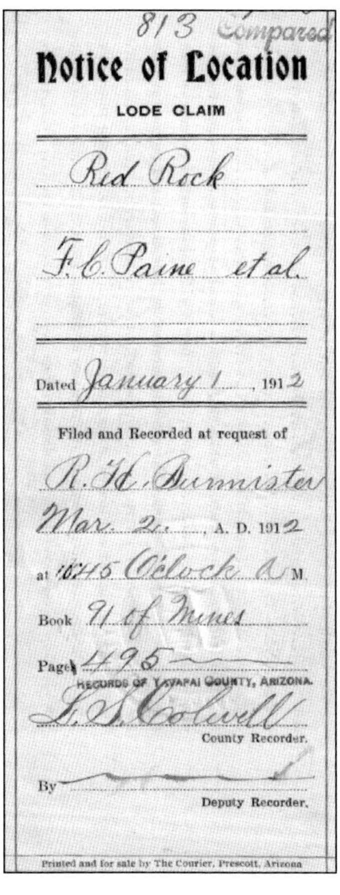

813 Compared

Notice of Location

LODE CLAIM

Red Rock

F. C. Paine et al.

Dated January 1, 1912

Filed and Recorded at request of

R. H. Burmister

Mar. 2, A. D. 1912

at 10:45 O'clock a M.

Book 91 of Mines

Page 495

RECORDS OF YAVAPAI COUNTY, ARIZONA.

L. S. Colwell

County Recorder.

By

Deputy Recorder.

Printed and for sale by The Courier, Prescott, Arizona

This is a 1912 Red Rock lode claim. Countless claims were made in the area, many of which were sold or bartered for other items when the resources weren't available to mine them.

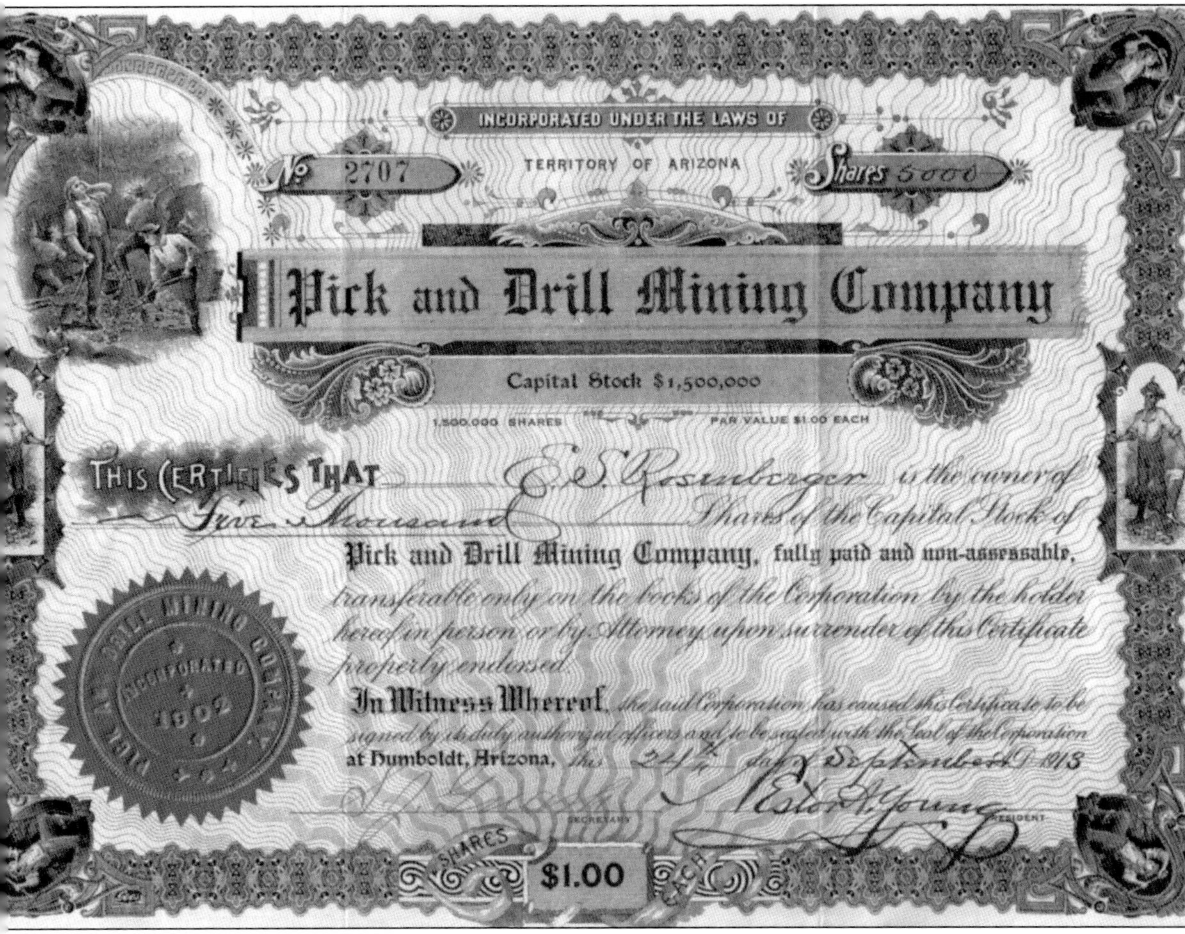

INCORPORATED UNDER THE LAWS OF

TERRITORY OF ARIZONA

No 2707 Shares 5000

Pick and Drill Mining Company

Capital Stock $1,500,000

1,500,000 SHARES PAR VALUE $1.00 EACH

THIS CERTIFIES THAT E. S. Rosenberger is the owner of Five Thousand Shares of the Capital Stock of Pick and Drill Mining Company, fully paid and non-assessable, transferable only on the books of the Corporation by the holder hereof in person or by Attorney upon surrender of this Certificate properly endorsed.

In Witness Whereof, the said Corporation has caused this Certificate to be signed by its duly authorized officers and to be sealed with the Seal of the Corporation at Humboldt, Arizona, this 24th day of September A.D. 1913

SECRETARY Nestor Young PRESIDENT

INCORPORATED 1902

SHARES $1.00 EACH

This is a 1913 certificate for 5,000 shares of Pick and Drill Mining stock. The company's president, Nestor Young, was a great-uncle of current Dewey-Humboldt Historical Society vice president John Charles Young.

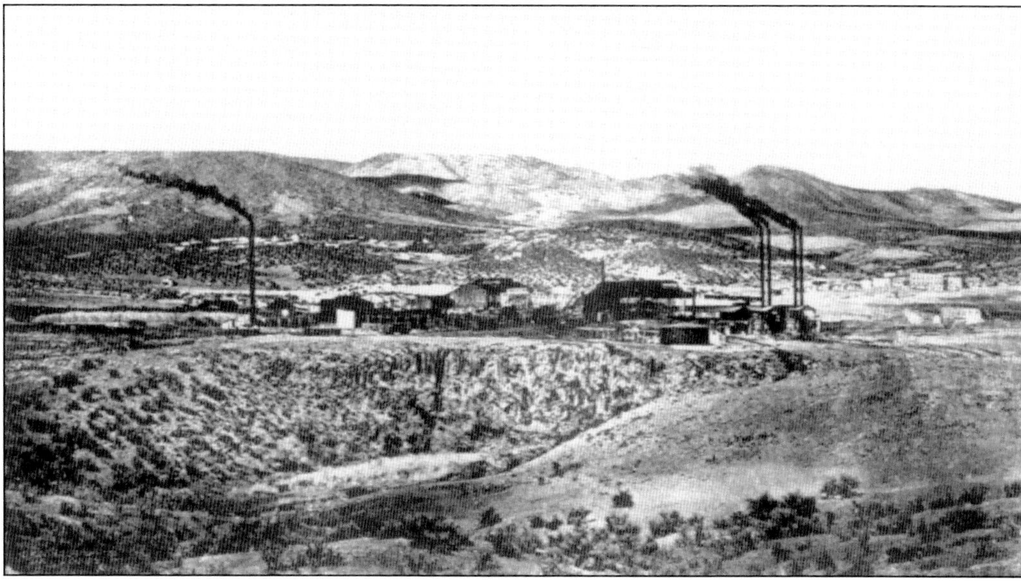

The Humboldt smelter is seen here in full operation sometime before 1905. Among the larger mines in the area were the Carroll on Yarber; Pick and Drill and Big Ledge on Brushy Wash; and the Bowman, Shylock, Iron King, and McCabe. There were many smaller ones as well. These mines created a need for a large smelter to refine the ore.

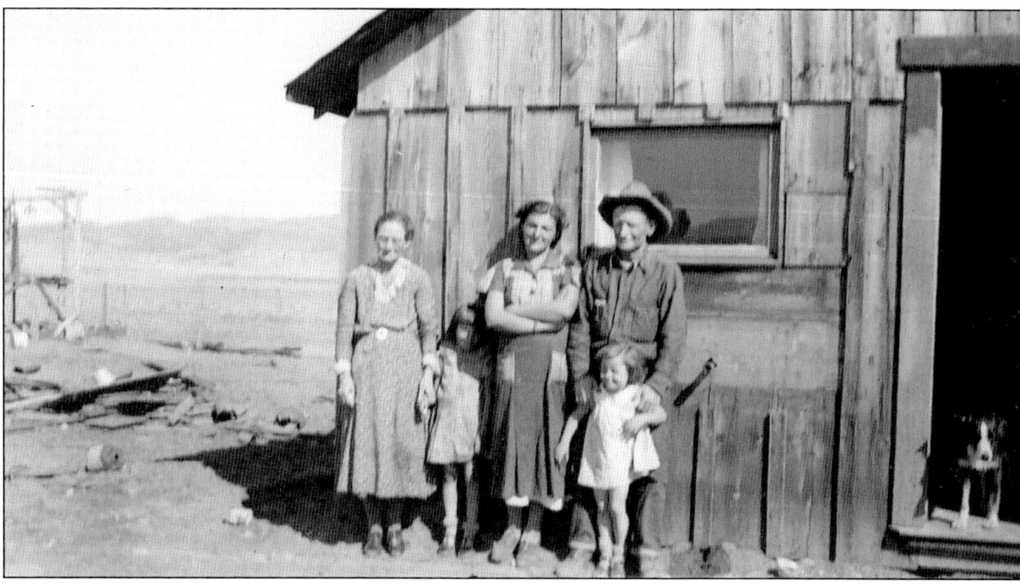

Jane Human became a widow when her husband passed away. She was left with four young boys and a ranch to run by herself. Unable to make her yearly tithing, her own grandfather, Parson Bristow, excommunicated her from the Lutheran church in the Verde Valley. This essentially cut her off from the close-knit society. She worked as a laundress in Cherry for the miners. Her boys carried the water by hand to help her earn her keep. Later, she married into the Jones family, whose members are seen here with Jane Human (left). They are, from left to right, Mary Lou, Mary, Edd, and Betty. The family never stepped foot in church again, preferring to do their worship and Bible study at home. Betty's grandson Jim Jones, however, founded the Humboldt Baptist Church and recently retired after over 30 years of service.

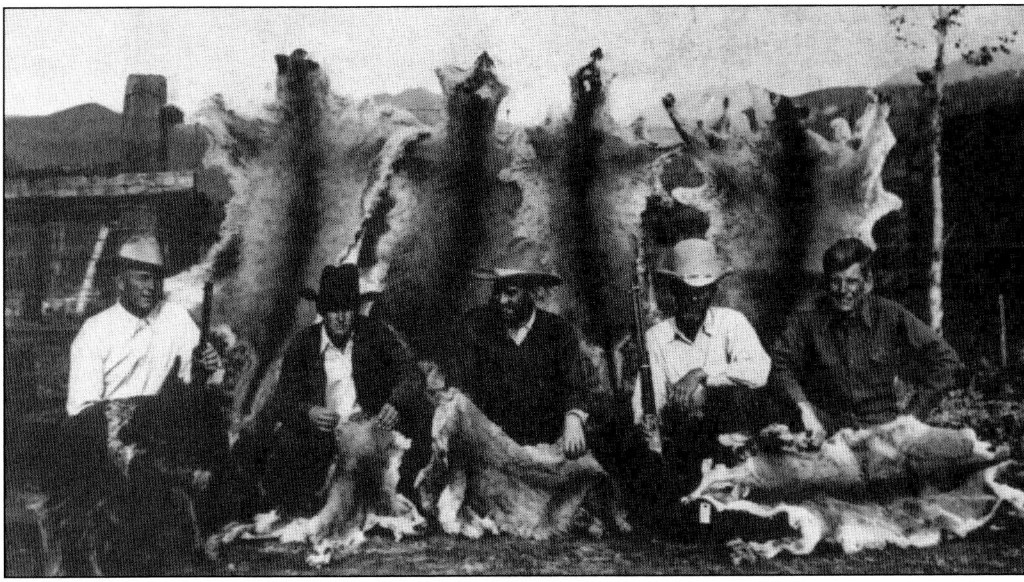

Giles Goswick (far left), one of the best lion hunters in the West, took a party of hunters into the hills of Yavapai County, with good results. Lions were known to attack cattle and young deer, so cattlemen and hunters joined together to exterminate them. Goswick, a government hunter, also sought mountain lions much of his life.

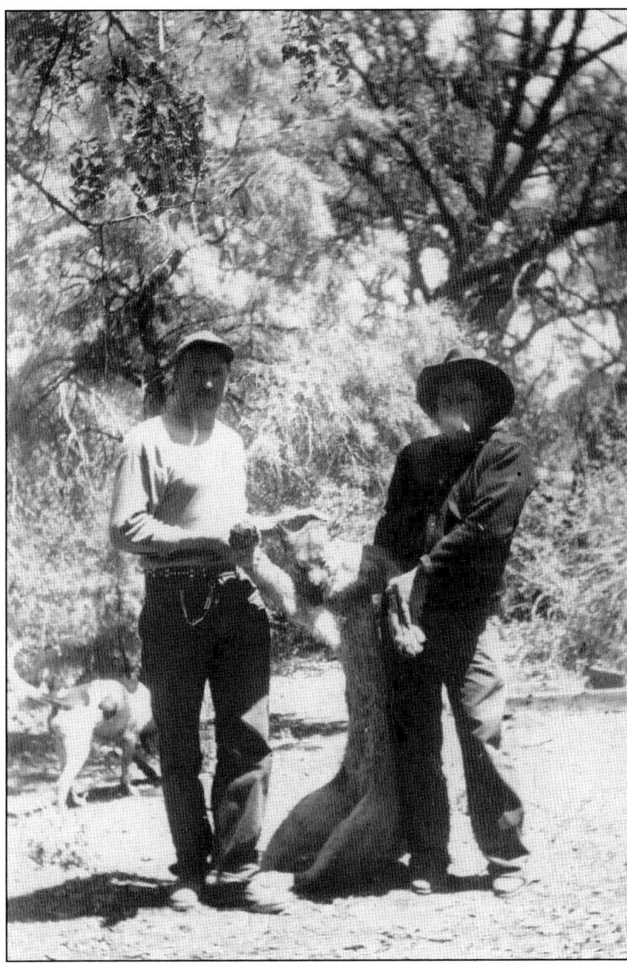

Giles Goswick (left) and a friend are pictured with a mountain lion. In the 1930s, a lion hunter got $135 a month plus food. By the 1950s, they received $95 for a female and $100 for a tom. The threat to area ranching was greater than the call to preserve these animals.

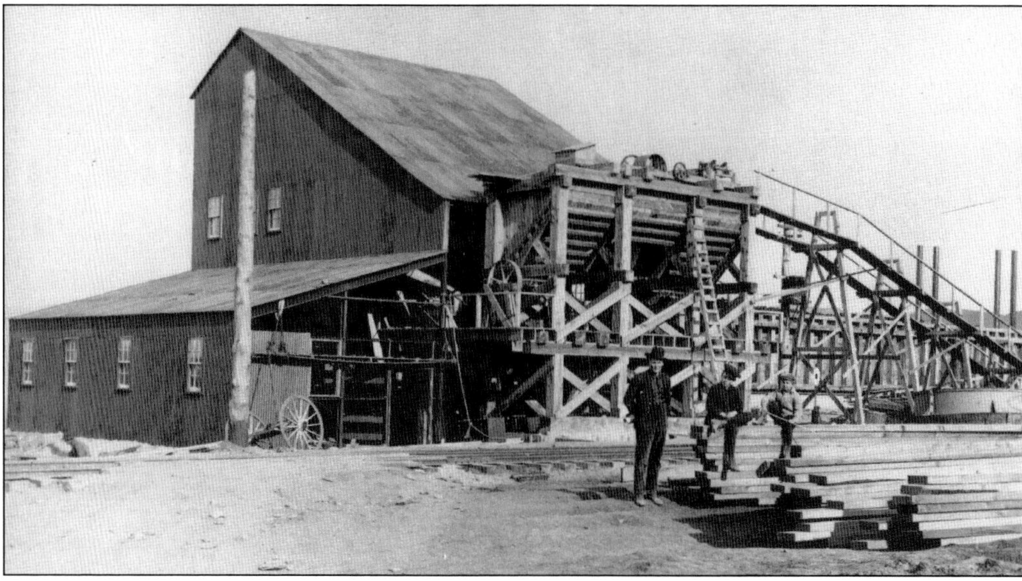

This is the Pick and Drill Mine. Fresh lumber shows the constant growth the mine had in the early days. This was once among the most successful mines in the area.

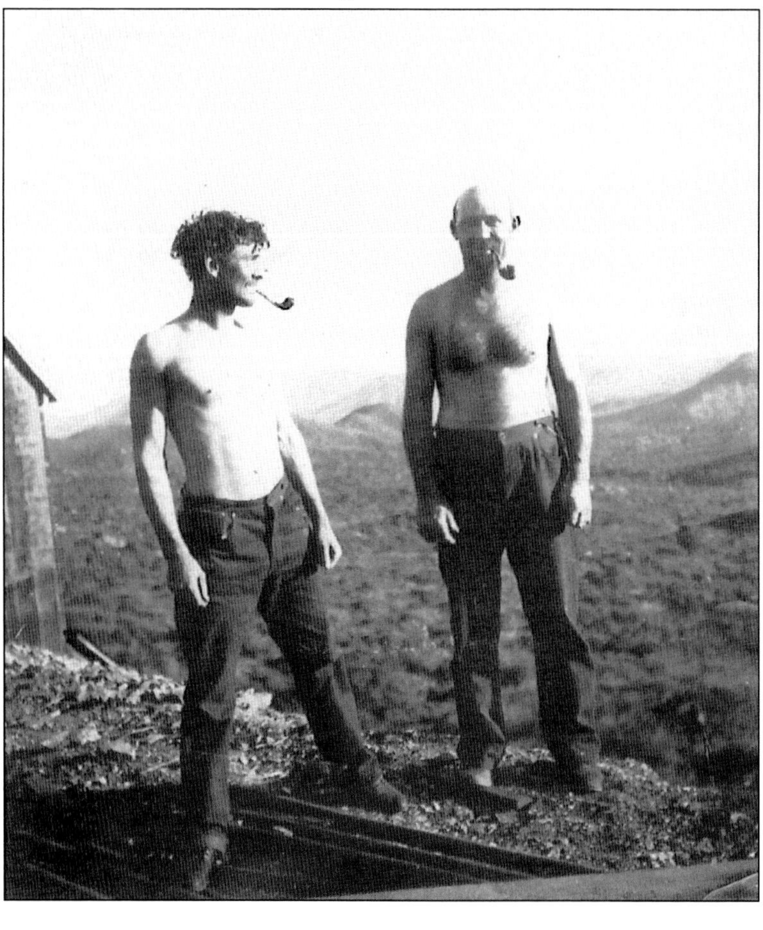

These Humboldt mine workers are blowing off steam after a long shift. Miners were known to play as hard as they worked, many spending their money at the bars and brothels on Prescott Street.

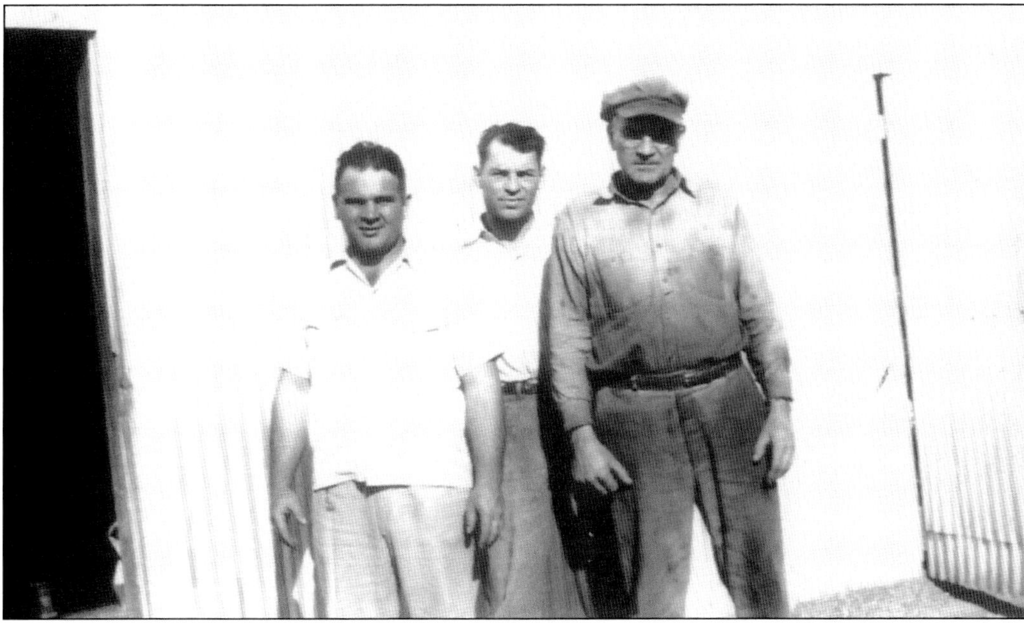

The Humboldt smelter workers pictured here are, from left to right, Walt Statler, Doug Thurman, and Joe Kaulok.

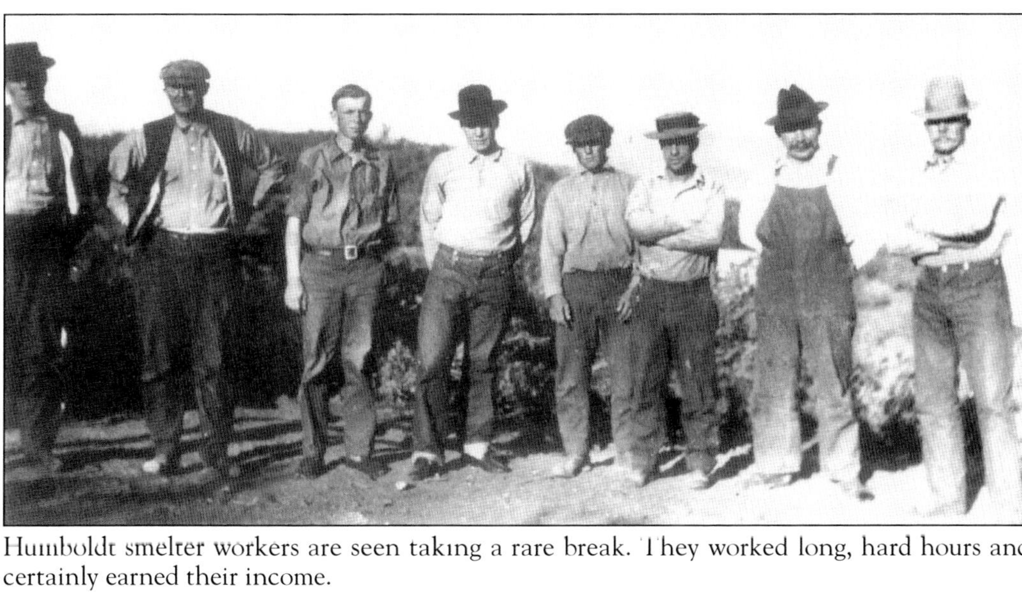

Humboldt smelter workers are seen taking a rare break. They worked long, hard hours and certainly earned their income.

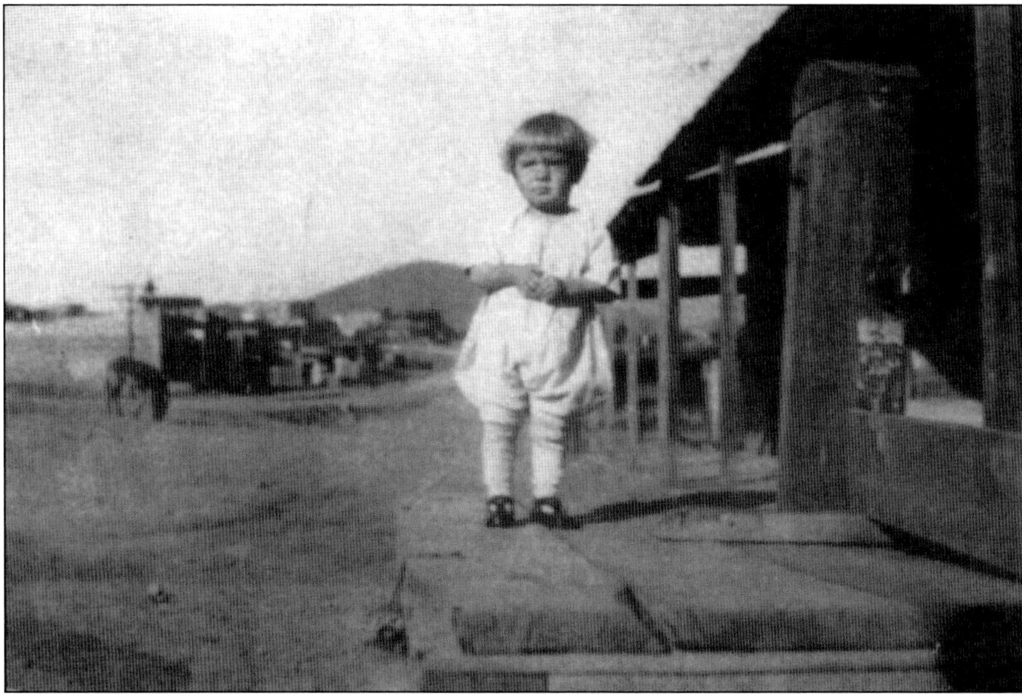

Mabel Brose Batt poses on the steps of her family's store, located on Prescott Street, in the early 1900s.

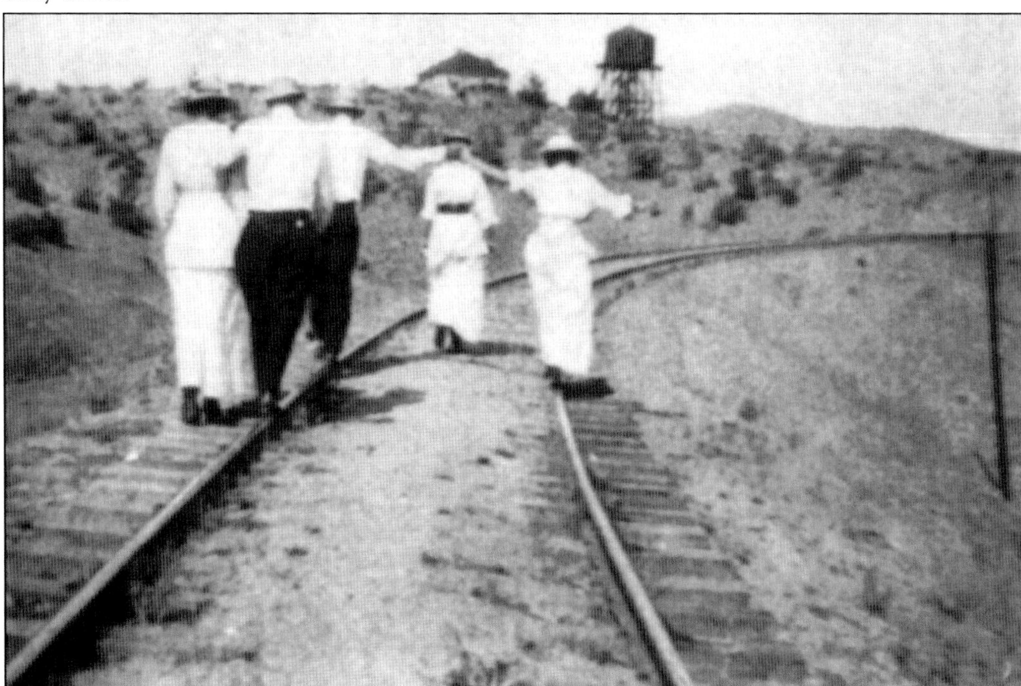

These people are walking along train tracks in Humboldt in 1912. The circumstances of this well-known photograph have never been determined, but it illustrates the carefree spirit of many of the youth who grew up around Humboldt.

The Humboldt station is seen here in 1912. This stop was added a few years after the Cherry Creek station was established, due to the growing number of passengers in the Humboldt area.

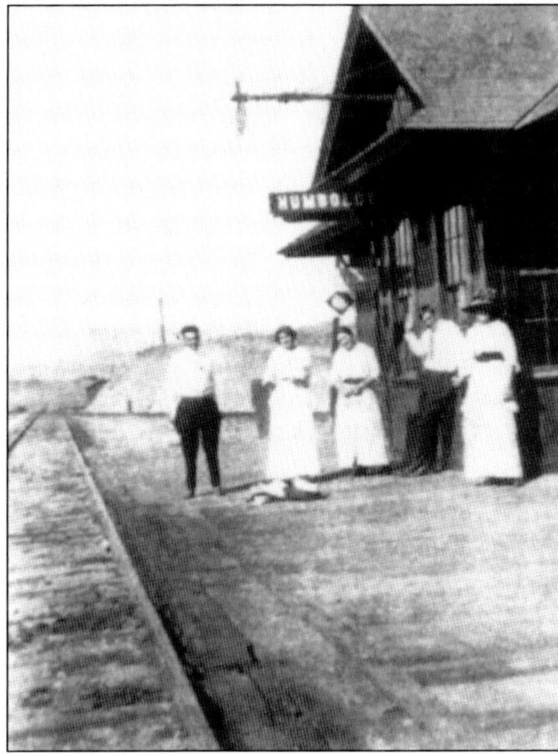

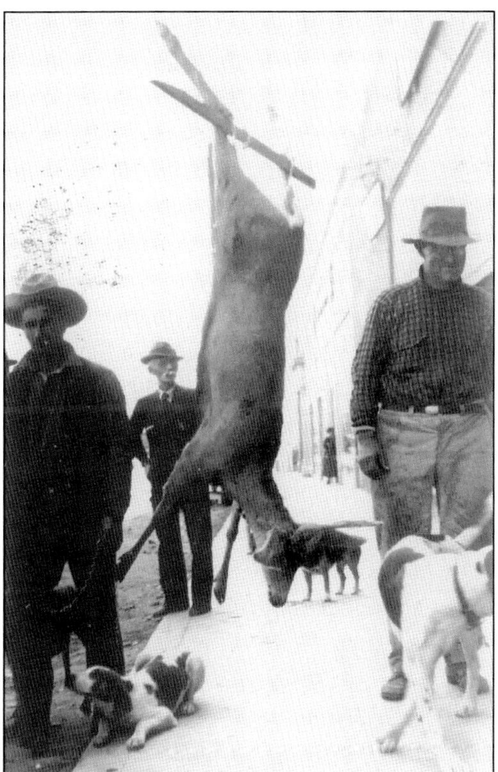

A member of the Goswick family (left) poses with friends in front of Wingfield's store following a successful hunt.

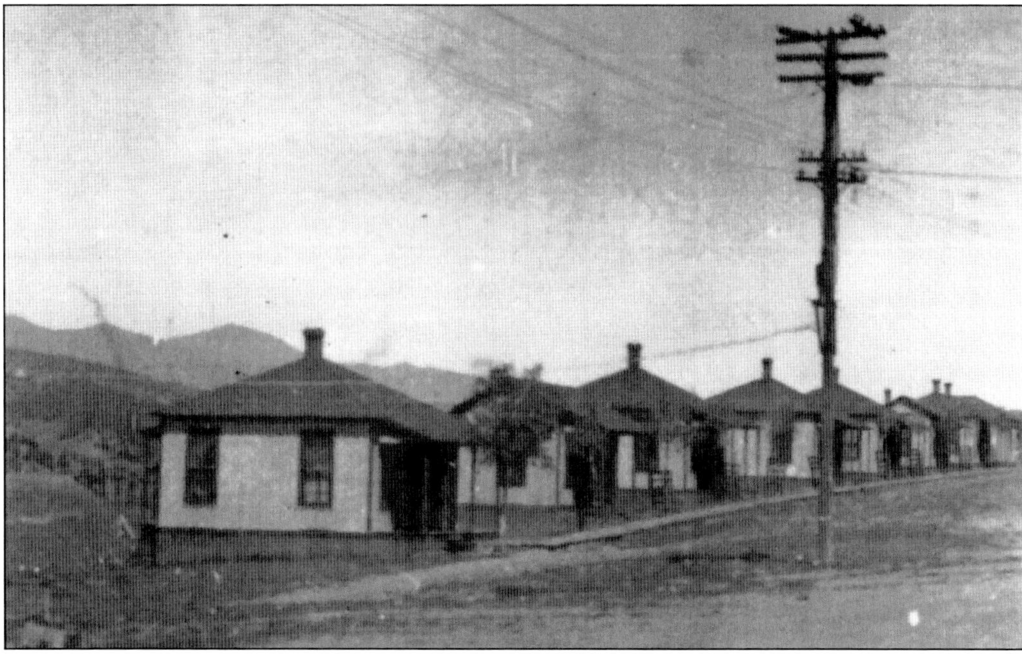

Shown here is mine-worker housing on Prescott Street in Humboldt. At the turn of the 20th century, the average house cost about $100, with some being advertised for as low as $20. Still, many mine workers lived in tents while they decided whether the mine job would be a long-term position. "Tent lots" were still available decades later.

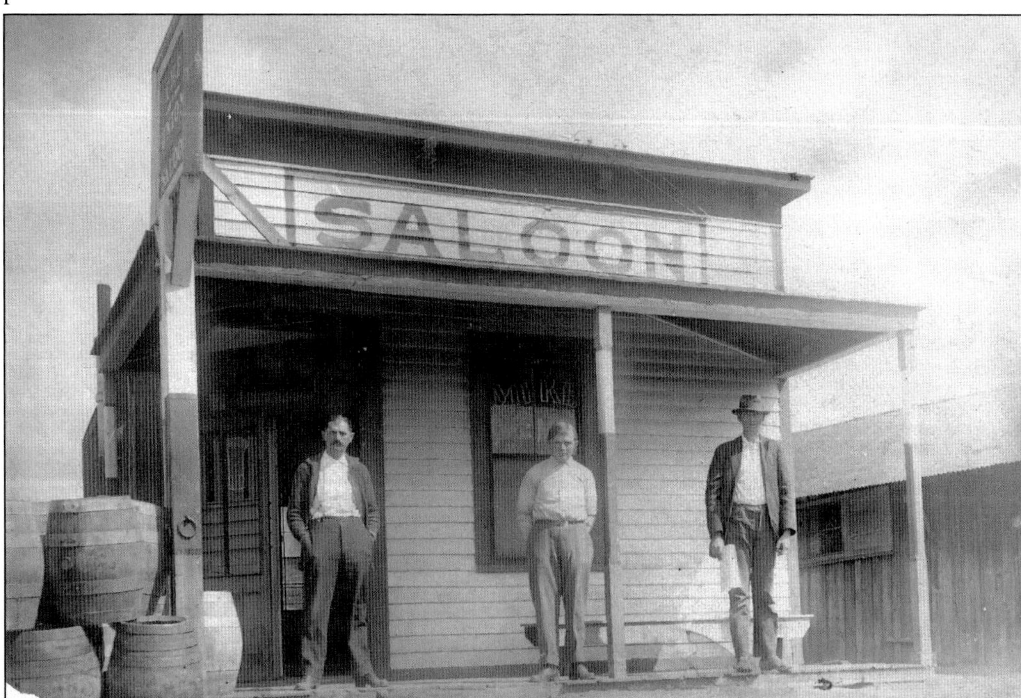

This is the first Chemas bar, on Prescott Street. It was listed on the roster of bars as early as 1911. The Chemas family had four bars in the area, including Billy Jack's, still open along Highway 69.

Seen here is the second Chemas bar, also on Prescott Street. All bars had to be located on Prescott Street, since bars and brothels weren't allowed on Main Street.

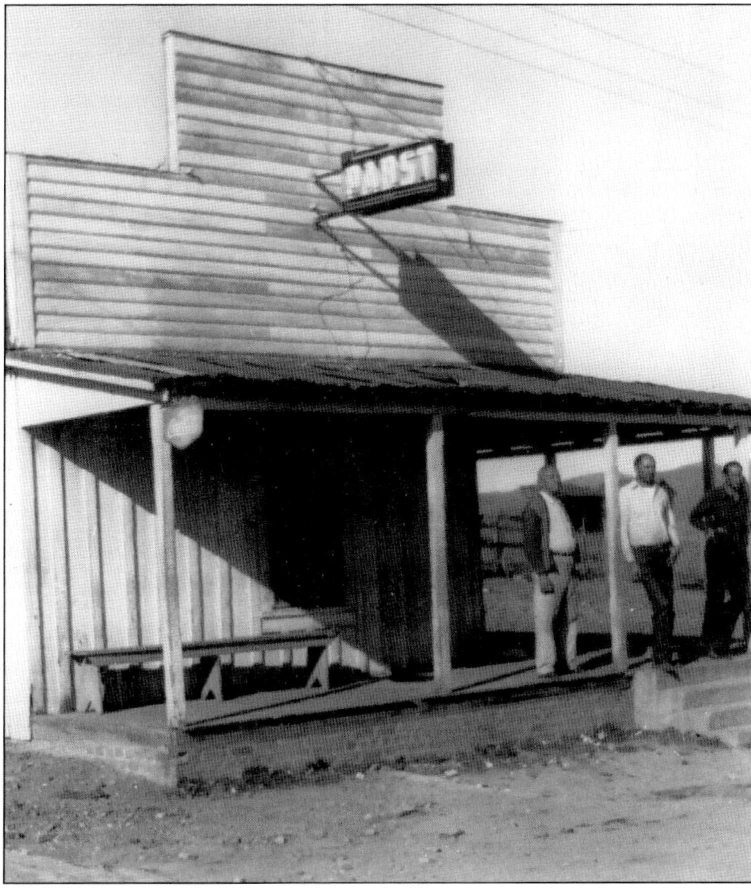

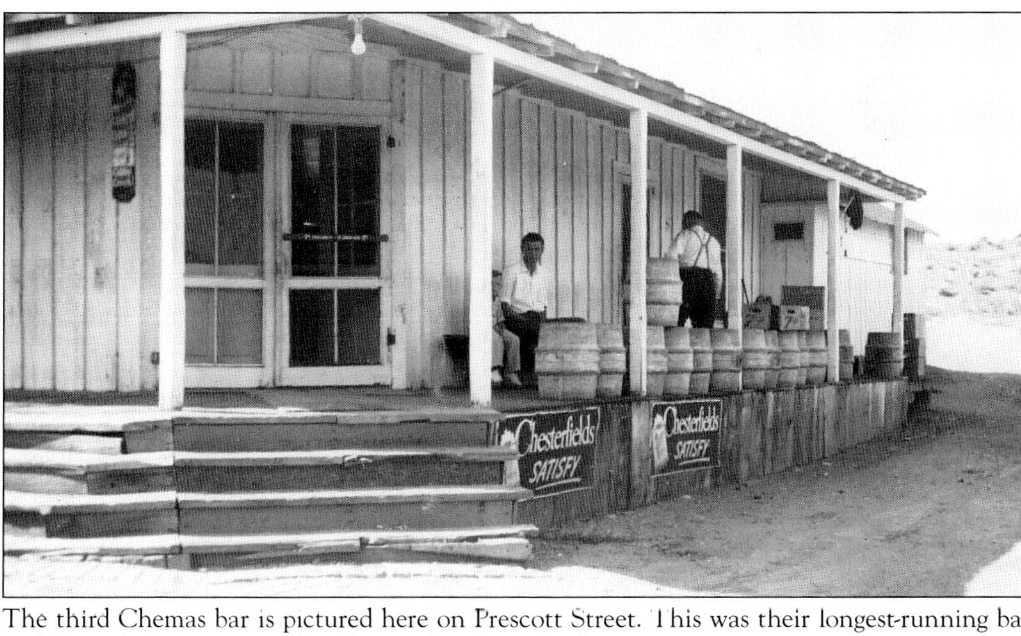

The third Chemas bar is pictured here on Prescott Street. This was their longest-running bar and showed the success of the Chemas family in this business.

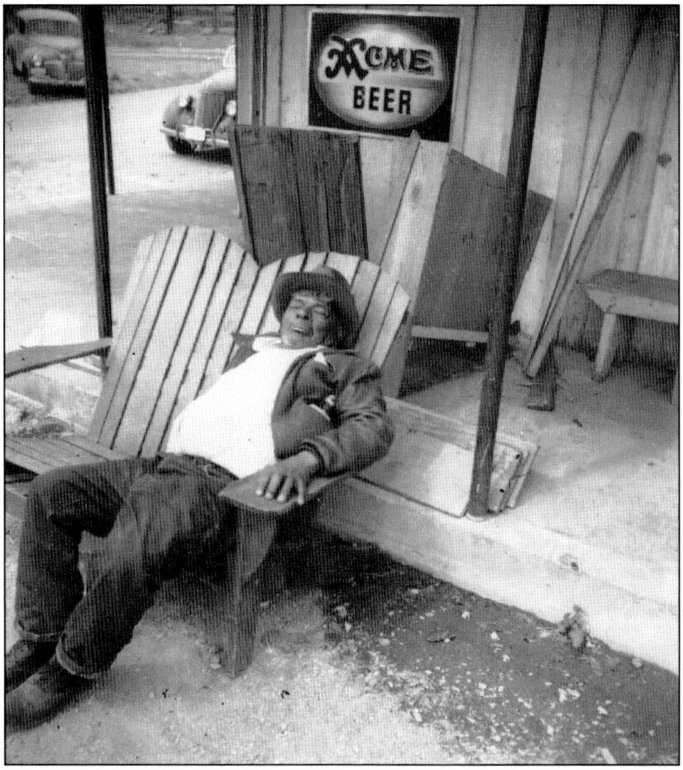

Jesus Gaitlan, town drunk, is seen here in the 1940s outside of the Chemas bar. Each night, his tiny wife, Truncalina, would come down with a switch and whip him until he ran home crying, with her hitting him the whole way.

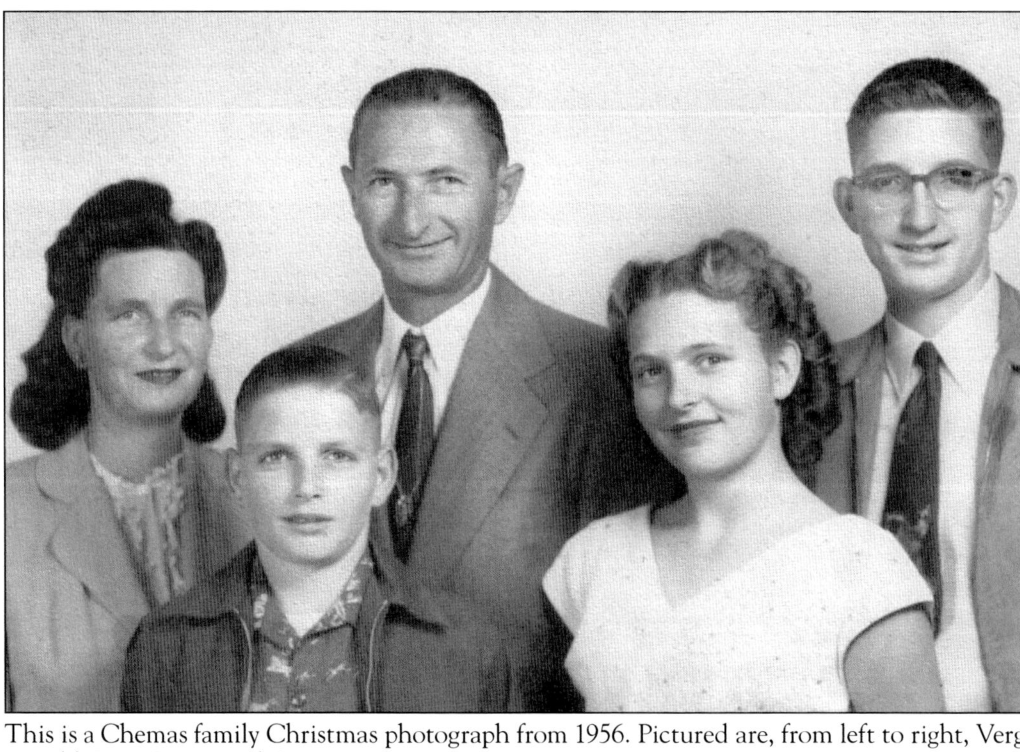

This is a Chemas family Christmas photograph from 1956. Pictured are, from left to right, Verg, Harold, Pete, Sonja, and George.

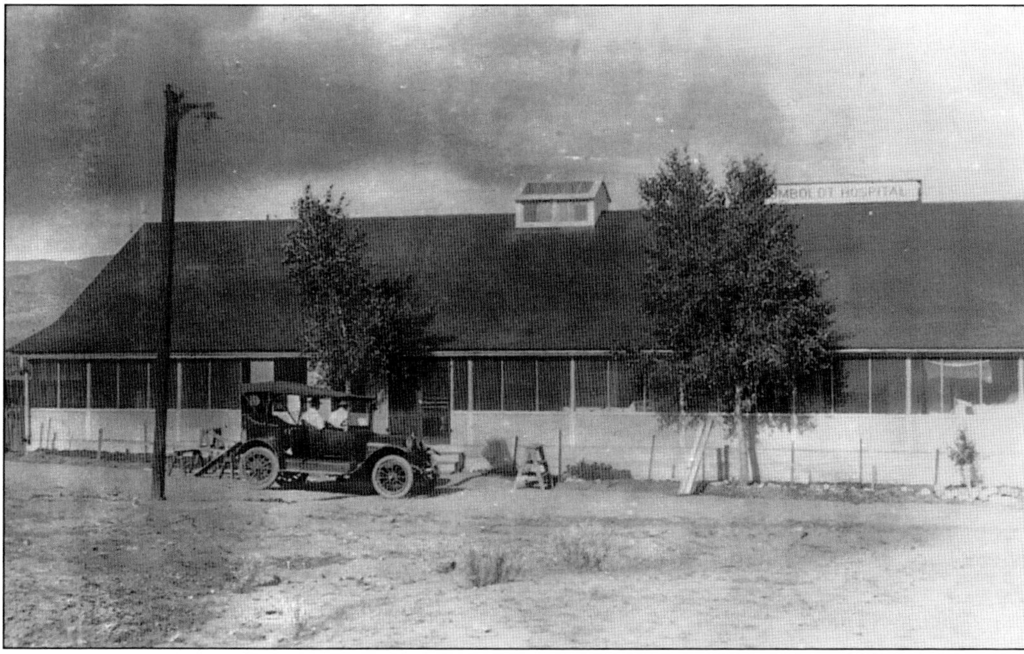

Built in 1900 as a mining company hospital, the six-ward hospital was owned by Dr. L.C. Toney. Considered a model of its kind, the facility advertised that it would "add much in the way of recommendations for the sick and injured of this prosperous camp as well as the surrounding country."

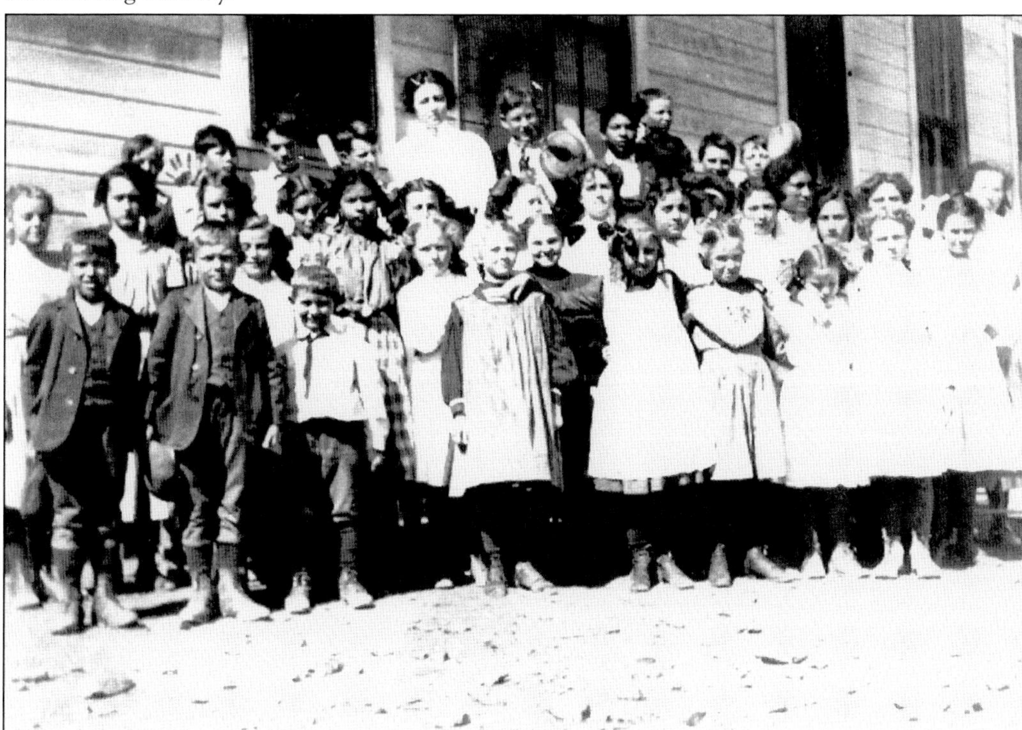

Students pose in front of the Humboldt schoolhouse in 1919.

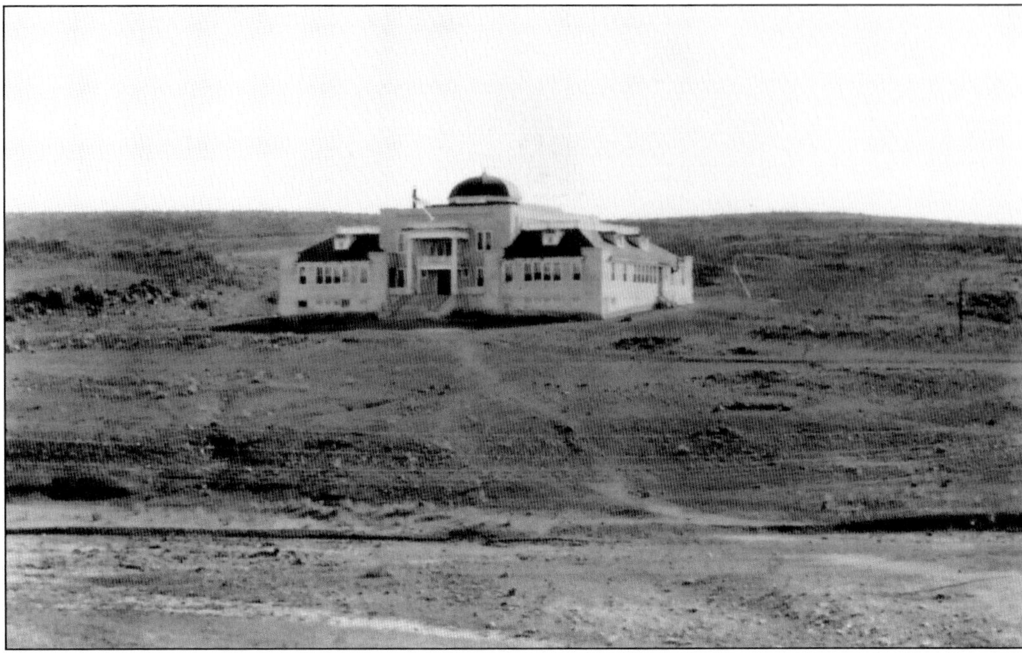

Students attended first through tenth grade at the Humboldt School between 1926 and 1934. The school was the crown jewel of the area. Built on Third Street, it solved the travel challenges of area students. The original Humboldt School started out as a one-room schoolhouse and grew to eight rooms with over 200 students, creating the need for a larger school.

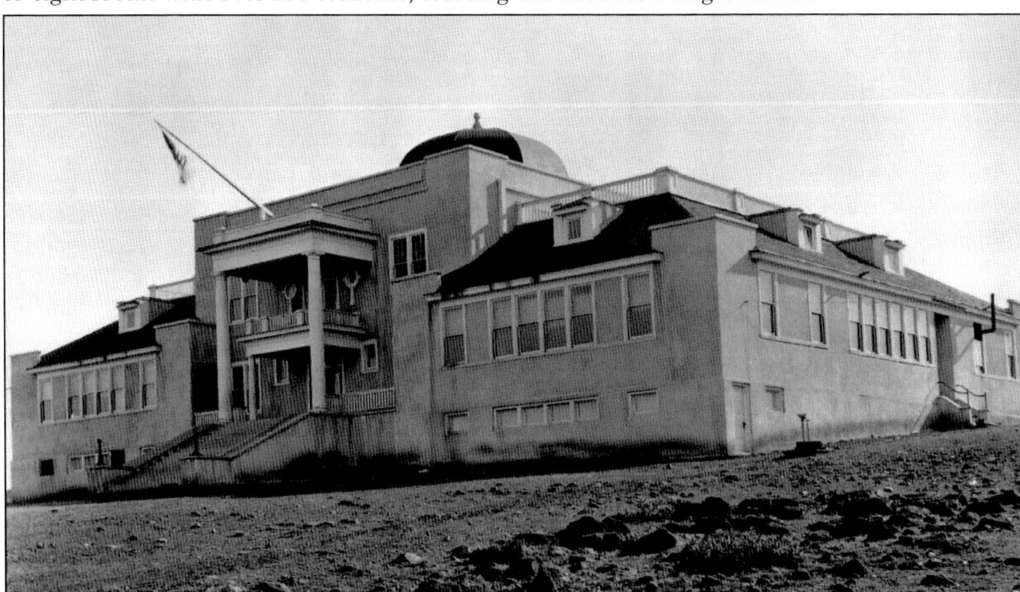

This c. 1919 photograph offers a closer view of Humboldt School around the time of its official opening. Local history books put the date of opening at 1926, but the *Arizona Weekly Journal-Miner* in Prescott documented the contract for the school at $50,000 in 1917 and its opening as taking place in the fall of 1919. The final figure for the cost of the school came in around $40,000, a large sum of money at the time.

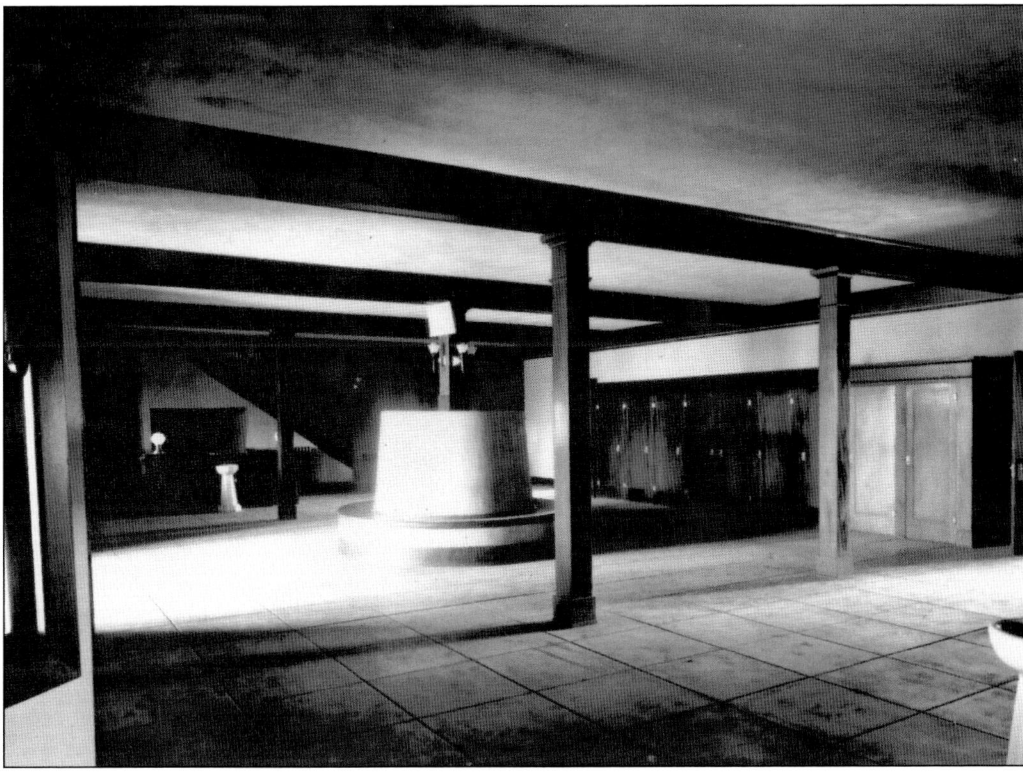

This photograph offers a glimpse into the Humboldt School's lobby area. It was considered state of the art for its time and was a source of considerable pride for the community.

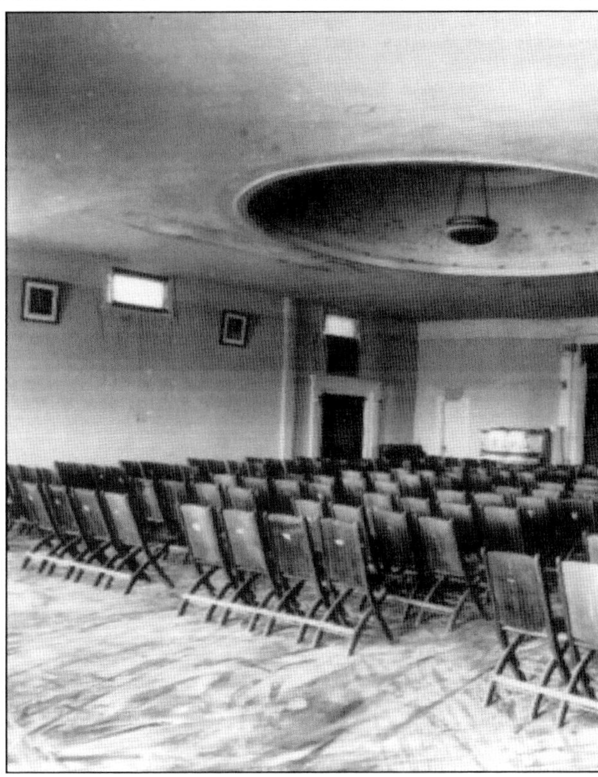

The auditorium at Humboldt School had a distinctive copper dome that could be seen for miles around. The dome included a school bell at the top. Costs soon overtook the ability of local residents to pay the relevant taxes, and the school mysteriously burned down in 1932, shortly after graduation. Among locals, it is commonly known that a group of residents burned it to the ground to relieve themselves of the heavy tax burden. The bell is the only thing to have survived, and it now sits atop Humboldt Elementary School.

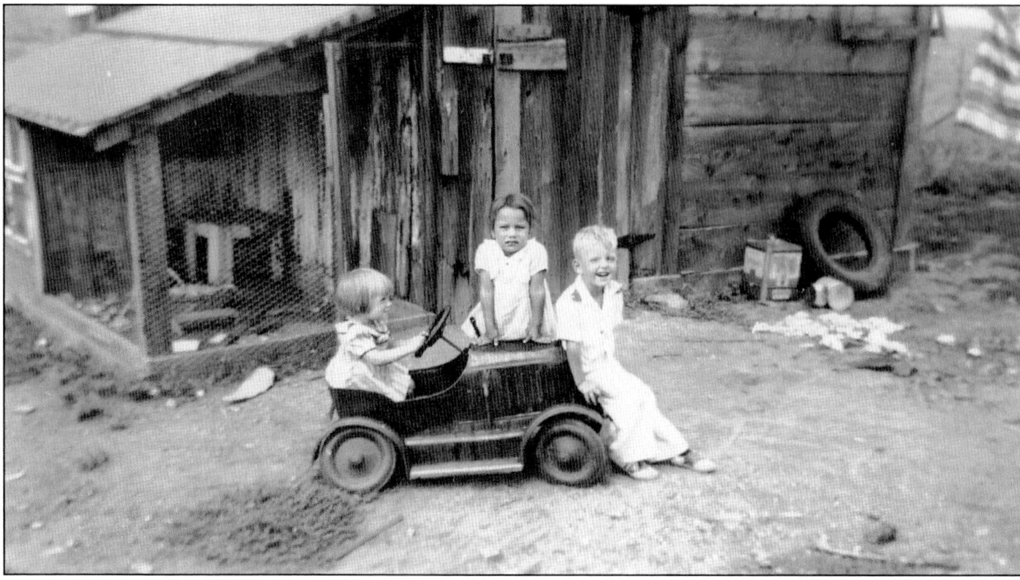

Sonja (seated in car) and George Chemas are seen playing jovially with Anna Lupno on the Chemas property in 1951.

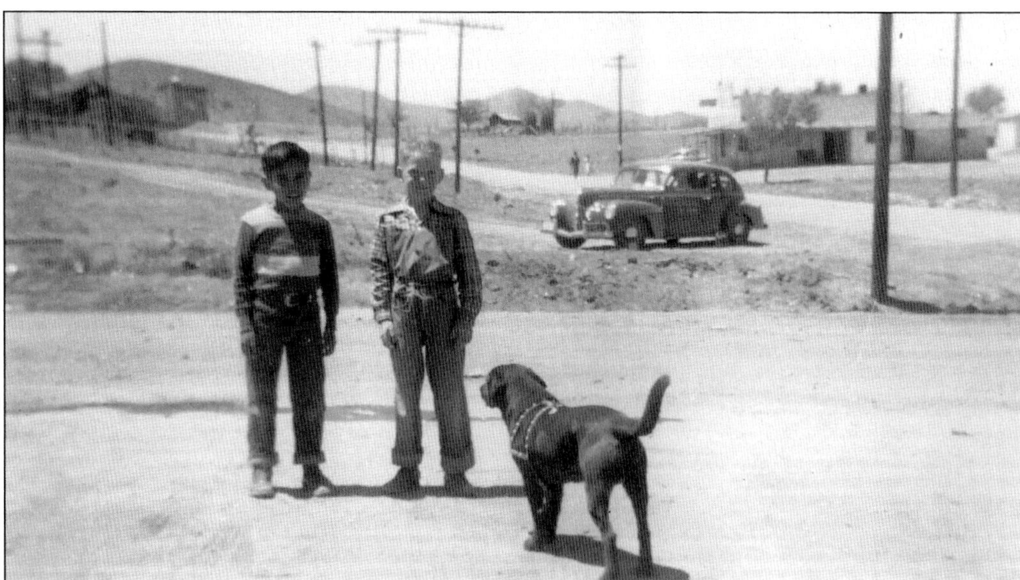

Porky Pedroza (left) and Harold Chemas greet Mike the dog on Prescott Street in Humboldt.

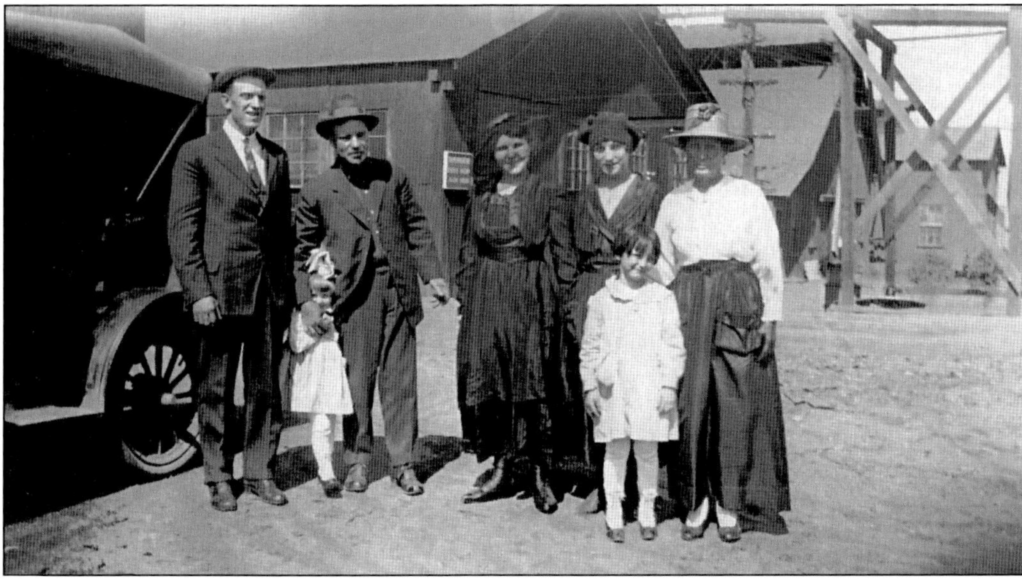

Pictured here in 1918 are, from left to right, Bill Barton, Vivian Riggs, Fred Wahalter (Vivian's stepfather), Bessie Wahalter, Lula Barton, unidentified, and "Grandma" Halloway.

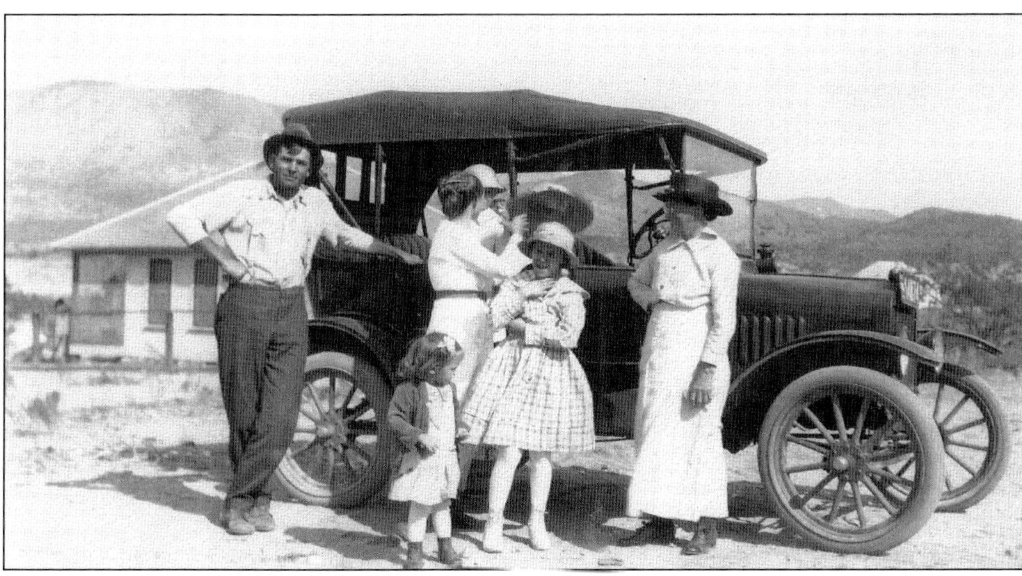

A local family is dressed up and ready to go on an outing. Great pride was taken in formal clothes in both Dewey and Humboldt, no matter the families' financial means.

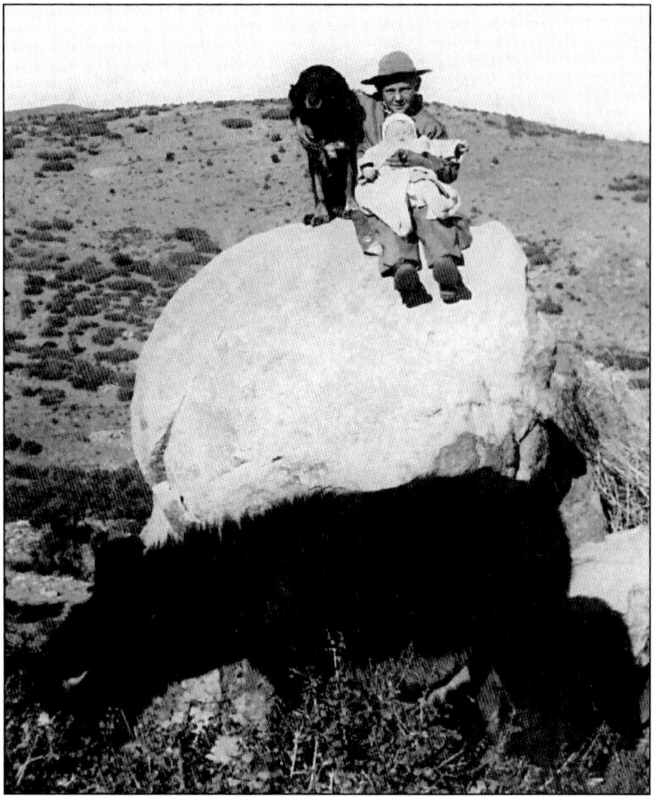

This photograph, taken in 1914 just outside of Humboldt, shows Vivian Riggs, age four months, being held by Sidney F. Buckels (Vivian's half brother). A family dog and a burro have come along to keep them company.

The Goswick family, longtime residents of the area and generous contributors to the community, are gathered at their "old house" on Big Bug Creek. Shown here are, from left to right, Giles Goswick, Merle Goswick, Edna Richards, Dick Richards, George Goswick, Marie Williams, Lou Goswick, Ted Schultz, Rink Goswick, Jewel Williams, Carl Goswick, Sam Williams, and Bitt Goswick.

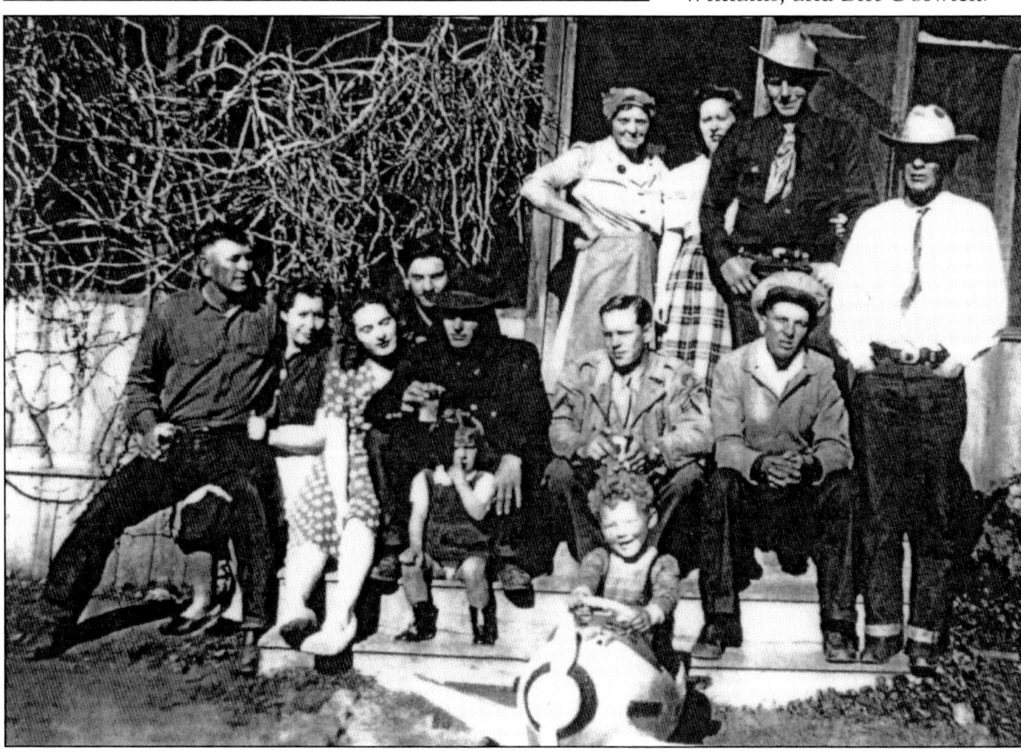

Rudy Chemas (left) and George Goswick pose with their latest mountain lion kill. This photograph was likely taken in the mid-1940s.

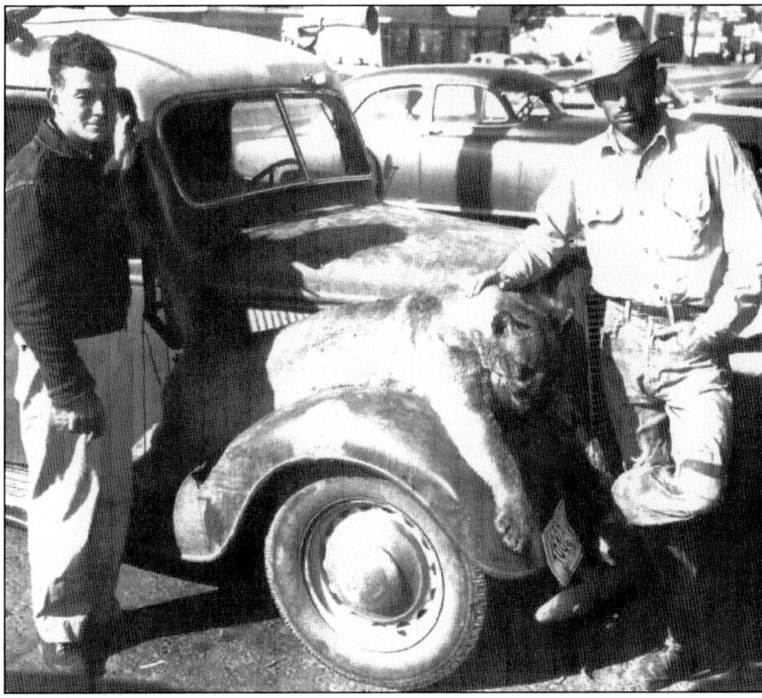

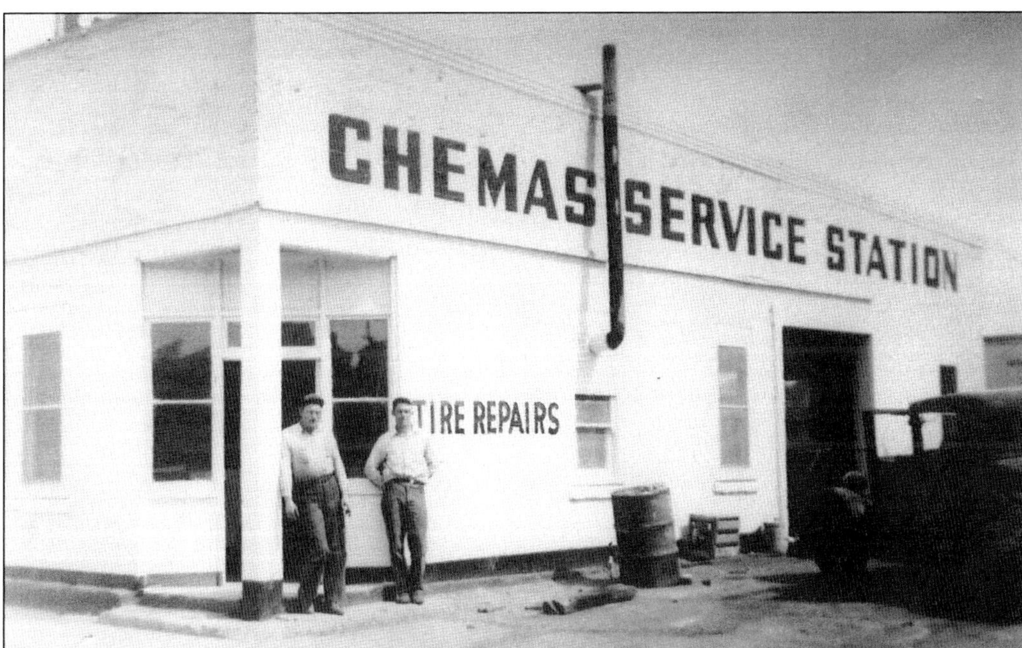

The Chemas Service Station is seen here. For decades, the Chemas family served the community through its service station and bars.

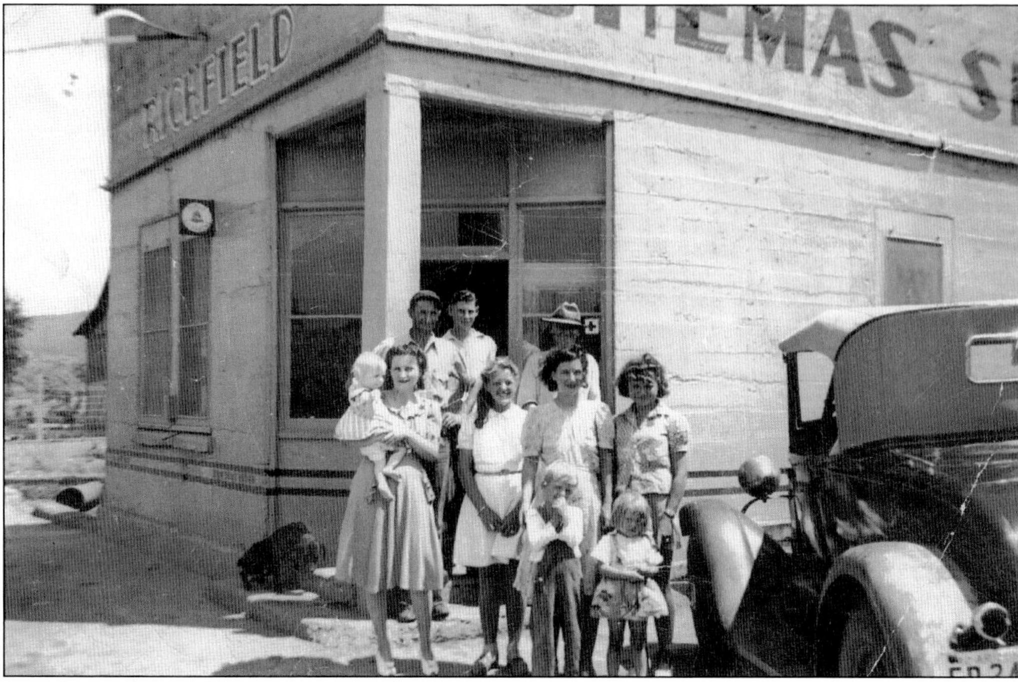

Members of the Chemas family and their friends pose for a photograph outside their service station in Humboldt. Among those pictured are Sonja, George, and Harold, all of whom still live in the family home.

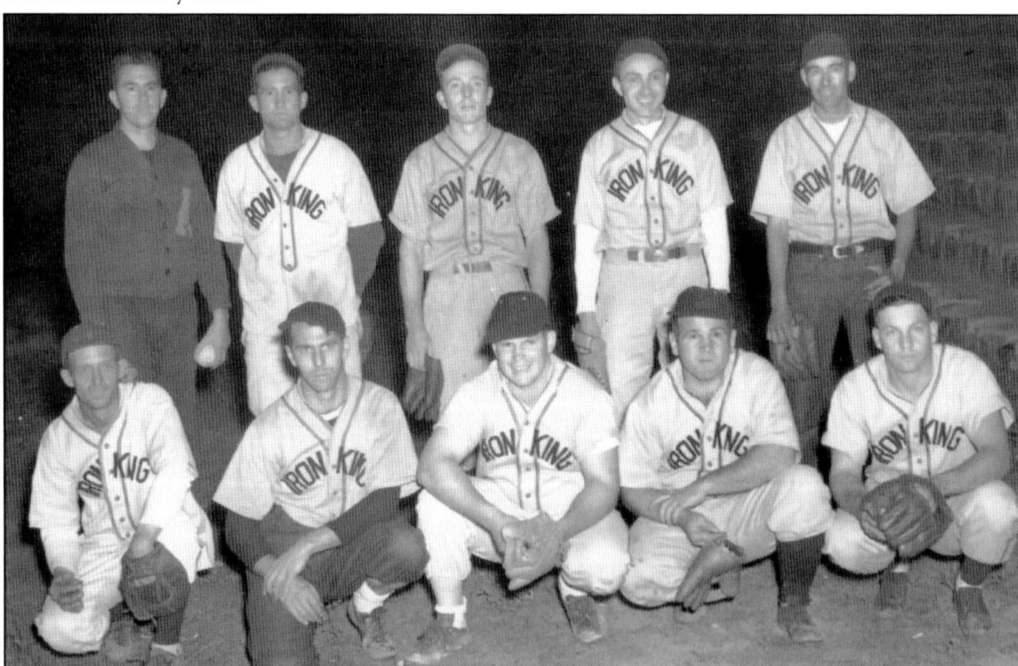

Here is an early photograph of the Iron King baseball team. Among its players were Dick Richards, Walt Statler, Johnny Malyjurek, Andy Zenkel, George Goswick, Nacho Mora, Lonnie Bombardiere, and coach Joe Miller.

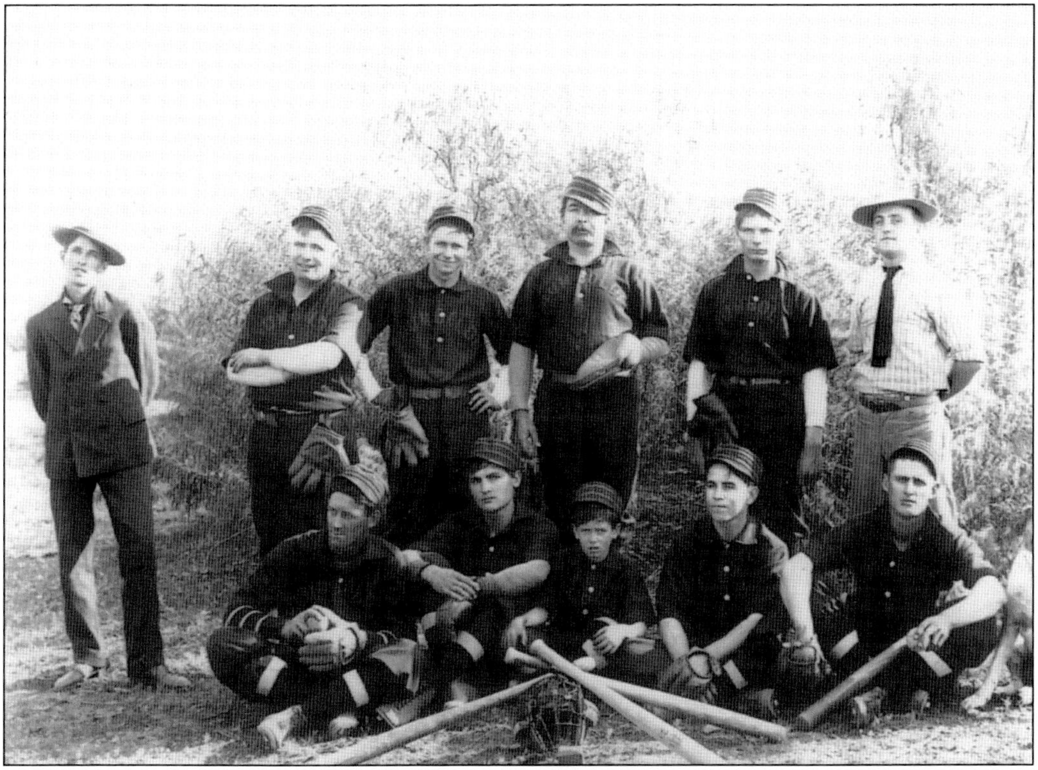

This undated photograph shows the Humboldt baseball team. Coach Carl Bybee, wearing a suit, is at left.

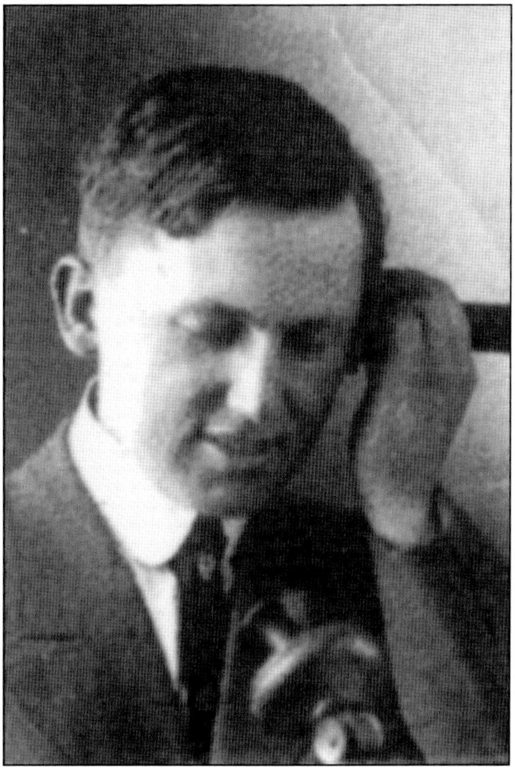

Humboldt had the first dialing telephone system in the region. The man shown here is probably a supervisor or maintenance worker. Operators at the time were exclusively women.

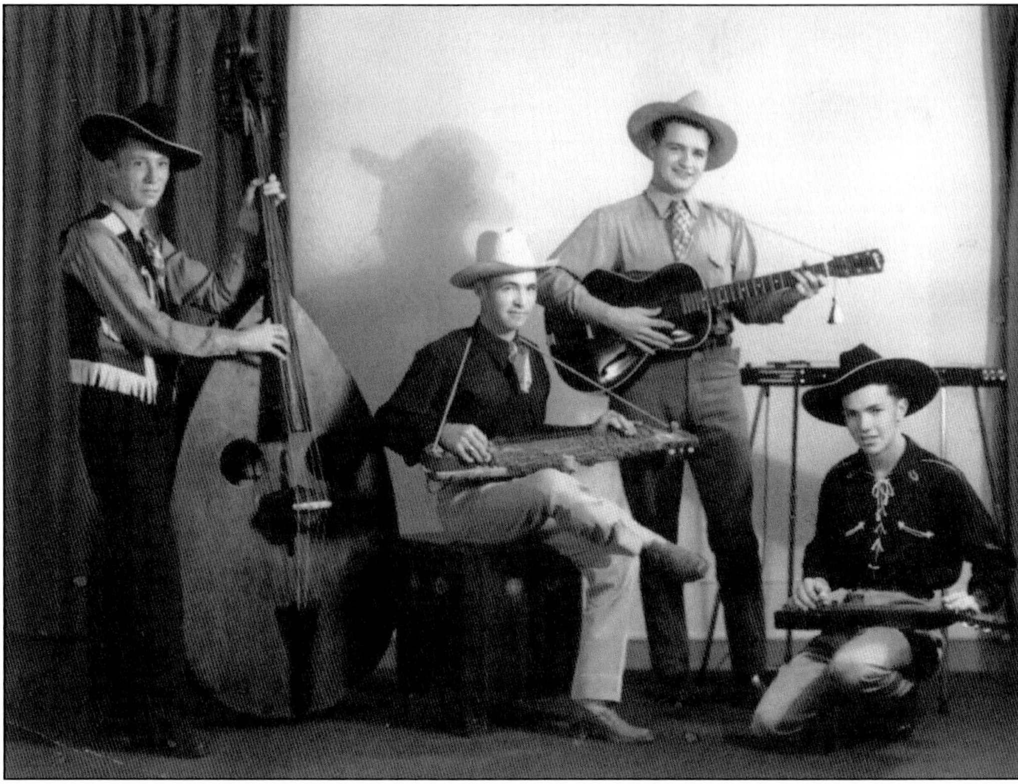

Members of an early Humboldt band pose for a photograph. Art Wilcox is on steel guitar, Leonard Owens is on lead guitar, and Ted Bronson is on dobro. The man at left is unidentified.

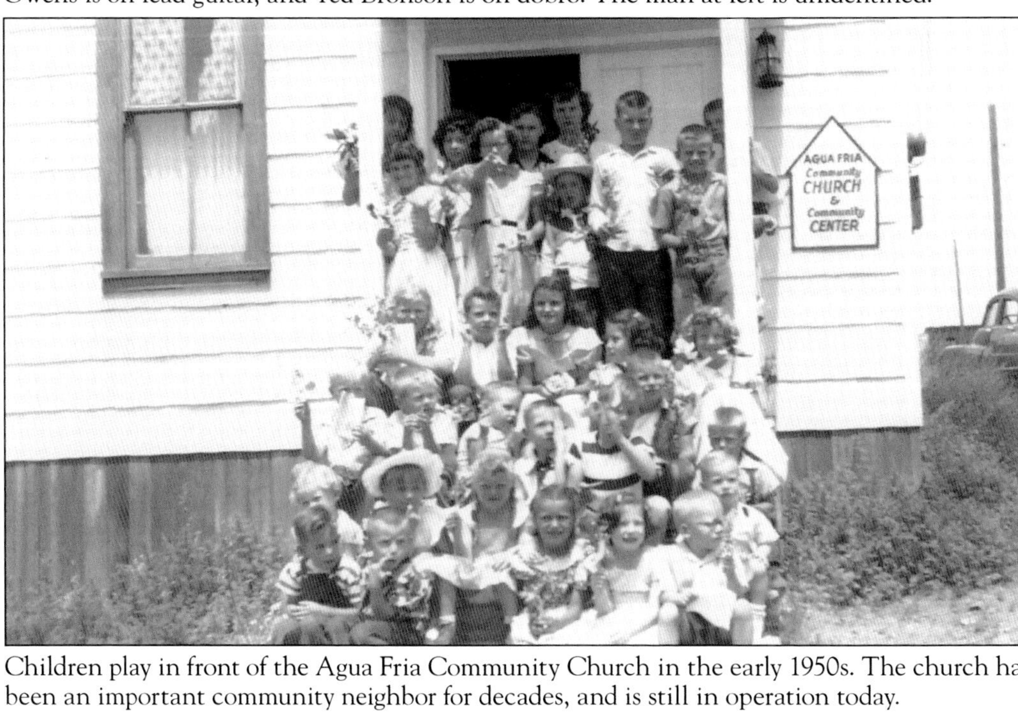

Children play in front of the Agua Fria Community Church in the early 1950s. The church has been an important community neighbor for decades, and is still in operation today.

Humboldt resident Pvt. Charles G. Wilson is pictured here. He was a member of Battery D, 80th Field Artillery at Camp Oglethorpe, Georgia, from 1917 to 1918.

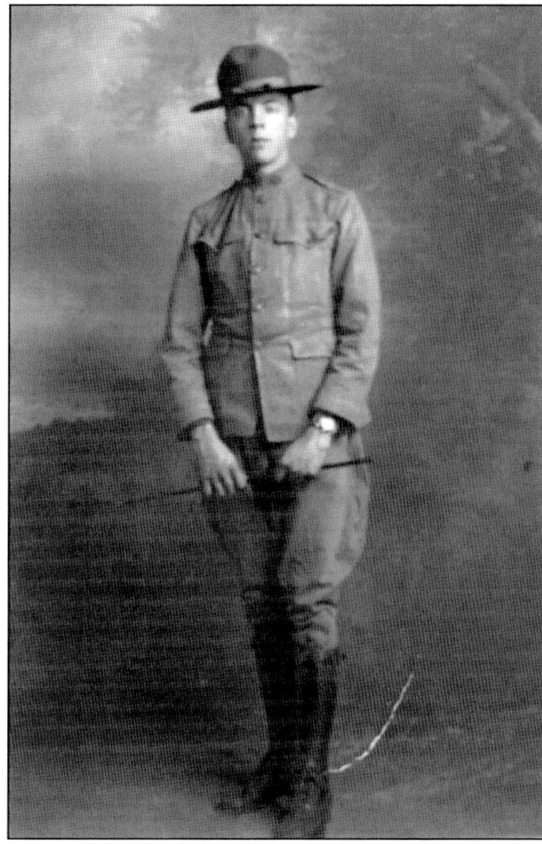

This is a scene from the McCabe Mine in the 1940s. It was one of the first mines in the area. Mining in the McCabe-Gladstone area began as early as 1870 on the Silver Belt claim. Mr. Hatfield and Mr. Slaughter originally prospected along Galena Gulch between 1863 and 1865. In 1879, Frank McCabe arrived and traded Hatfield a horse for his right to claim the property.

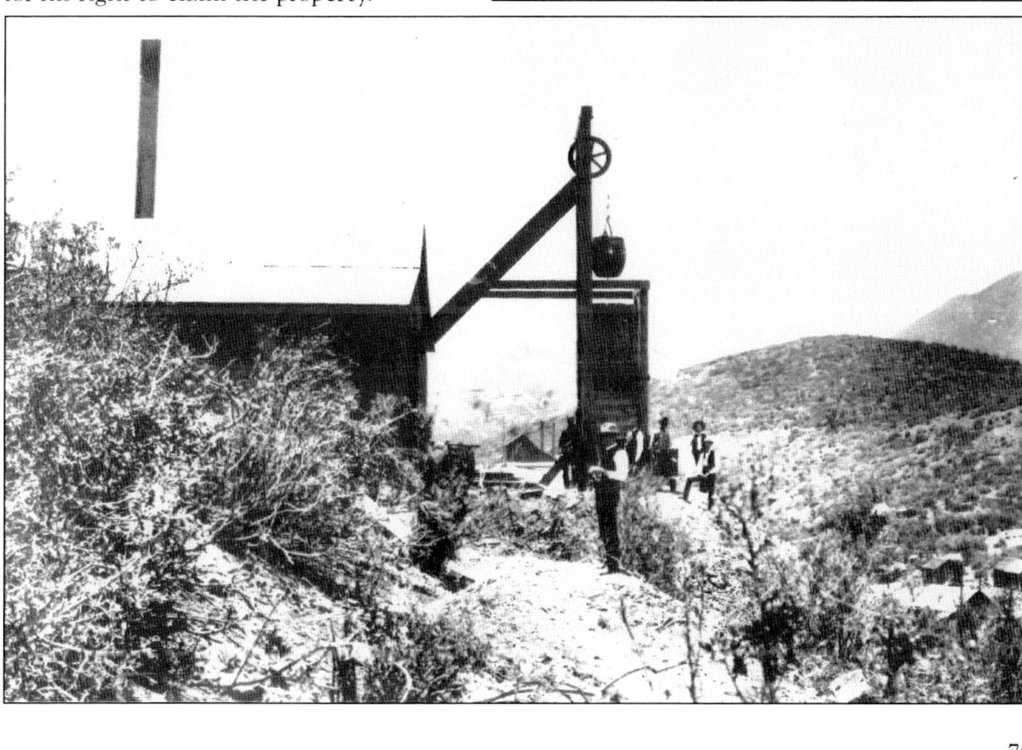

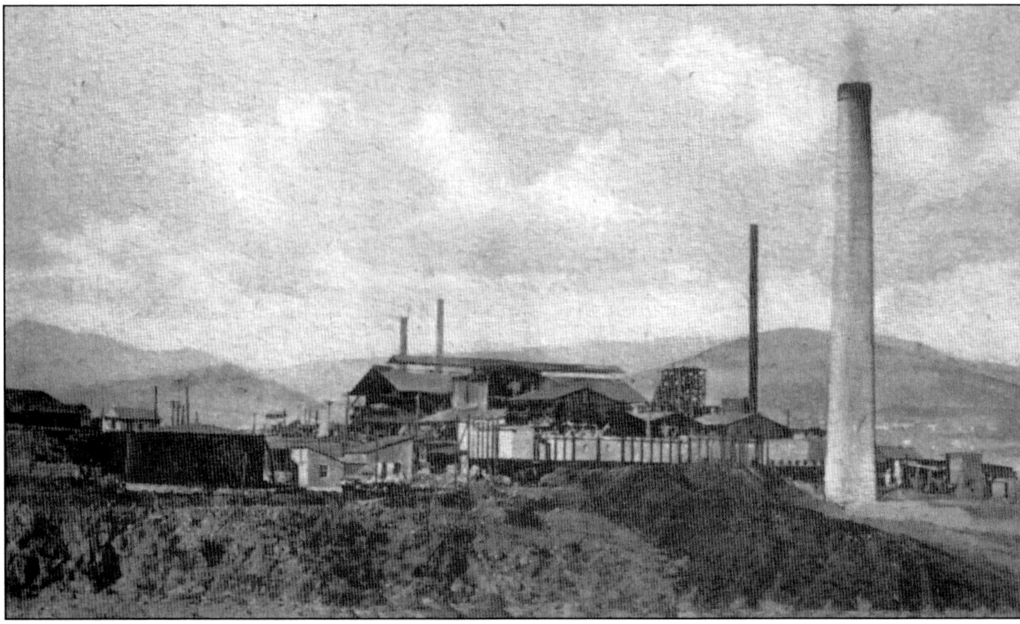

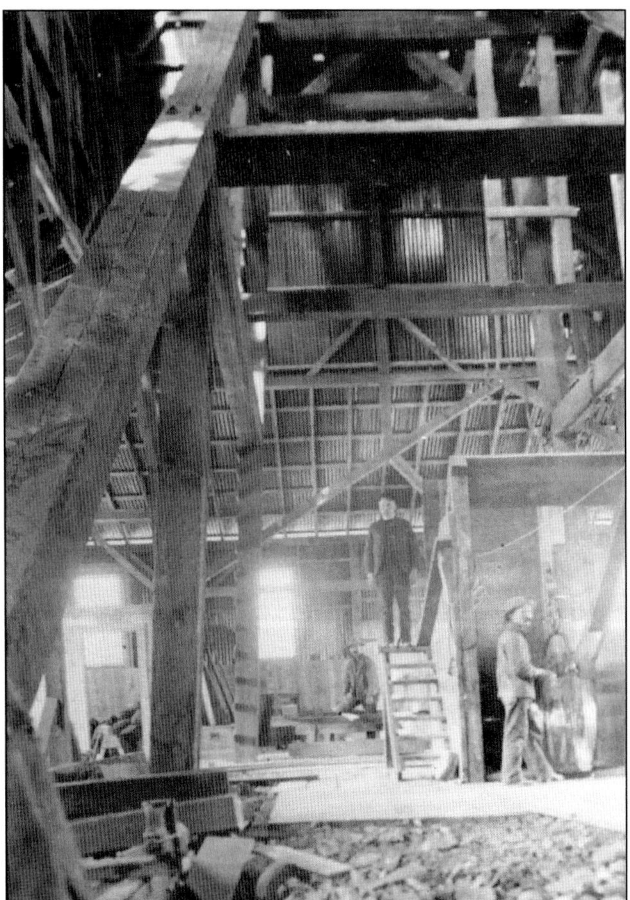

This photograph shows the Humboldt smelter in the late 1890s. A new smelter was built in 1905, quadrupling the daily capacity. The smelter stack, shown here, remained standing until 1955, and the new stack, while not in use, still stands today in the community.

A rare look inside the bustling Humboldt smelter from 1917 attests to the nation's economic demand for copper. Workers were hired to run shifts around the clock. The mine employed over 400 at its peak.

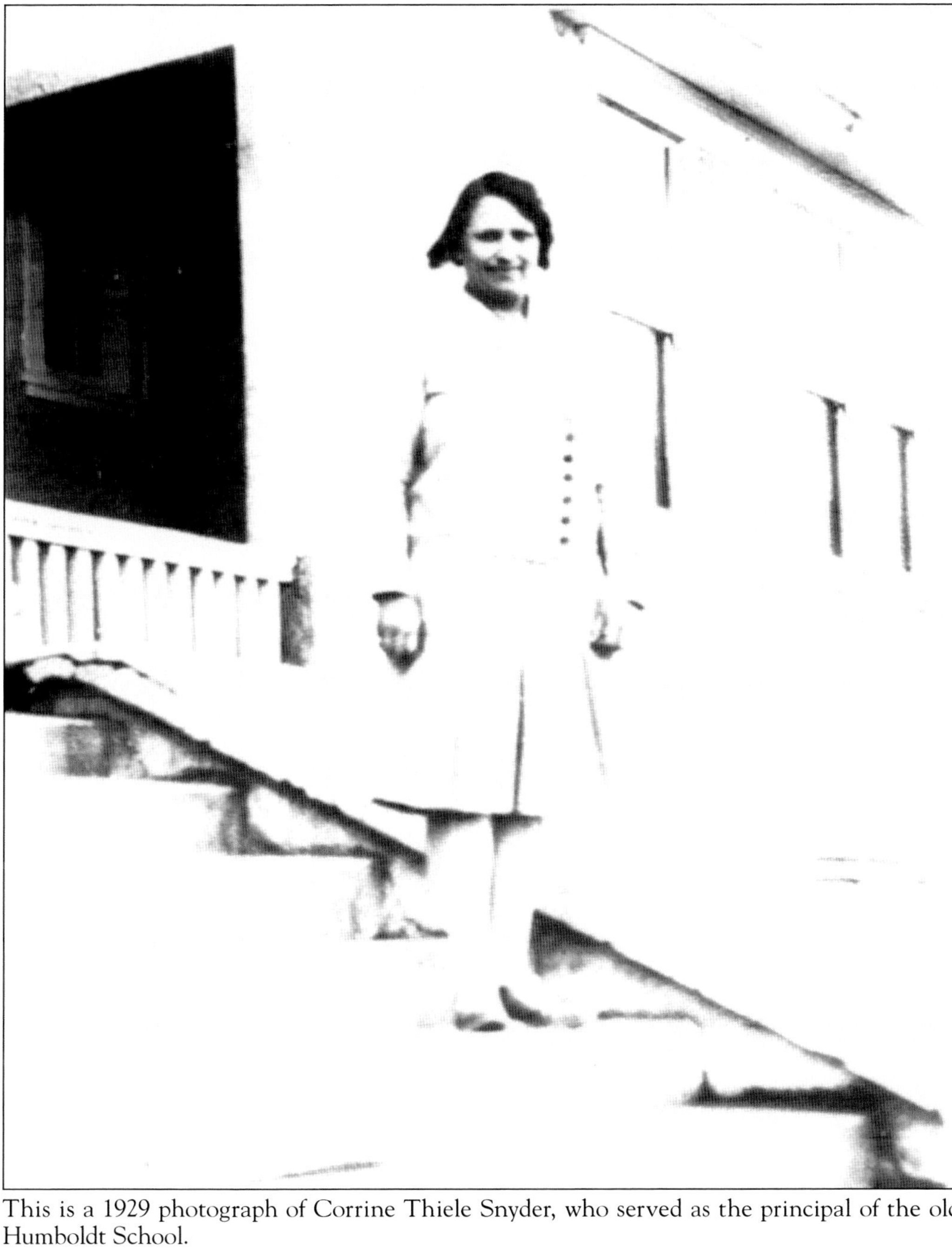

This is a 1929 photograph of Corrine Thiele Snyder, who served as the principal of the old Humboldt School.

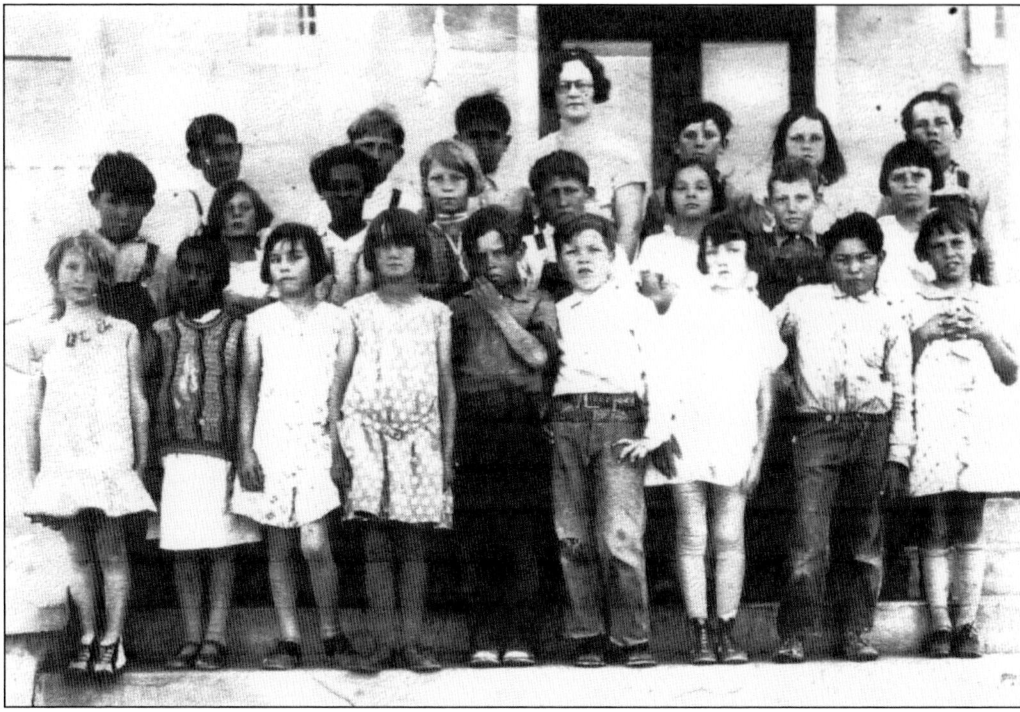

These students and their teacher were photographed in front of the original Humboldt School taking a break from their studies.

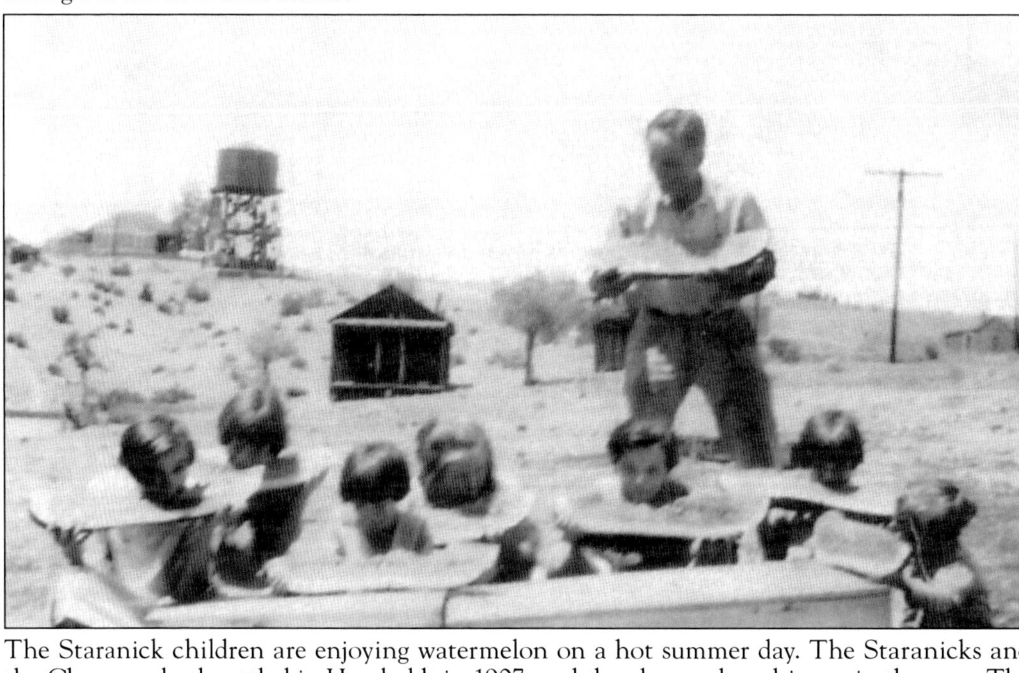

The Staranick children are enjoying watermelon on a hot summer day. The Staranicks and the Chemases both settled in Humboldt in 1907, and they have a long history in the area. The Staranicks homesteaded 320 acres at the Yarber Wash area and started the original Humboldt school to provide their children with an education. All of Joe and Mary Staranicks' children grew up to be outstanding citizens in the community.

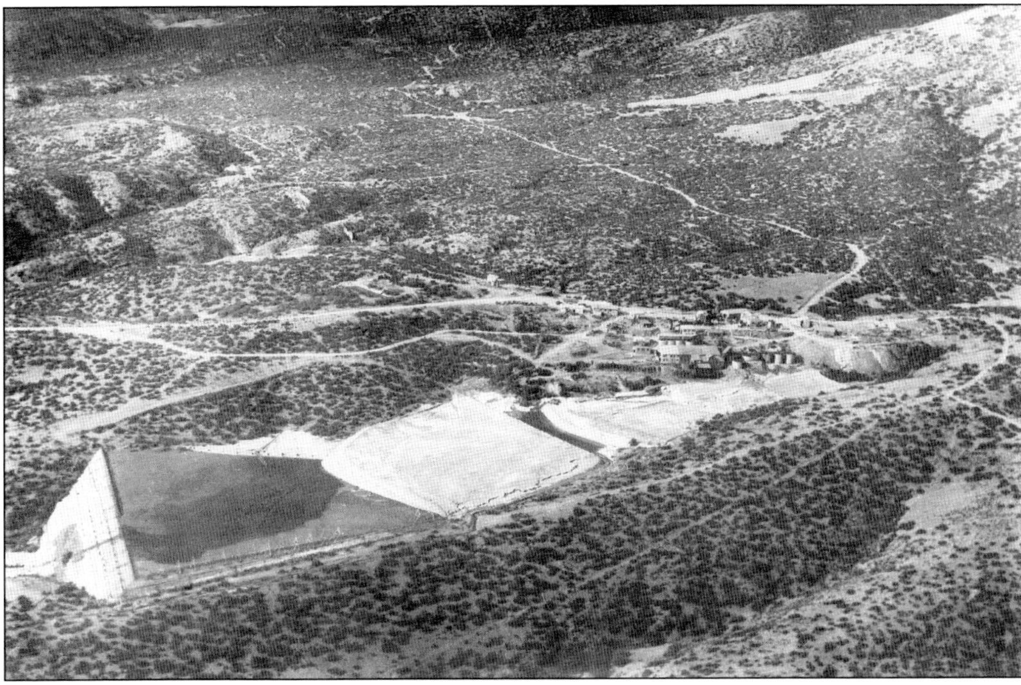

The Iron King Mine shipped out approximately $120,200,000 in gross value ore during its operation. It operated from the late 1800s until the early 1960s and was a periodically active mine for gold, silver, copper, lead, and zinc.

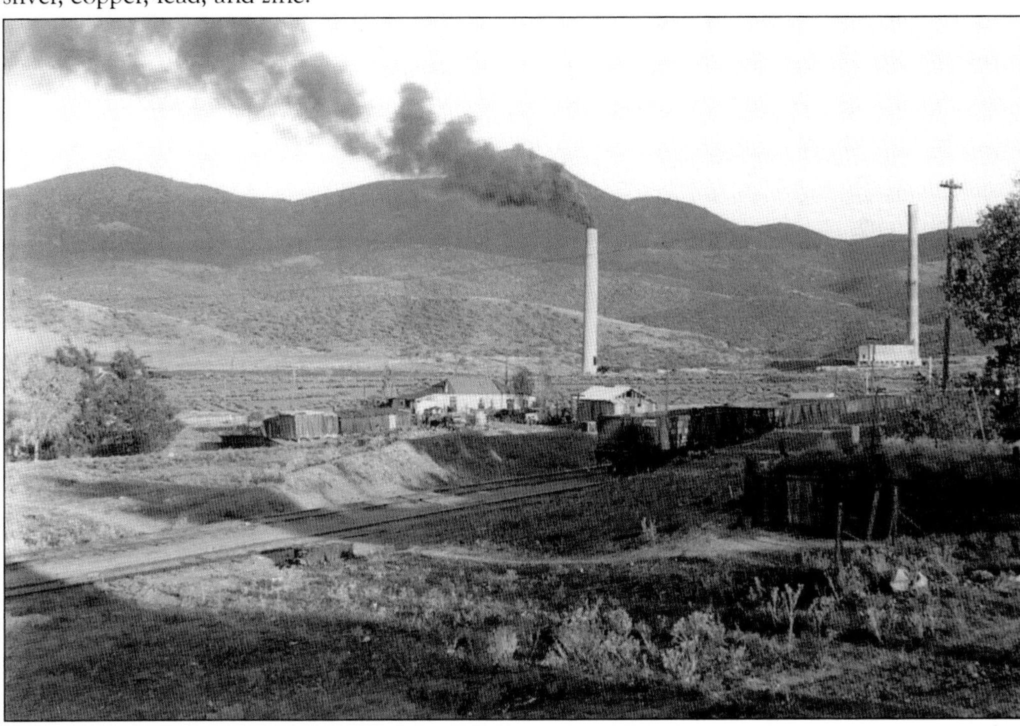

Pictured is the original Humboldt smelter, used prior to 1905. At that time, operations switched to a much more efficient and higher-capacity smelter.

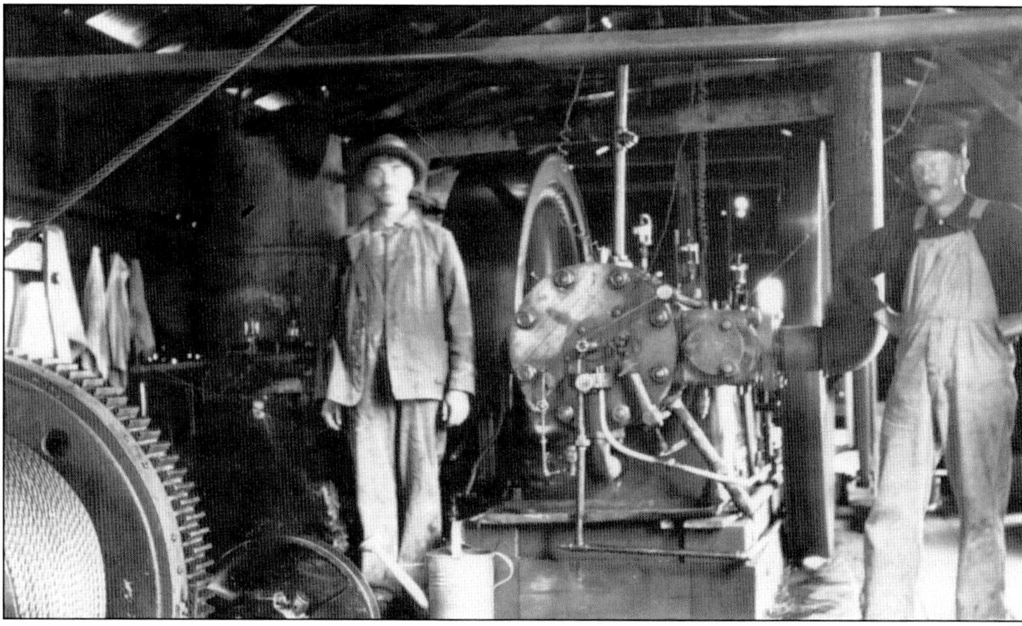

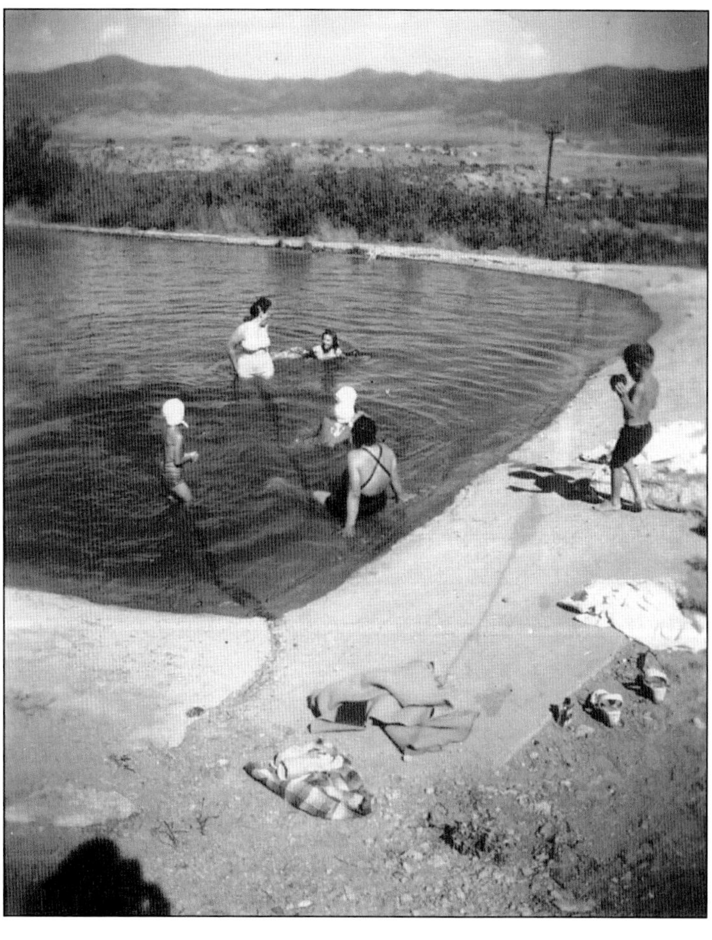

Iron King Mine workers are pictured here around 1920.

The Iron King community pool was a welcomed amenity for all residents. More than any other mining operation, the Iron King company deeply invested in the community, including running this pool for local residents, starting a Little League program for area kids, and other activities.

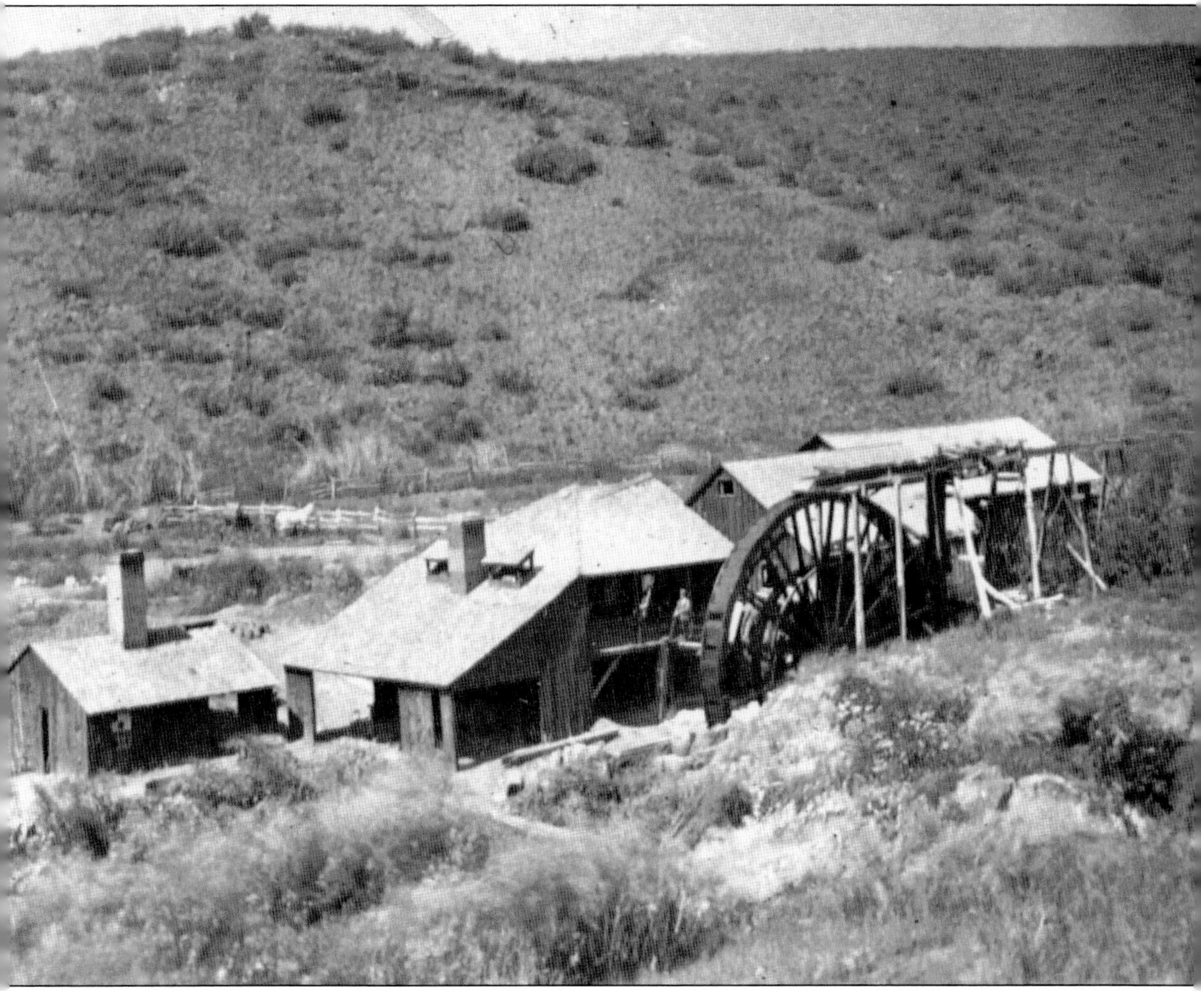

This is the Levi Bashford Mill, where Humboldt really began, around 1876–1878. Owner Levi Bashford sold the property in 1884 and became a prominent Prescott businessman. This was the first milling operation in the area to allow much higher quantities of ore to be processed.

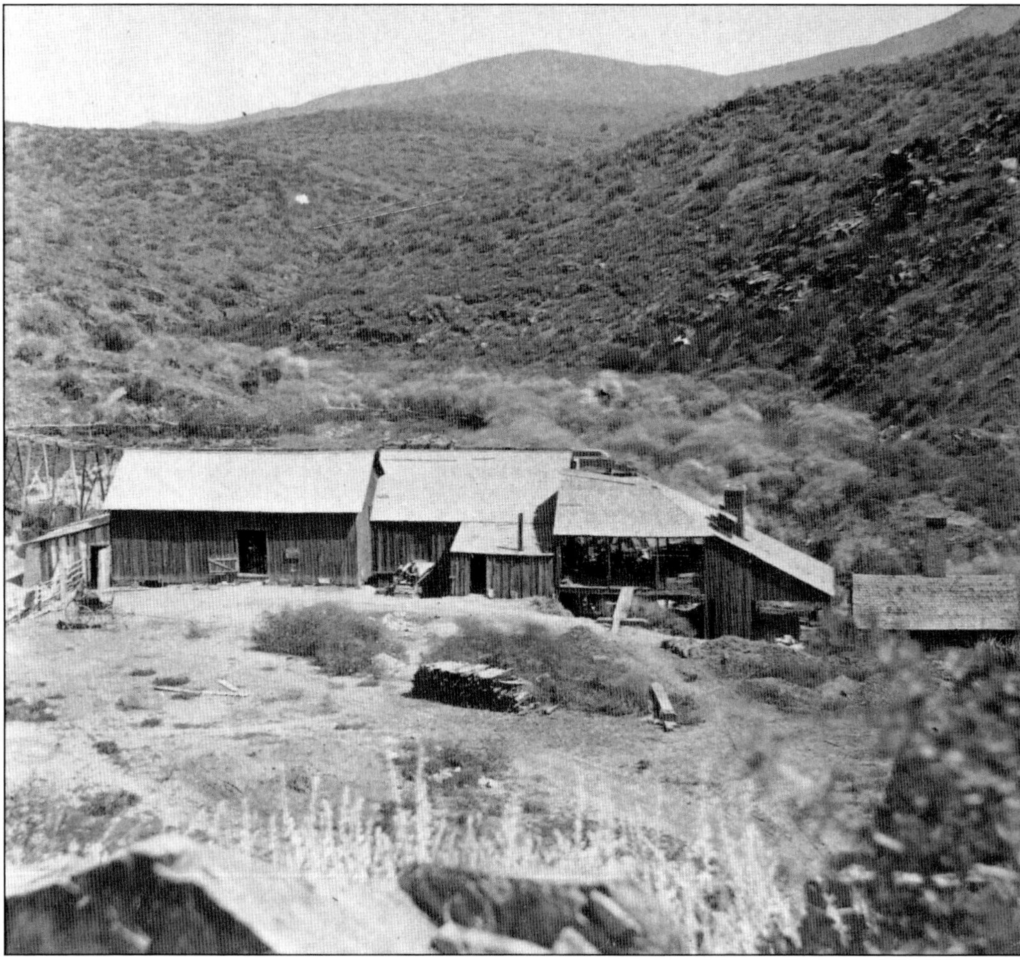

The backside of Bashford Mill is pictured here. With a capacity of 20 tons a day, it allowed the area to become a mining hotbed when it first opened. In 1938, a 140-ton mill was erected to crush ore. It later expanded to a 225-ton capacity.

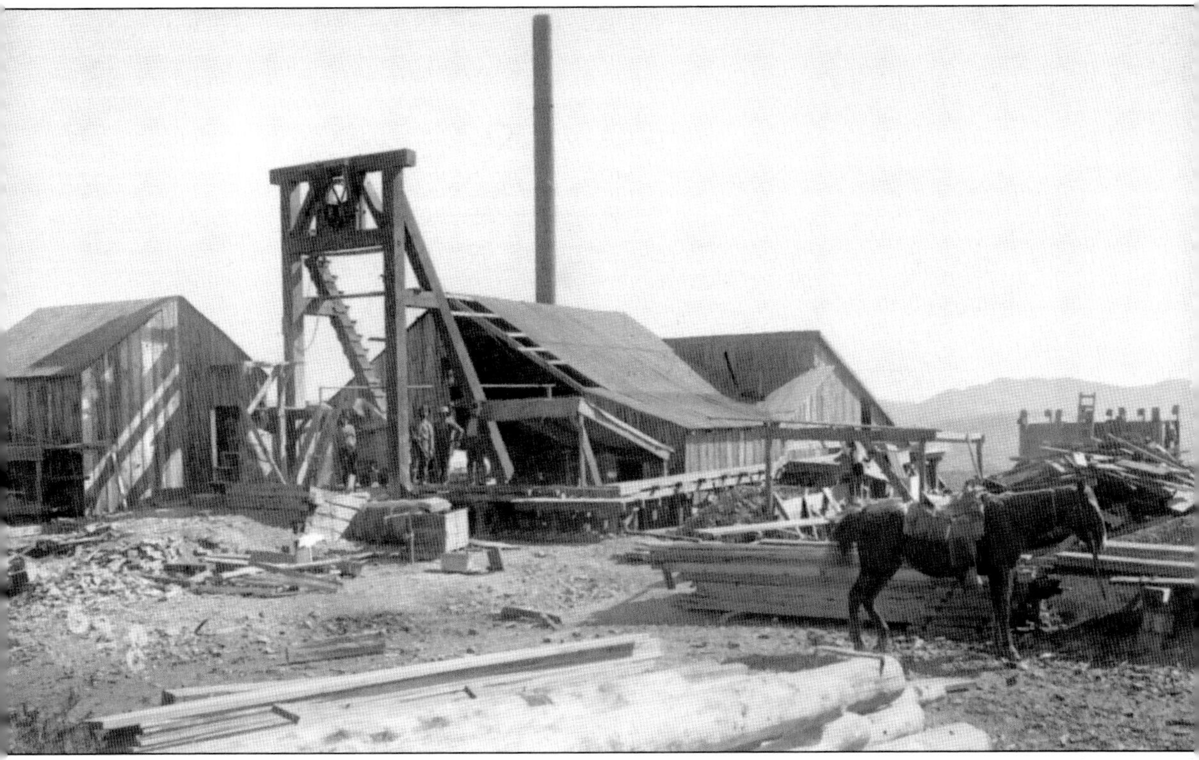

This 1890 photograph shows the Silver Belt mining operation. The Silver Belt claim spawned many mines on its property over the years.

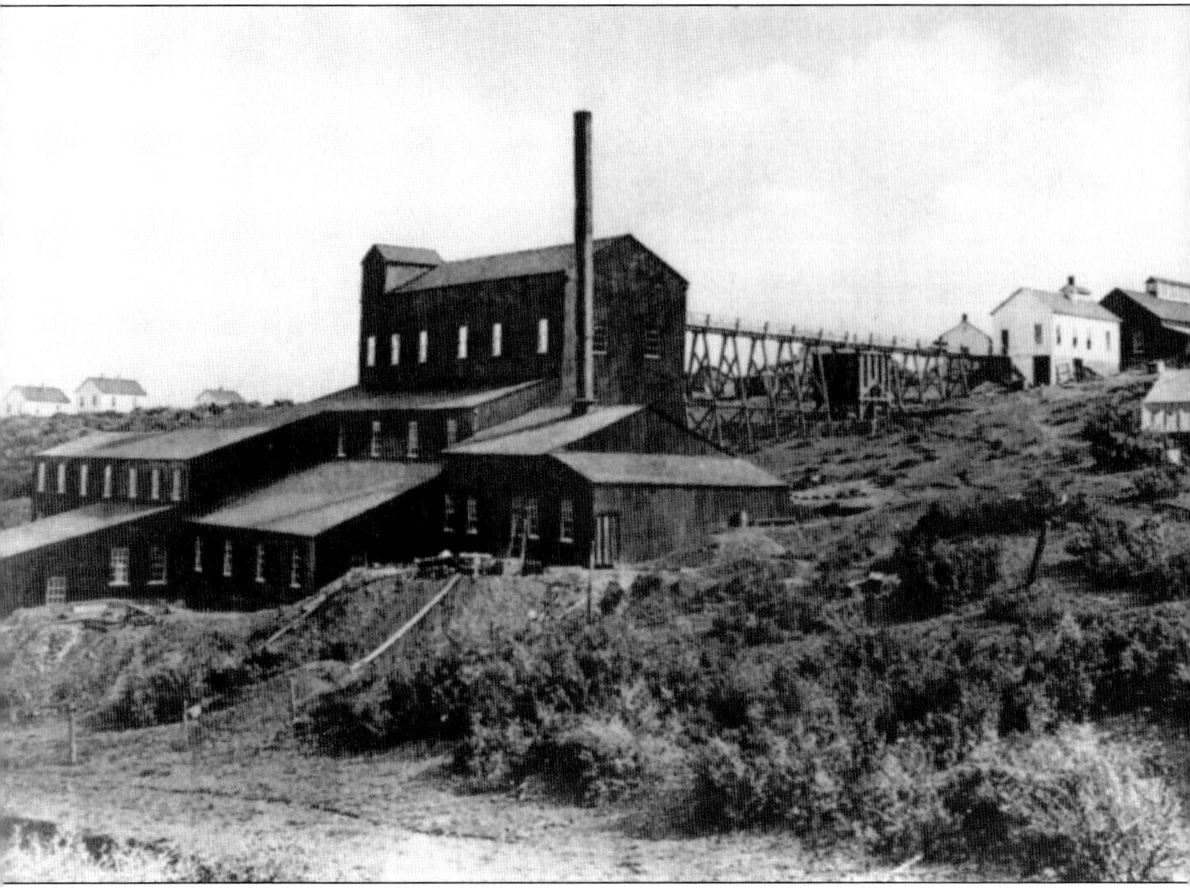

This is a 1900 photograph of the McCabe mining operation.

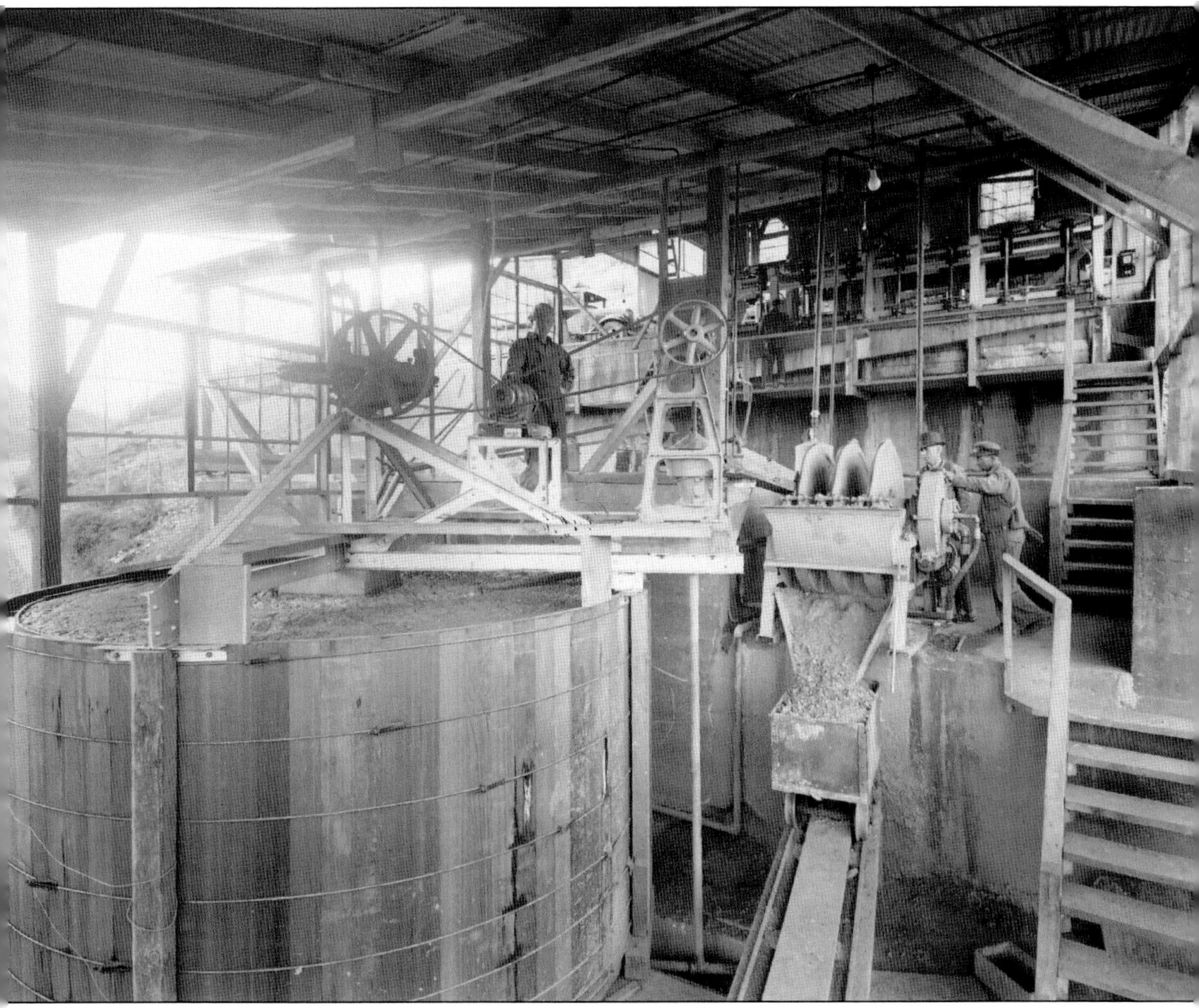

Several men are seen working in a slurry mill for Humboldt Mine in 1930.

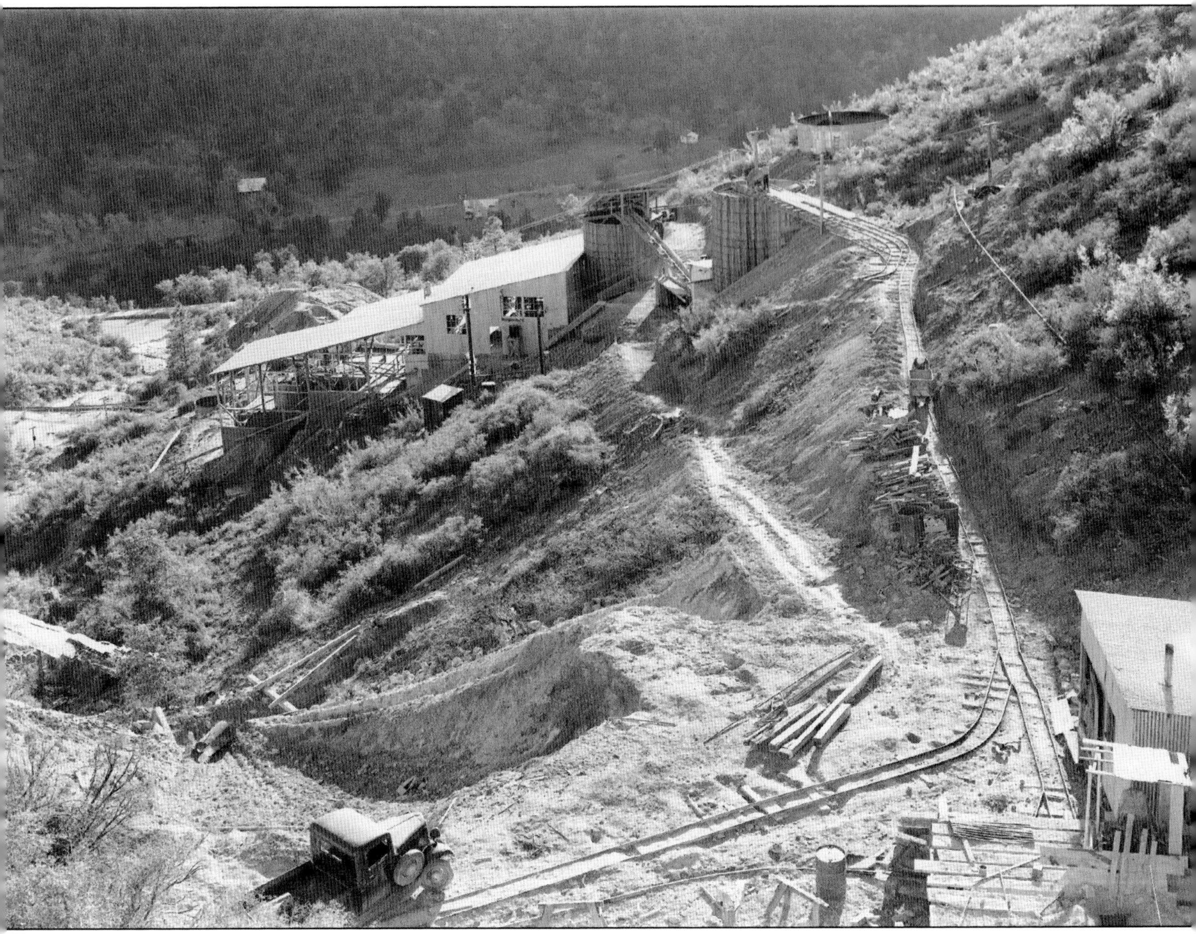

This is an overview of Iron King Mine around 1950. While starting as a gold mine at the turn of the century, the name derived from the heavy iron oxide outcropping that led to its discovery.

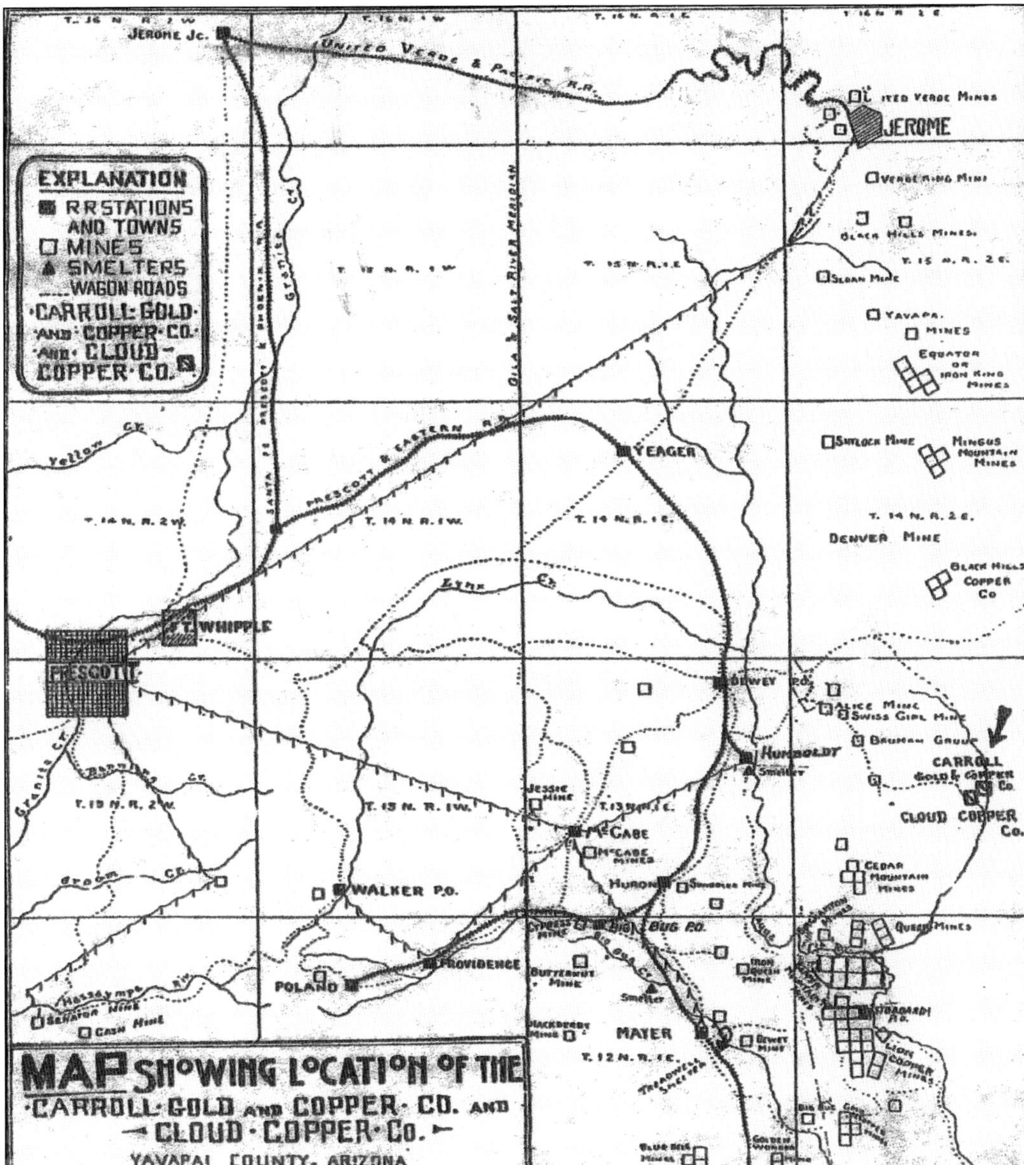

This is a Carroll Mining Company map from the 1910s. The Agua Fria mining district is clearly outlined.

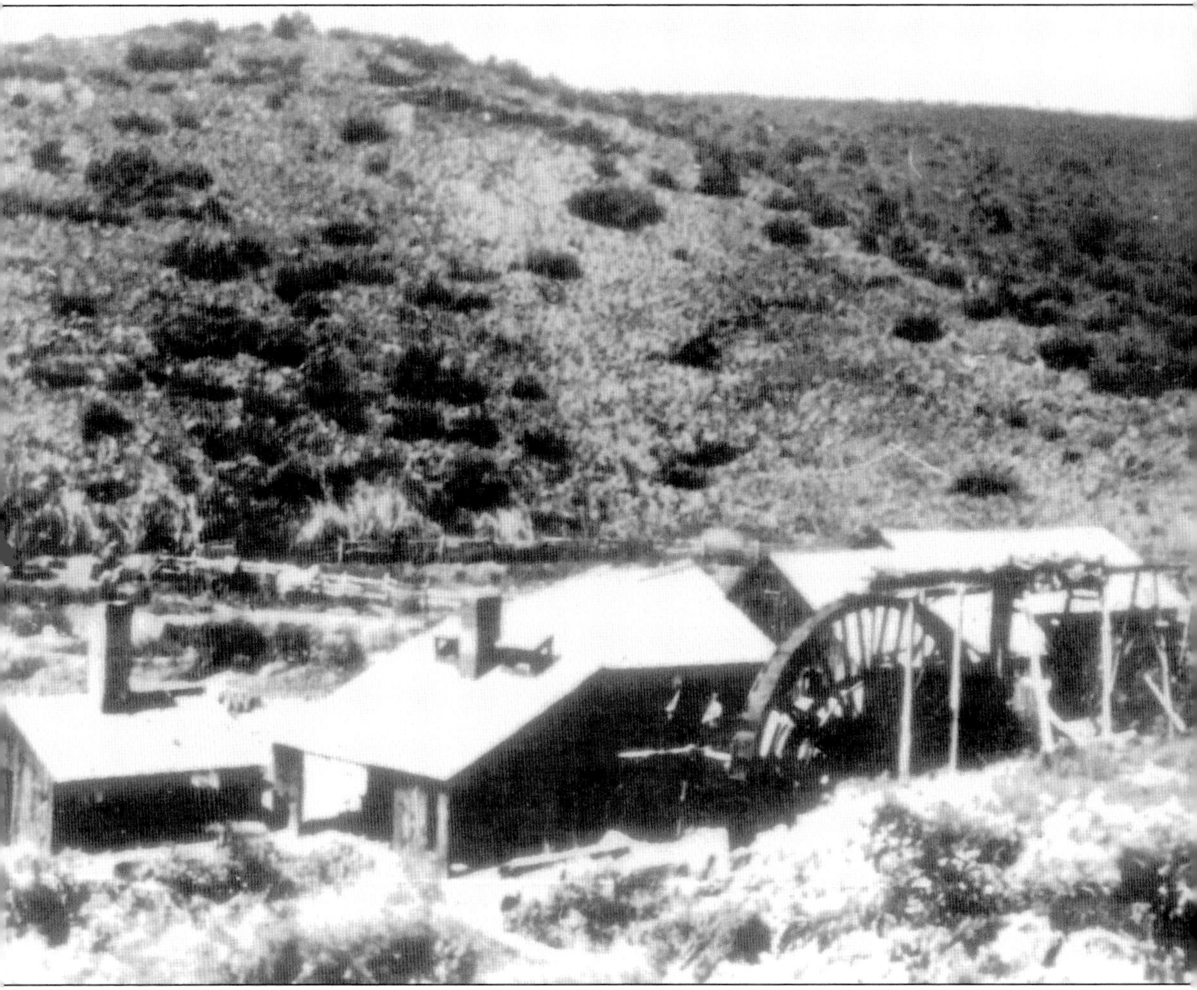

This is a much later view of the Bashford Mill, shortly before it closed in 1905.

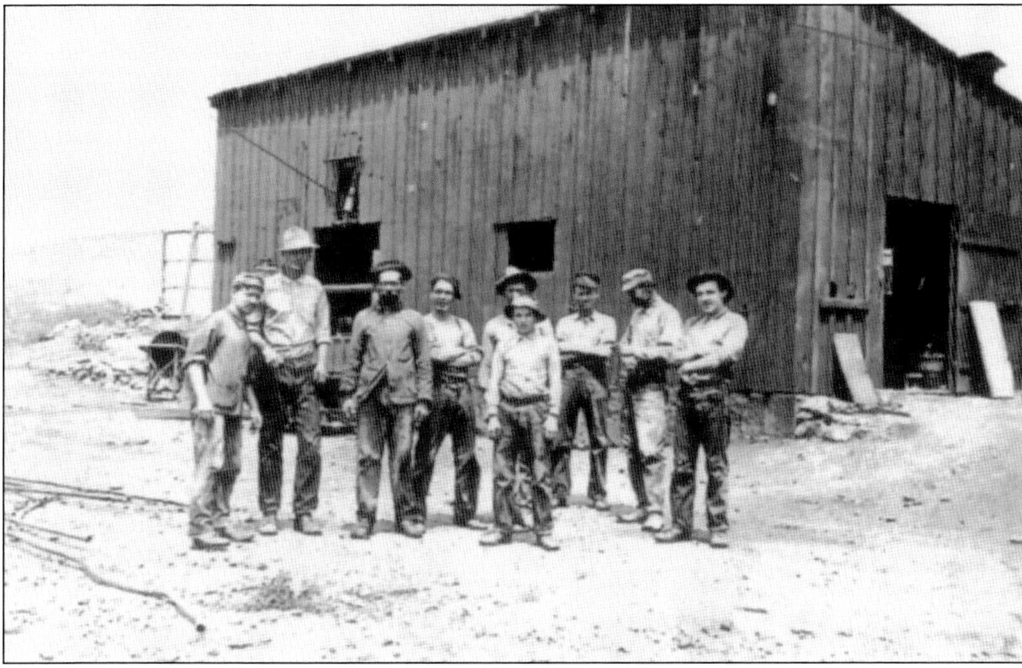

Workers at the Pick and Drill Mine are seen here in 1902.

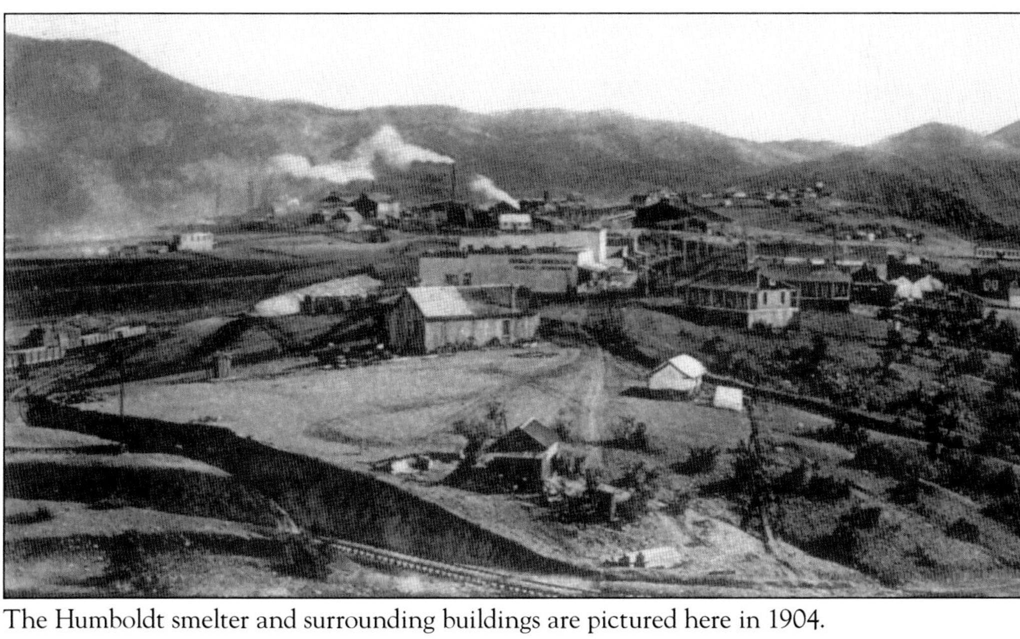

The Humboldt smelter and surrounding buildings are pictured here in 1904.

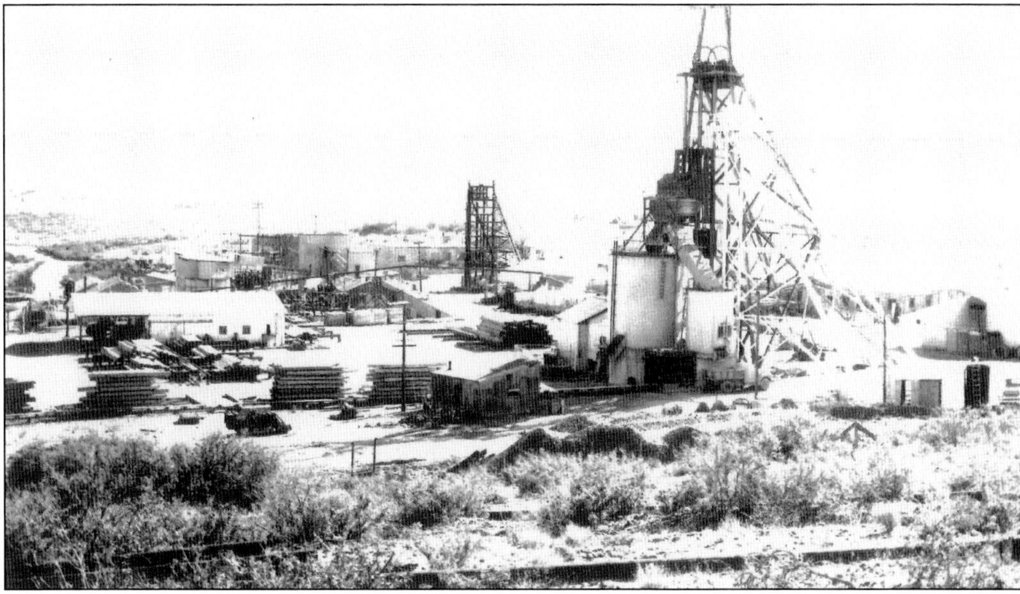

This 1950s photograph shows the Iron King Mine head frame hoist and plant. The mine was expanded in 1936 to remove metals from underground. In 1940, a cyanide processing plant was added to the site to treat the mill tailings and to enhance precious-metal recovery.

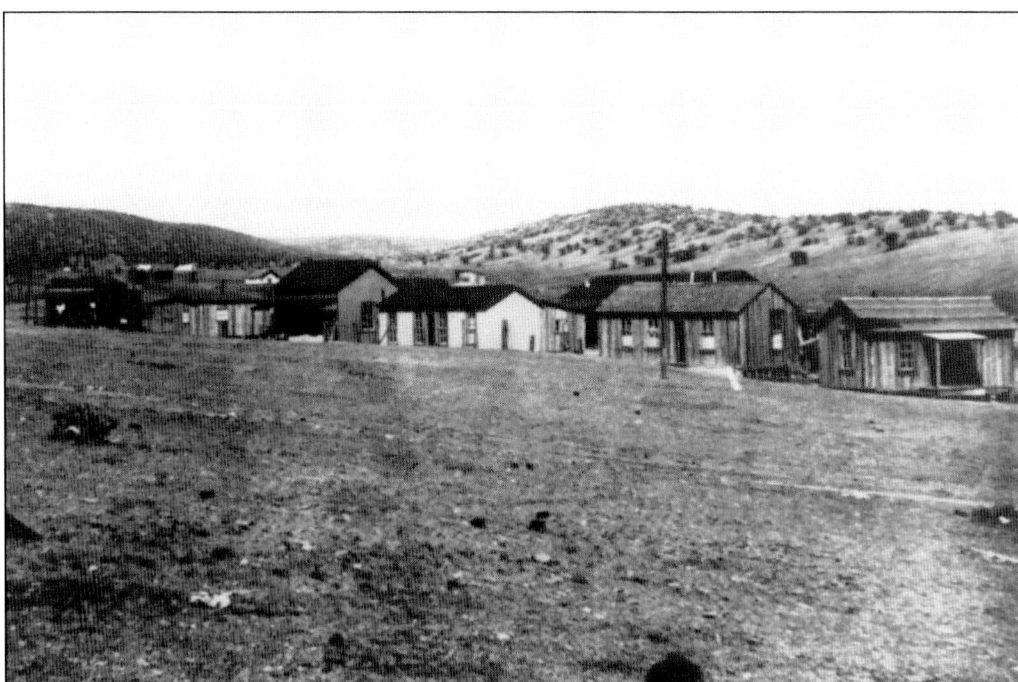

Construction of housing for miners and their families is taking place along Prescott Street in the late 1890s. Many of these houses were moved to other areas when the mining work subsided.

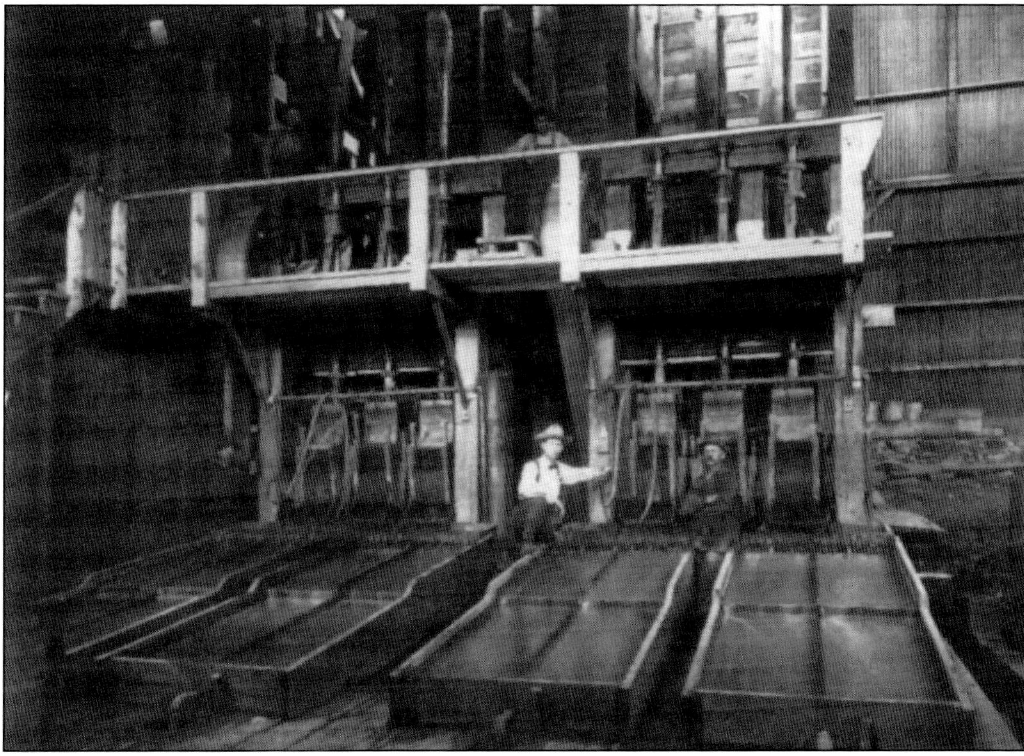

Mine workers are photographed concentrating ore. This photograph was most likely a publicity shot, considering the workers' clean clothes.

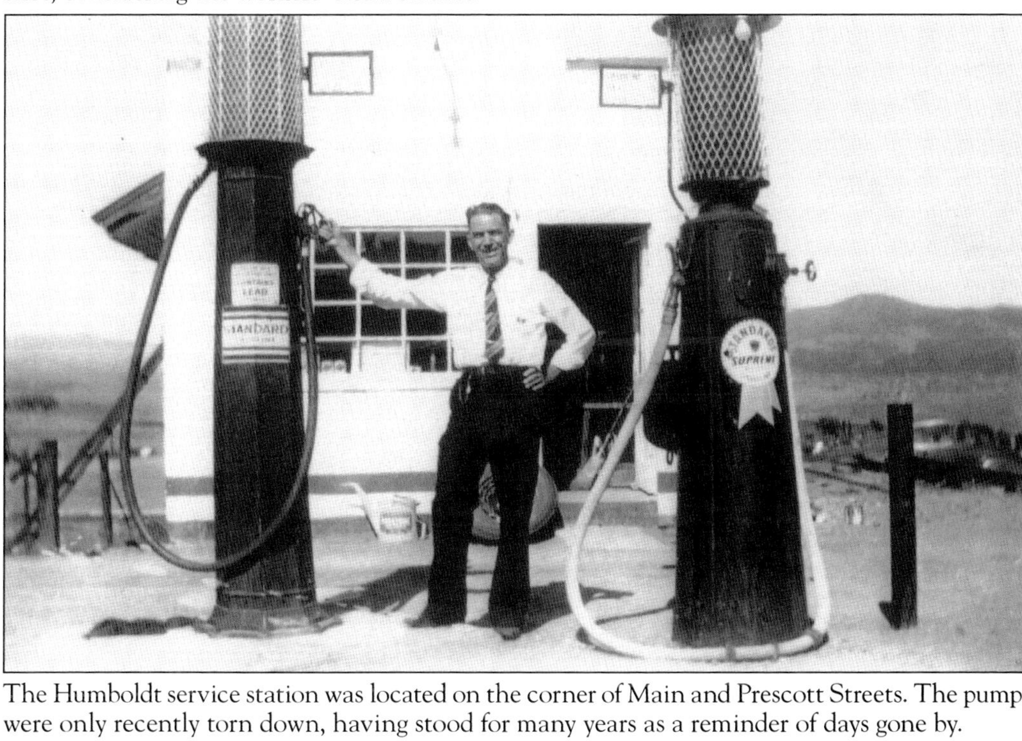

The Humboldt service station was located on the corner of Main and Prescott Streets. The pumps were only recently torn down, having stood for many years as a reminder of days gone by.

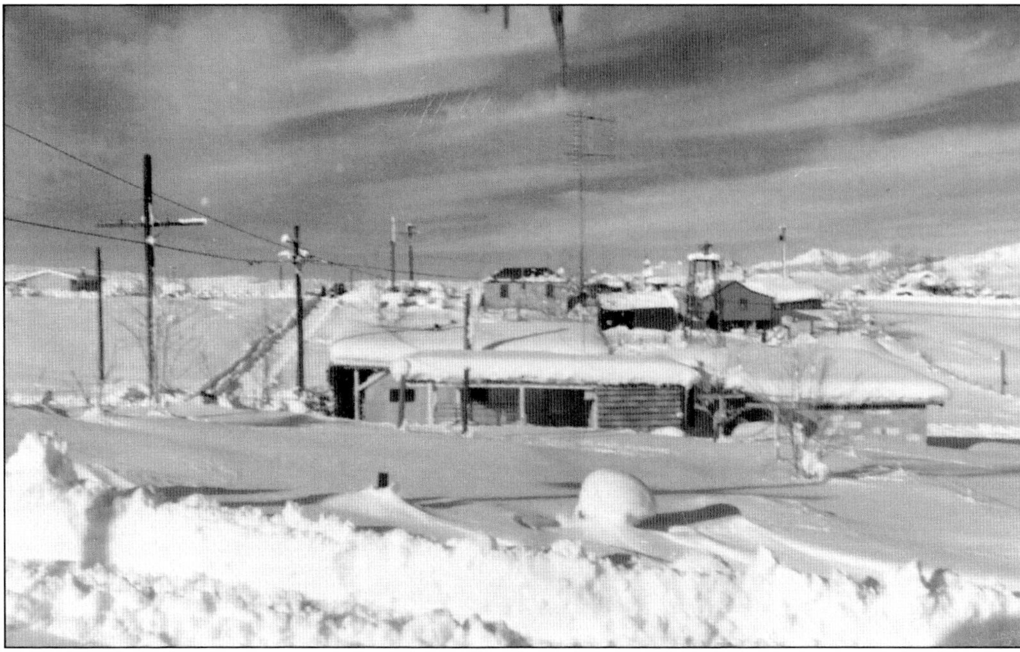

This photograph, taken in the winter of 1967, shows the Chemas front porch blanketed in snow following a heavy storm.

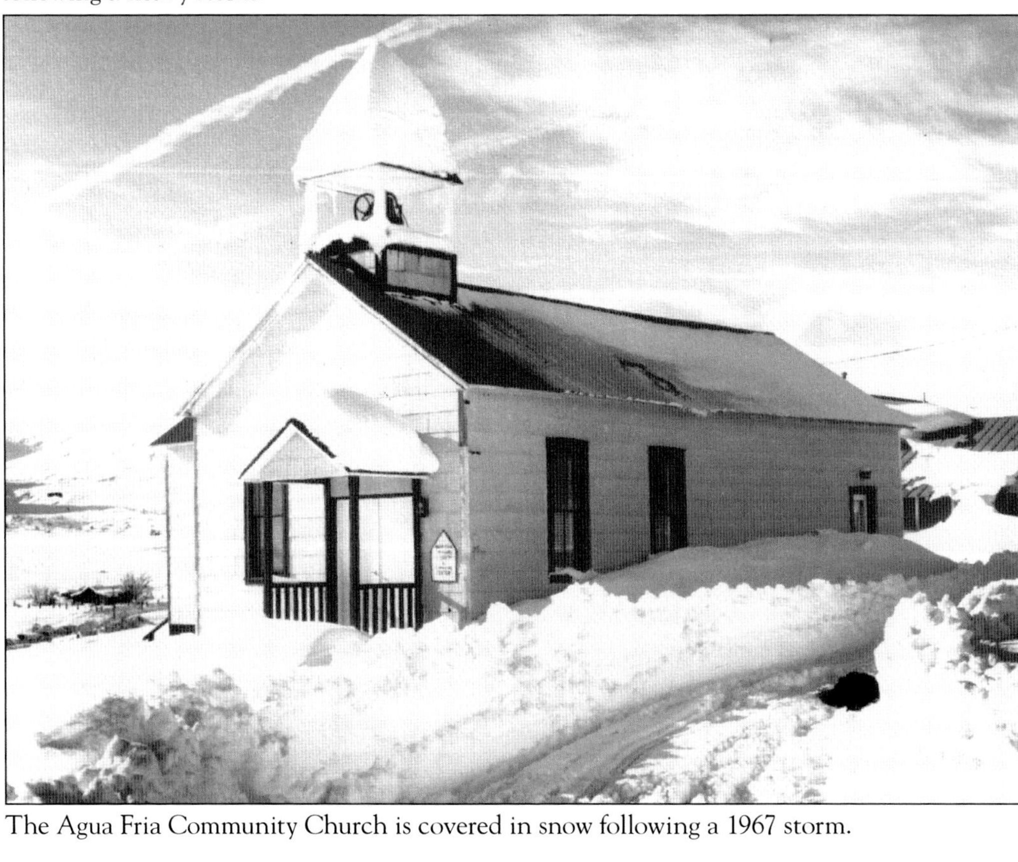

The Agua Fria Community Church is covered in snow following a 1967 storm.

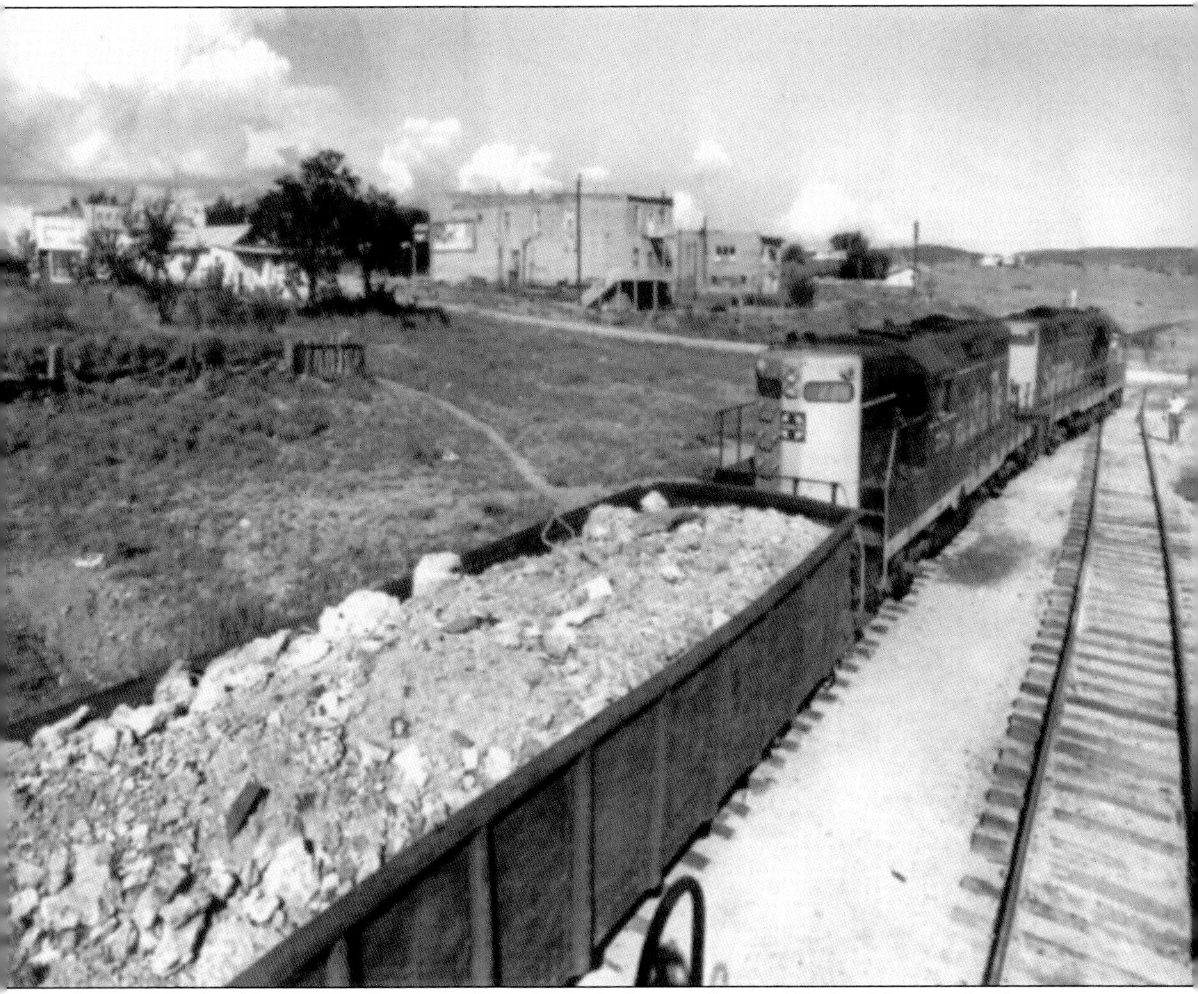

This was the final load of ore from Iron King Mine before its closing. The building in the distance at center still stands today, the home for Antiques and More.

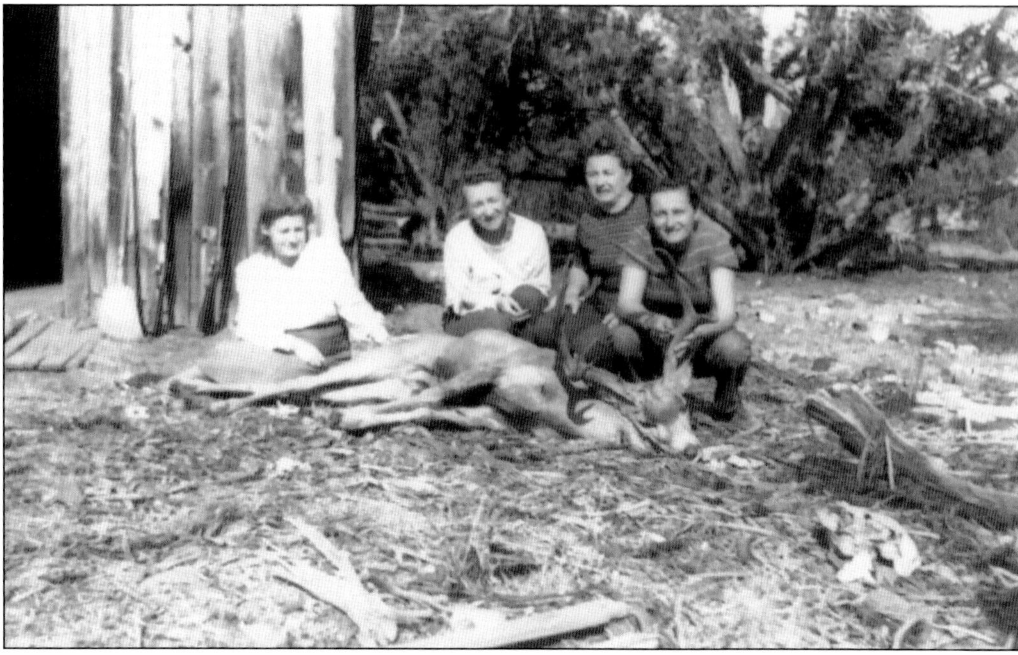

Several area residents proudly show off their hunting trophy on Prescott Street.

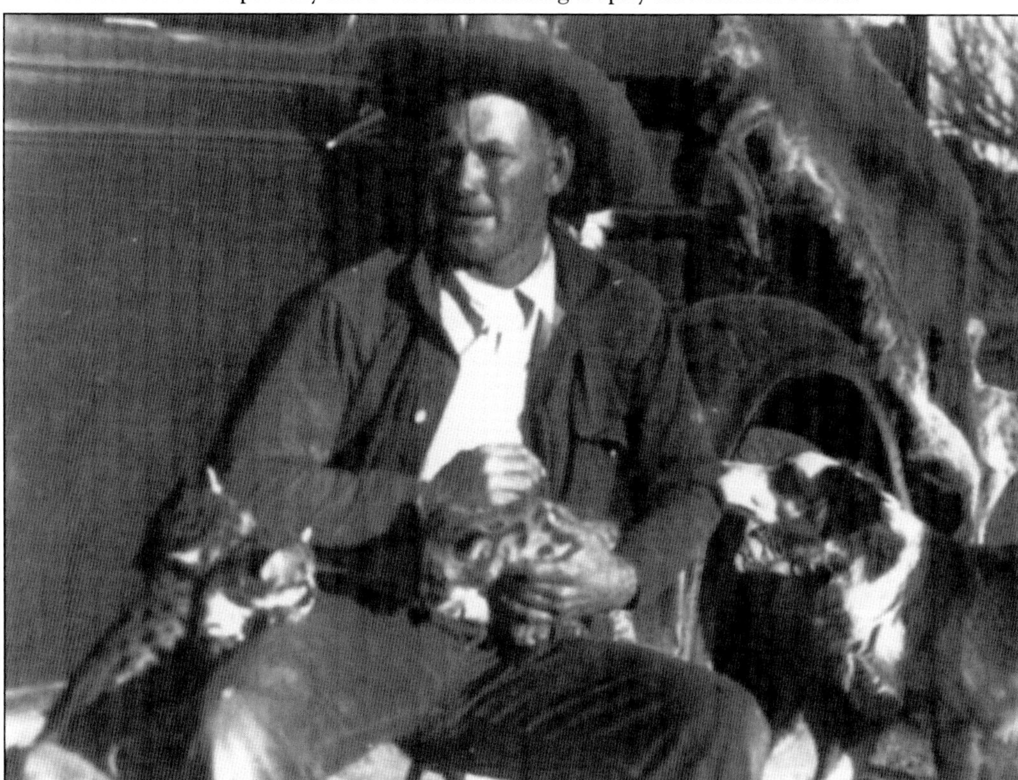

Giles Goswick was one of the best lion hunters in the West. He is pictured here with wild cubs and a curious dog.

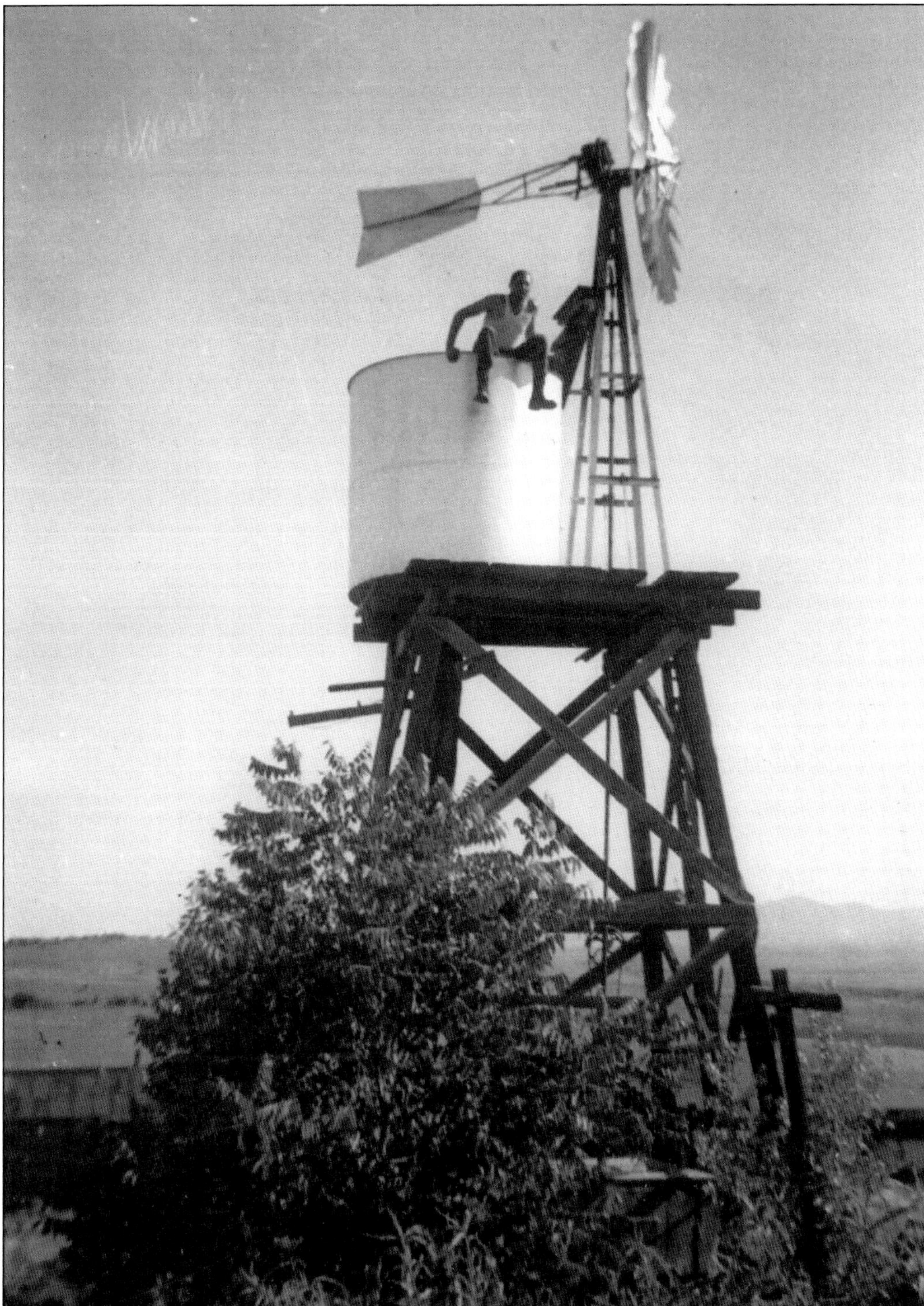

It was a typical sight for residents to see Rudy Chemas clowning around on the family water tank, as seen here.

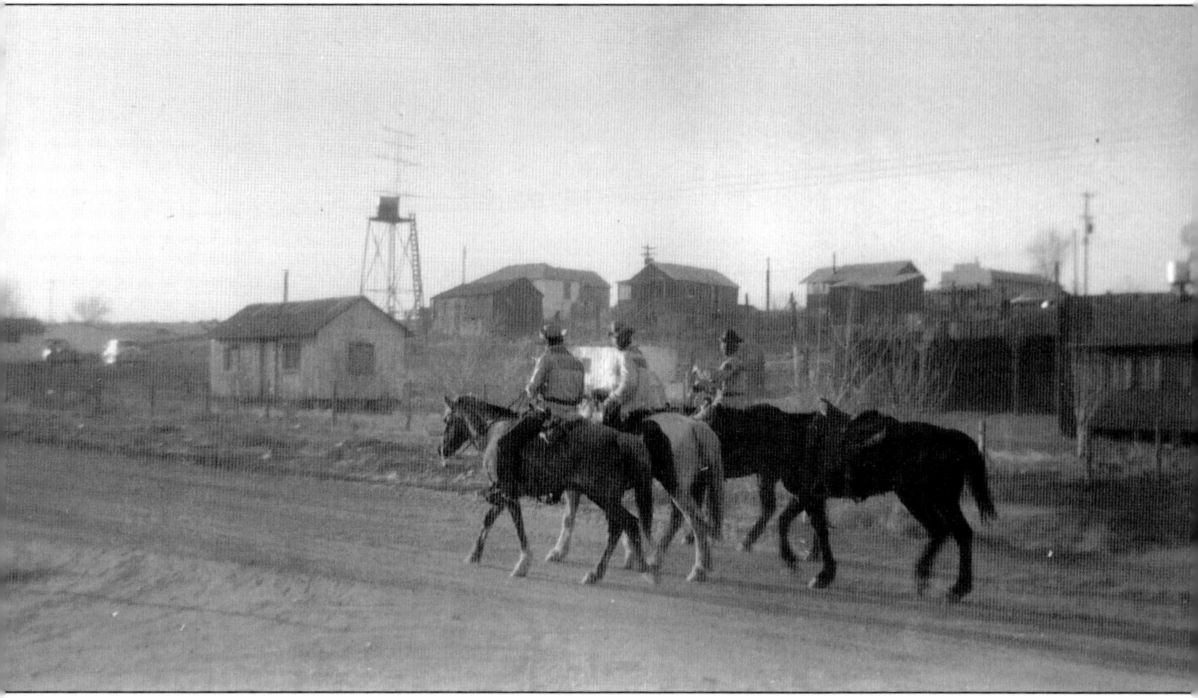

A gathering of Bill Williams's mountain men takes place on Prescott Street. This group still exists today. It represents the town of Williams in countless parades and activities.

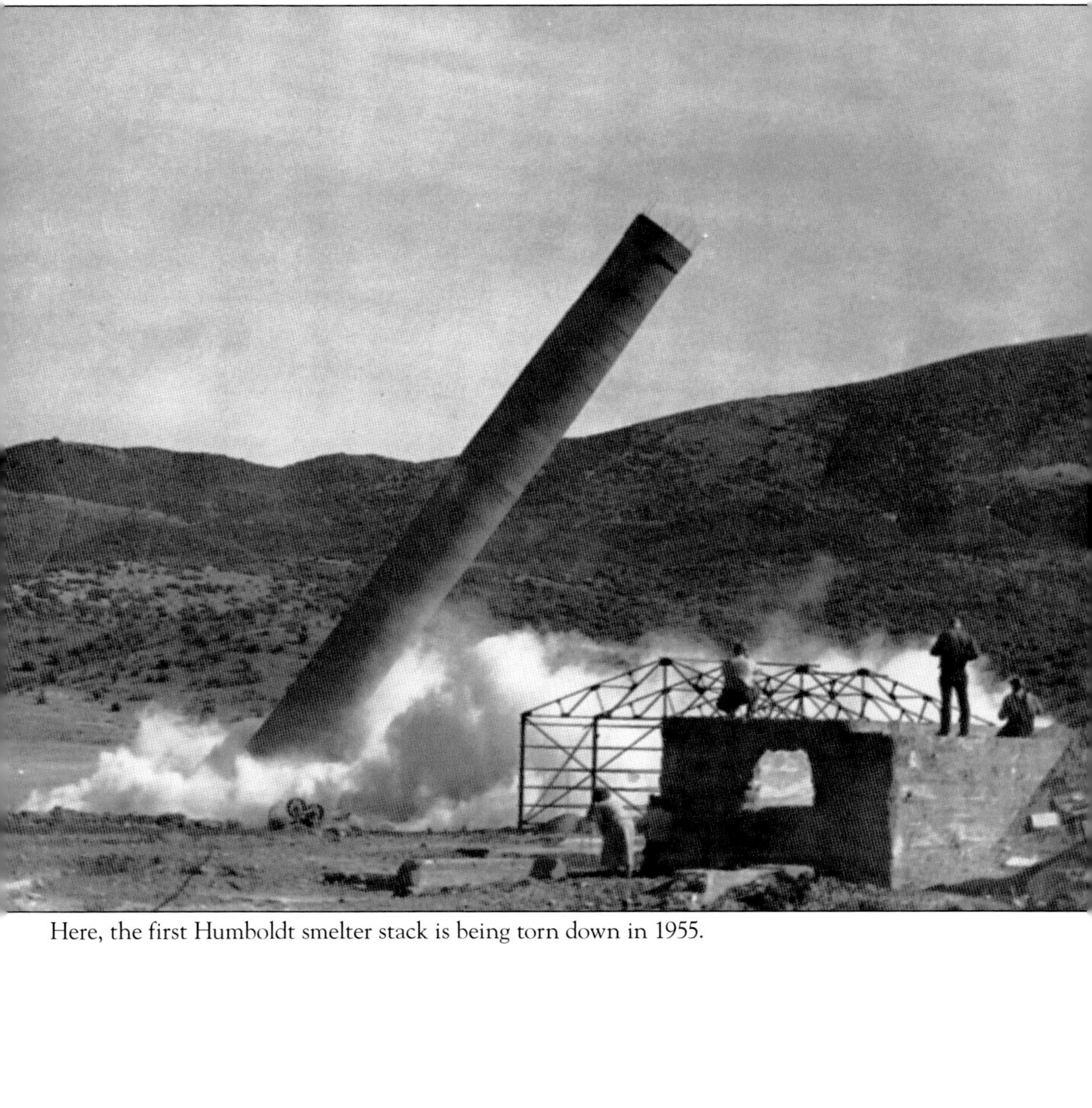

Here, the first Humboldt smelter stack is being torn down in 1955.

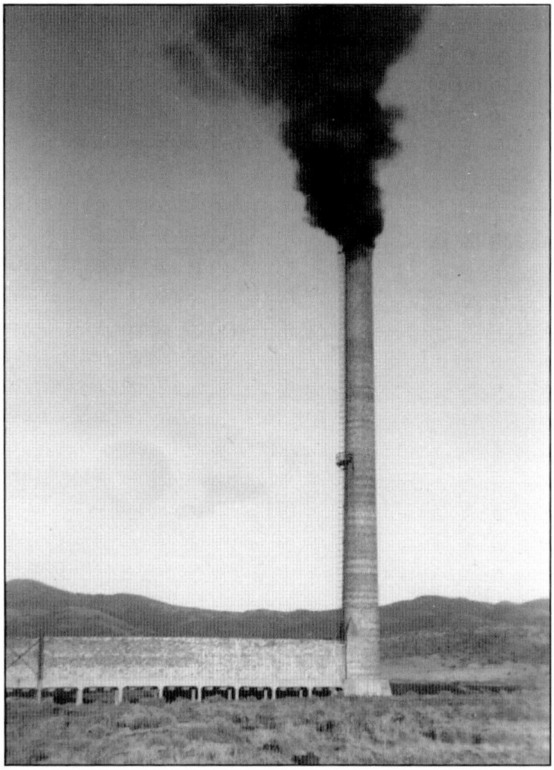

The Chemas kids appear to be burning tires in the old smelter stack. After the new smelter opened in 1905, area kids would climb to the top of the old one as a dare, or roll tires there and burn them, simulating the operation of the smelter.

This recent photograph shows the original water intake point for the Humboldt smelter.

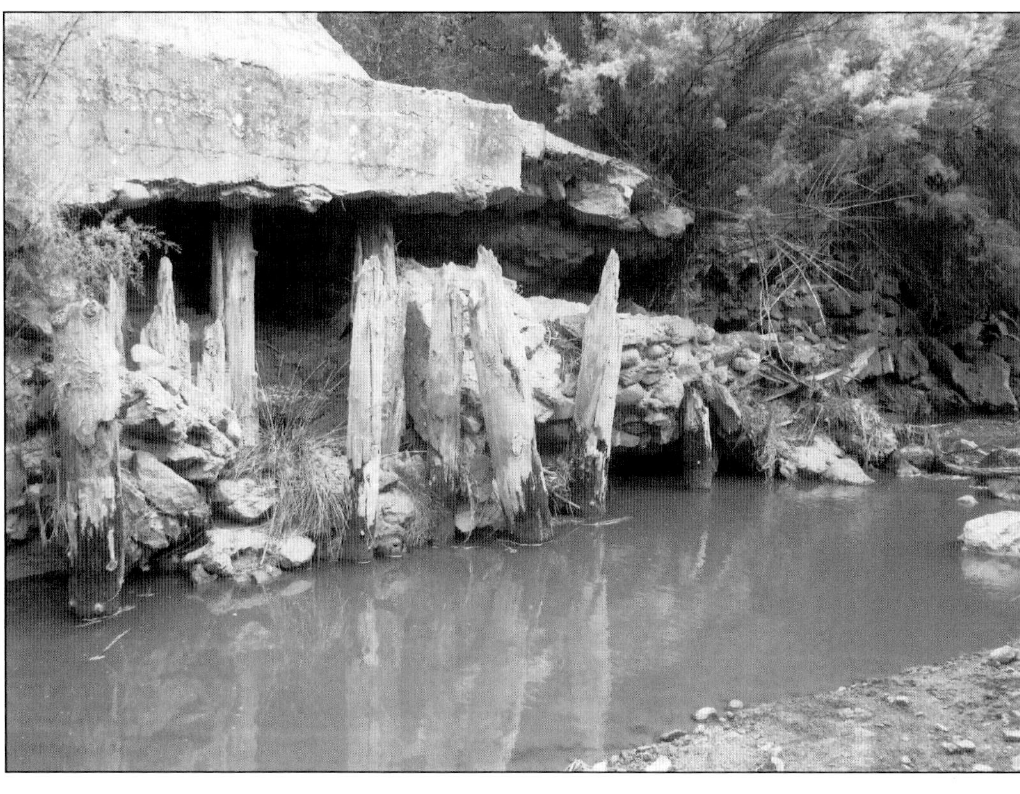

Three

Surrounding Areas
Cherry, Poland, Mayer, Cleator, Crown King, and Bumble Bee

While this book is primarily about the towns of Dewey and Humboldt and their important relationship to each other, it would be an injustice not to at least mention the other areas nearby that shared similar fates. Cherry Creek (now Cherry), Poland (now Poland Junction), Big Bug Station (now Mayer), Cordes Junction, Cleator, Crown King, and Bumble Bee all celebrated and suffered similar fates, most much smaller in population than when mining ruled these mountains. Other towns no longer in existence, such as Stoddard, McCabe, Huron, Chaparral, and others, are but footnotes now in the exciting history of settlement and mining that will forever mark the road one travels when studying the roots of this area. Those who stayed, and those who have moved here more recently, will agree on one thing. It is a great place to live and raise kids, and the weather and the neighbors are usually quite bearable indeed.

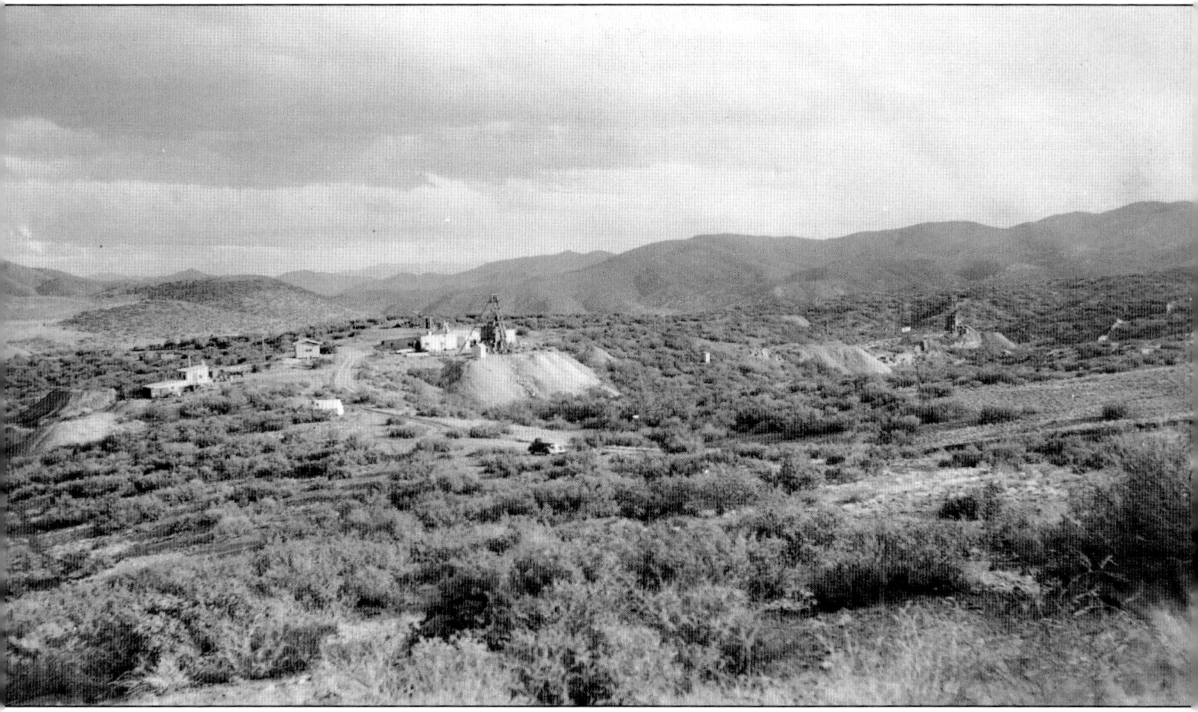

Crown King, the largest mine in the Bradshaw Mountains, later lent its name to a local settlement, Crowned King Mine. Years later, the name was shortened to its current form, Crown King. The first claim located in the Crown King group was the Buckeye, by Rod McKinnon, on July 1, 1875.

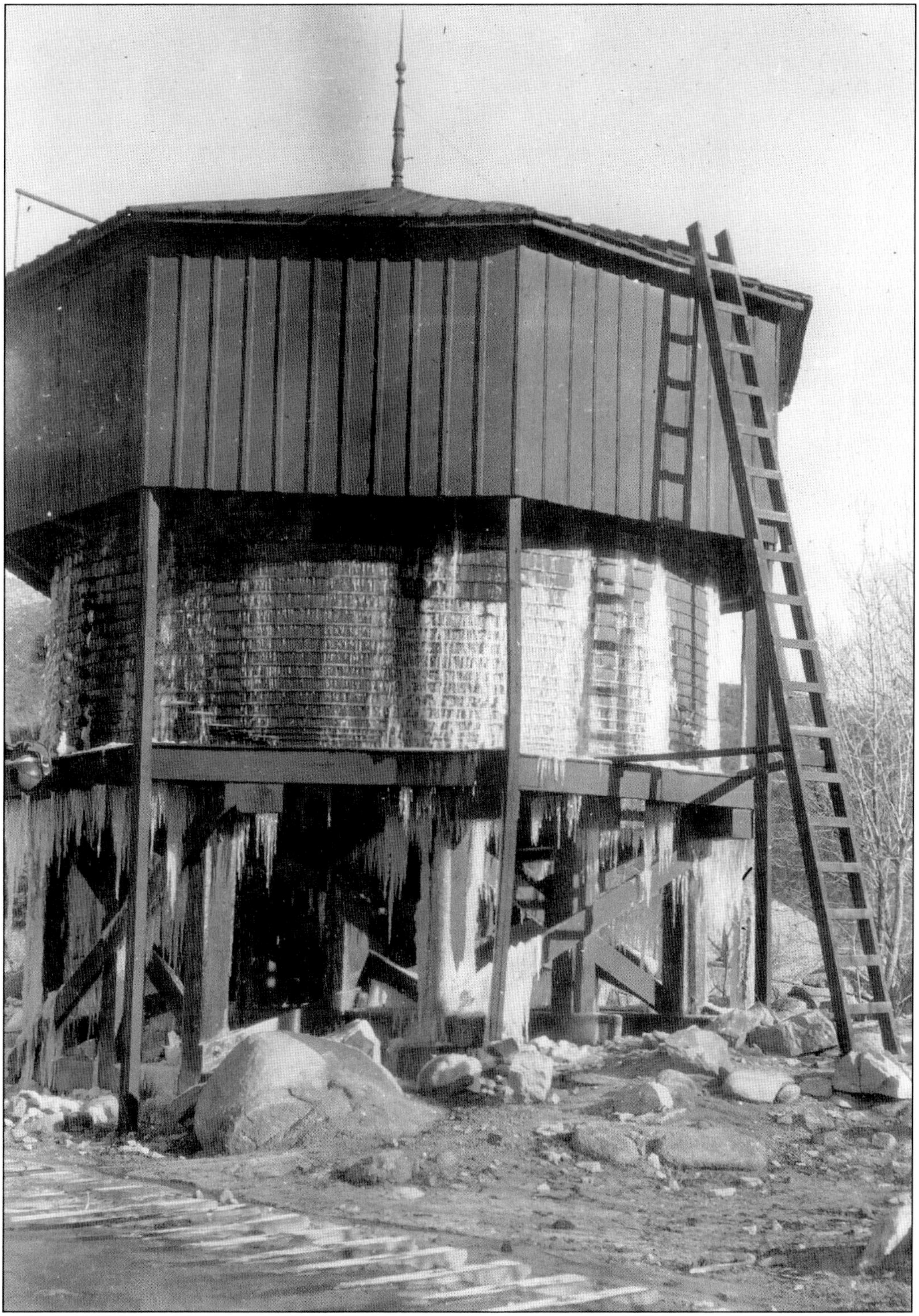

This is the famous Crown King water tower, which provided water to the growing area as the mines rapidly expanded.

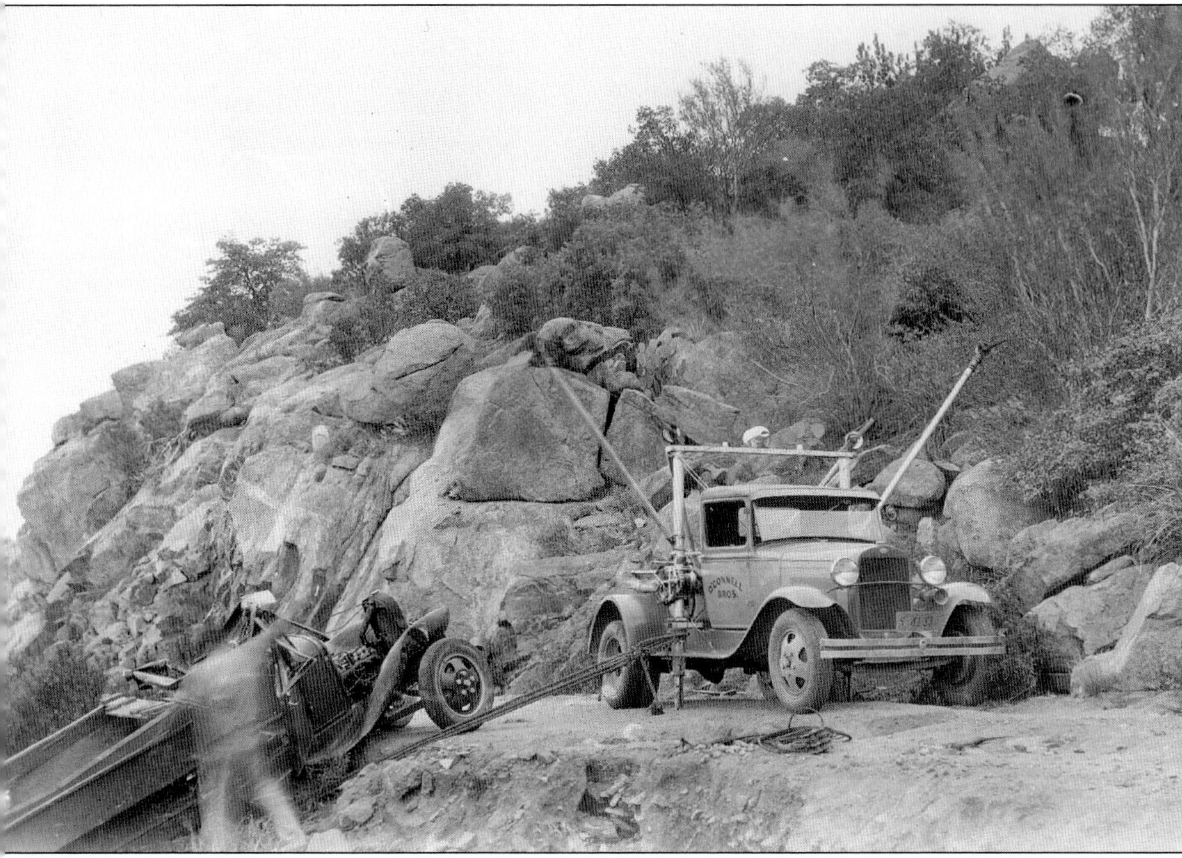

The O'Connell Brothers Towing Company uses heavy machinery to pull a wrecked car out of a tough spot. The location depicted is on the road to Crown King.

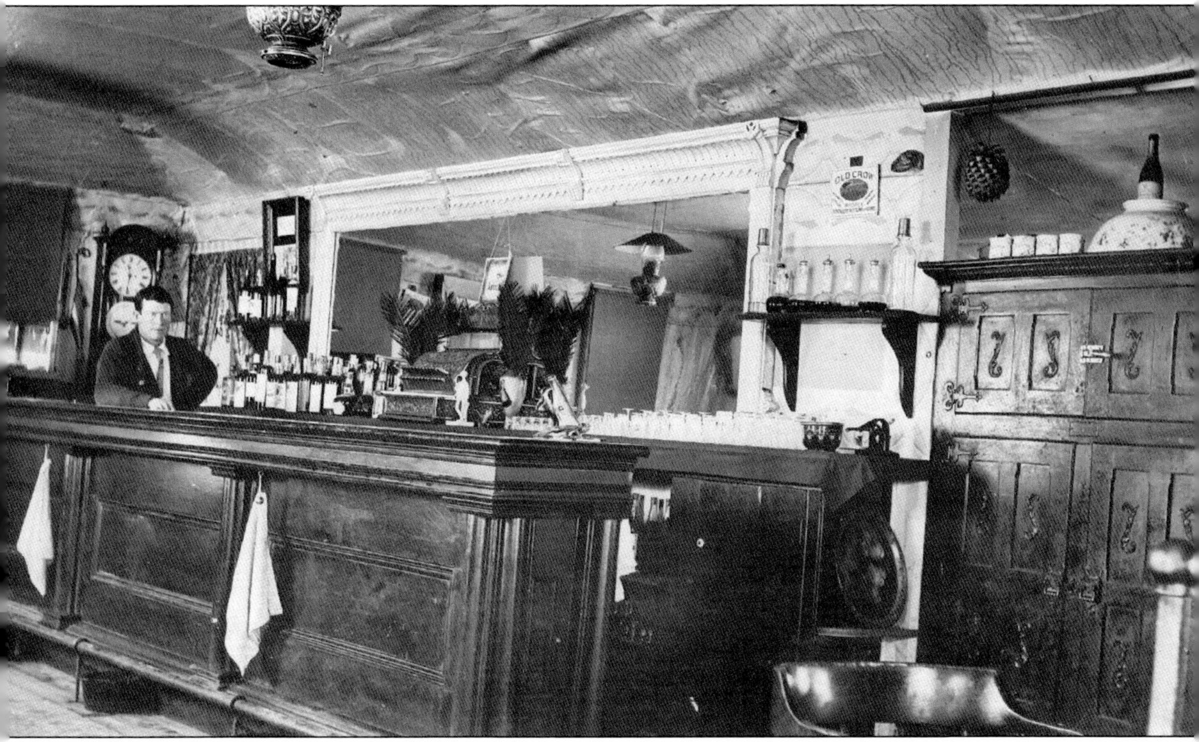

"Doc" Tyler is seen behind the bar at his Granite Saloon in Crown King, around 1890. All that remains of this bar is the foundation.

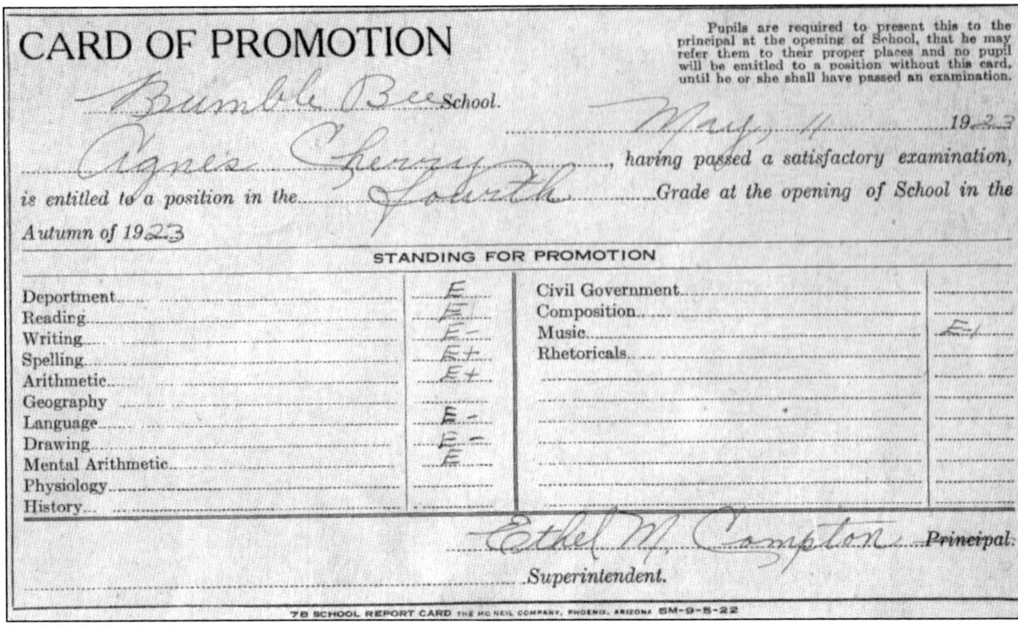

CARD OF PROMOTION

Pupils are required to present this to the principal at the opening of School, that he may refer them to their proper places and no pupil will be emitted to a position without this card, until he or she shall have passed an examination.

Bumble Bee School. May 11 1923

Agnes Cherry, *having passed a satisfactory examination, is entitled to a position in the* Fourth *Grade at the opening of School in the Autumn of 1923*

STANDING FOR PROMOTION

Subject	Grade	Subject	Grade
Deportment	E	Civil Government	
Reading	E	Composition	
Writing	E-	Music	E+
Spelling	E+	Rhetoricals	
Arithmetic	E+		
Geography			
Language	E-		
Drawing	E-		
Mental Arithmetic	E		
Physiology			
History			

Ethel M. Compton, *Principal.*

Superintendent.

78 SCHOOL REPORT CARD THE McNEIL COMPANY, PHOENIX, ARIZONA 5M-9-5-22

This is a 1923 report card for Agnes Cherry, younger sister to Esther Cherry Henderson. Agnes attended the Bumble Bee School. Around the turn of the 20th century, young kids in Humboldt went to Bumble Bee School, many riding horses and mules. High school students went to Prescott.

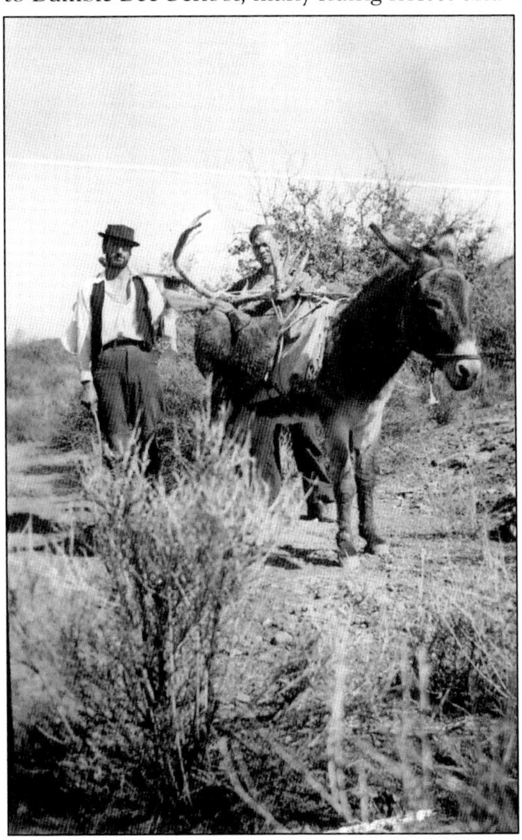

These men pose with their elk kill in Bumble Bee. An adult elk could feed a family for quite some time and was considered a nice trophy.

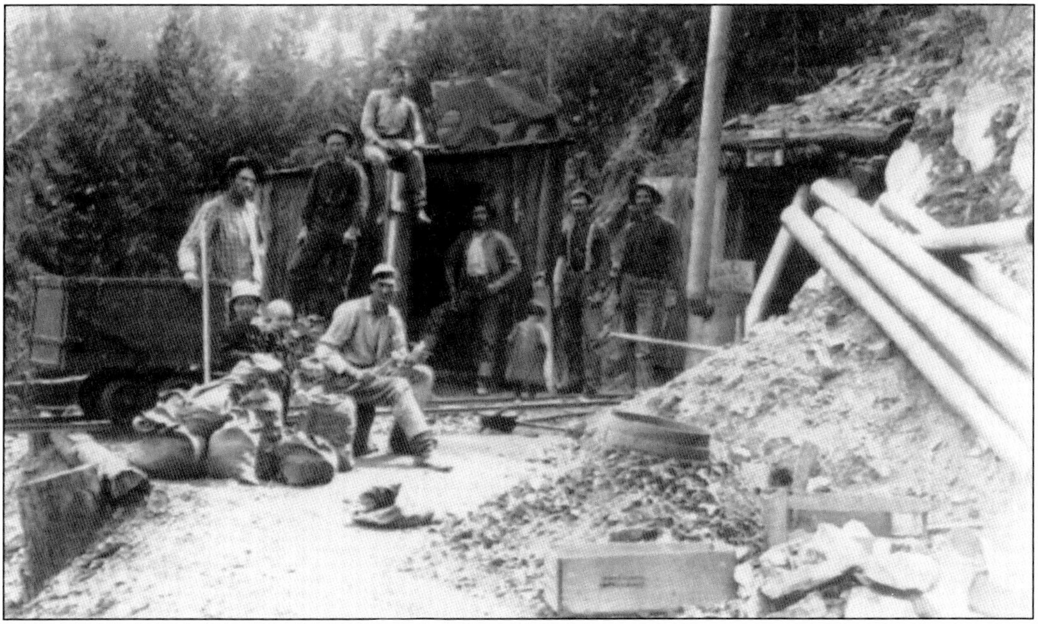

Poland Mine workers are seen here taking a rare break. Poland's post office was established in 1901 and was discontinued on February 15, 1913. The town is named after the mine discoverer Davis Robert Poland, who located the claim in 1872.

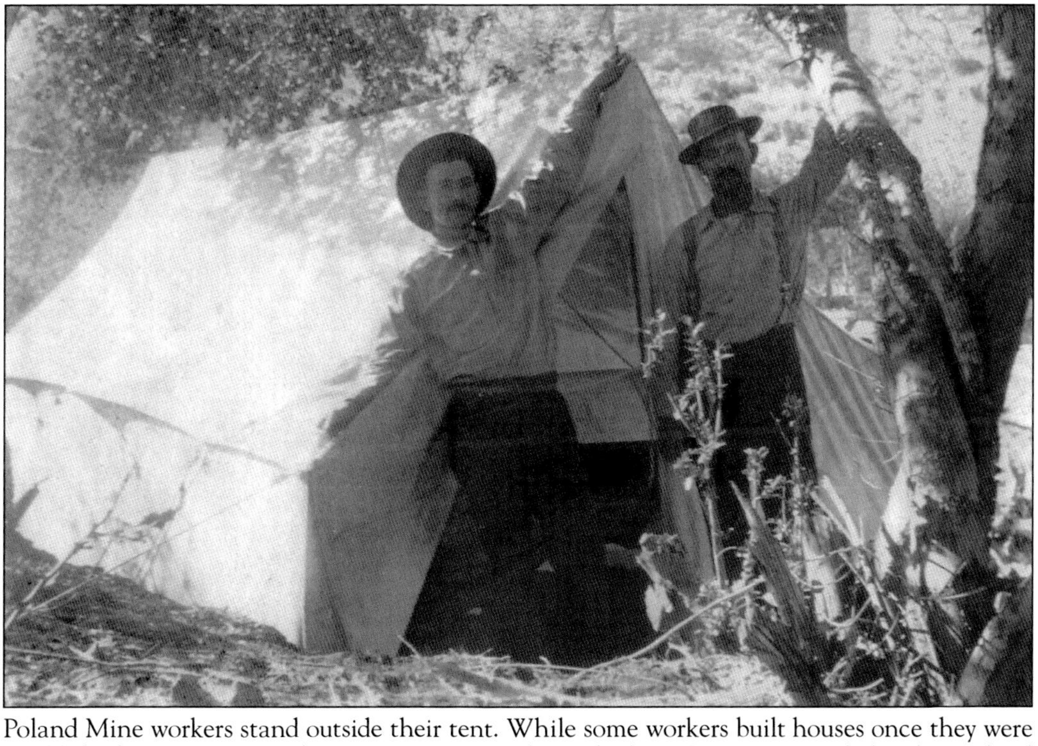

Poland Mine workers stand outside their tent. While some workers built houses once they were established, tents were much more common in the early days. Over 800 people lived in Poland in 1902, and the town boasted a fine lodging house with 14 rooms. A tunnel was dug two miles through a mountain to the town of Walker to aid in ore transport.

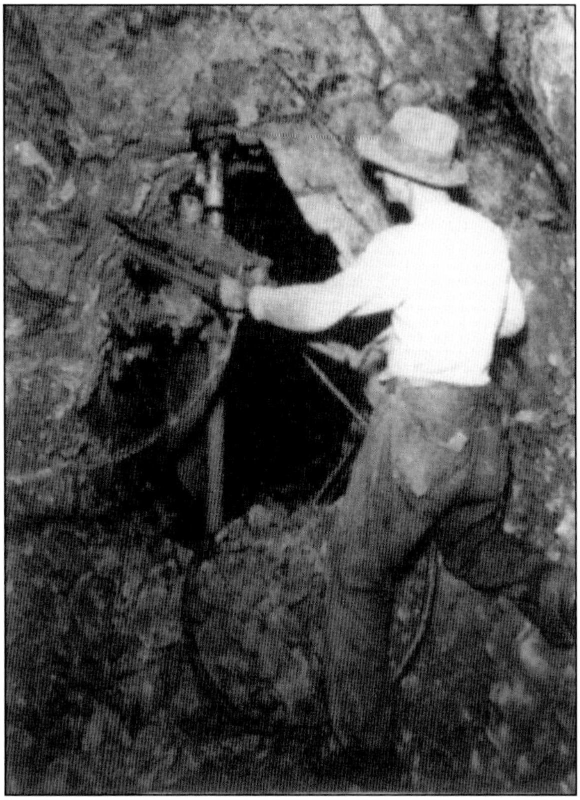

A Poland Mine worker labors with equipment deep underground. Miners in Poland were paid $2.25 per day, which did not include food or lodging, which cost $1 per day. Eventually, miners struck for higher wages and received $4 per day.

Pictured here are early Poland Mine workers busy extracting ore by hand alongside their burros. The tunnel to Walker opened up the ability to process more ore from the mine.

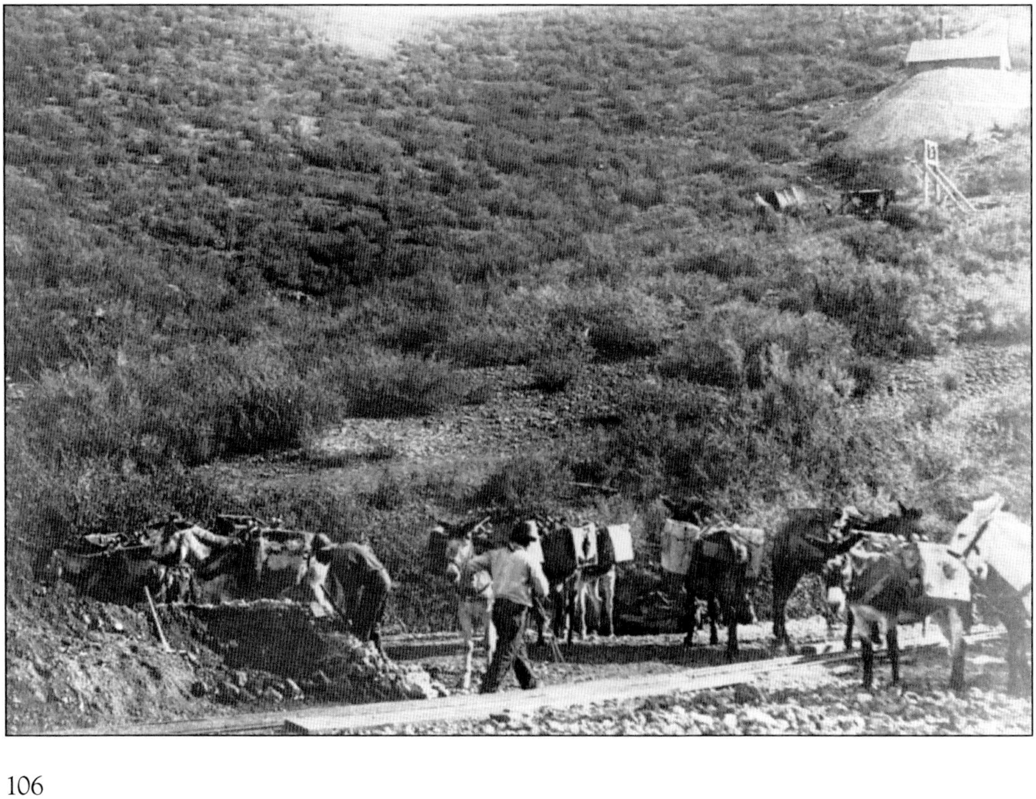

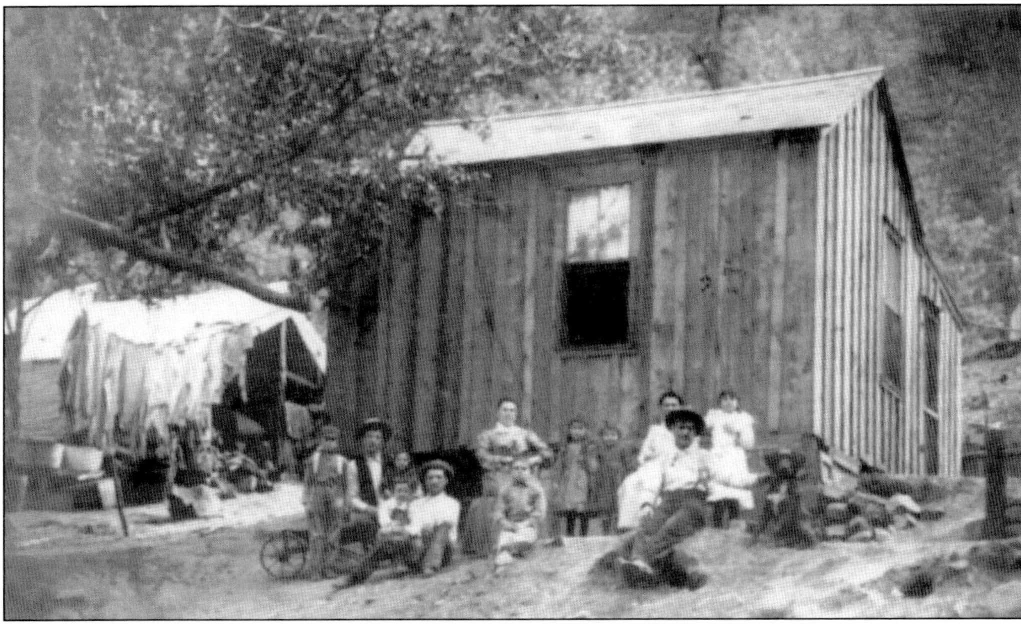

This is an early house for a Poland (Junction) Mine worker family. The tent at left was a product of earlier use or served to house an expanding family. Many families lived in tents until determining that they would have long-term employment.

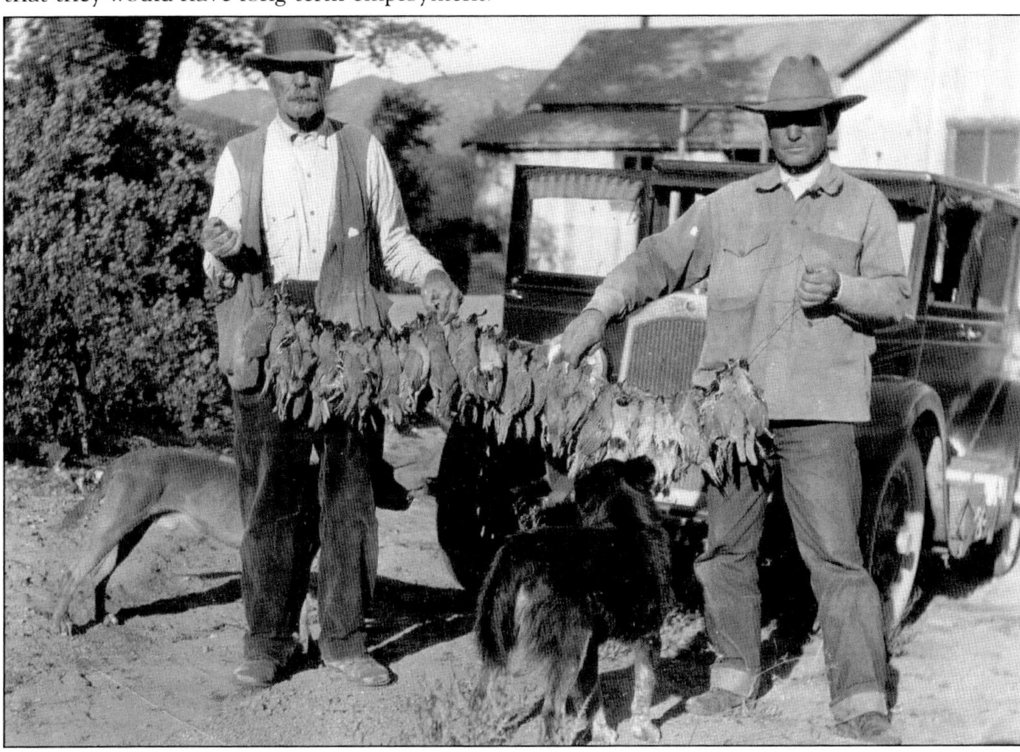

Here, Spencer (left) and Norval Cherry are displaying their day's hunt. This photograph was taken in Cherry Creek, currently the town of Cherry. Game was plentiful at the time, so food was rarely a concern for those who had time to go out on hunting expeditions.

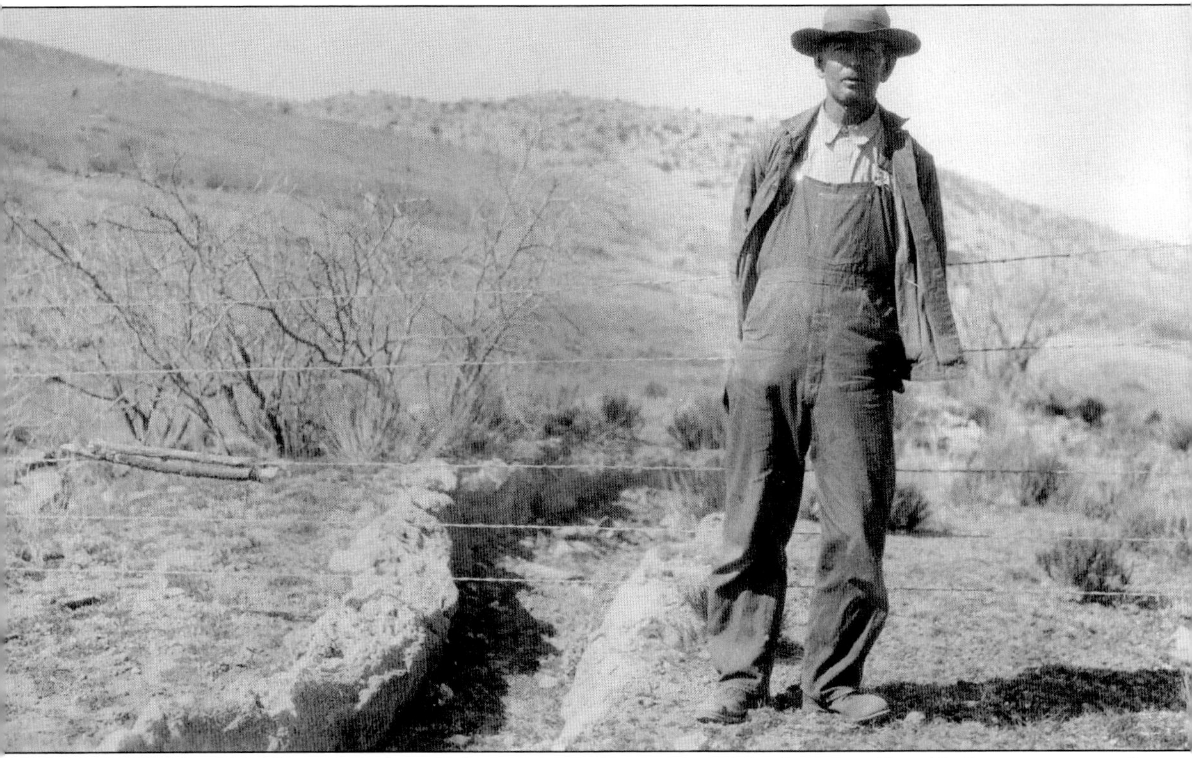

This was Bumble Bee and its early irrigation system, used for farming. Bumble Bee was named for nearby Bumble Bee Creek. Established in 1863, the town served as a stagecoach stop and an outpost for the US cavalry. The post office was established in 1879.

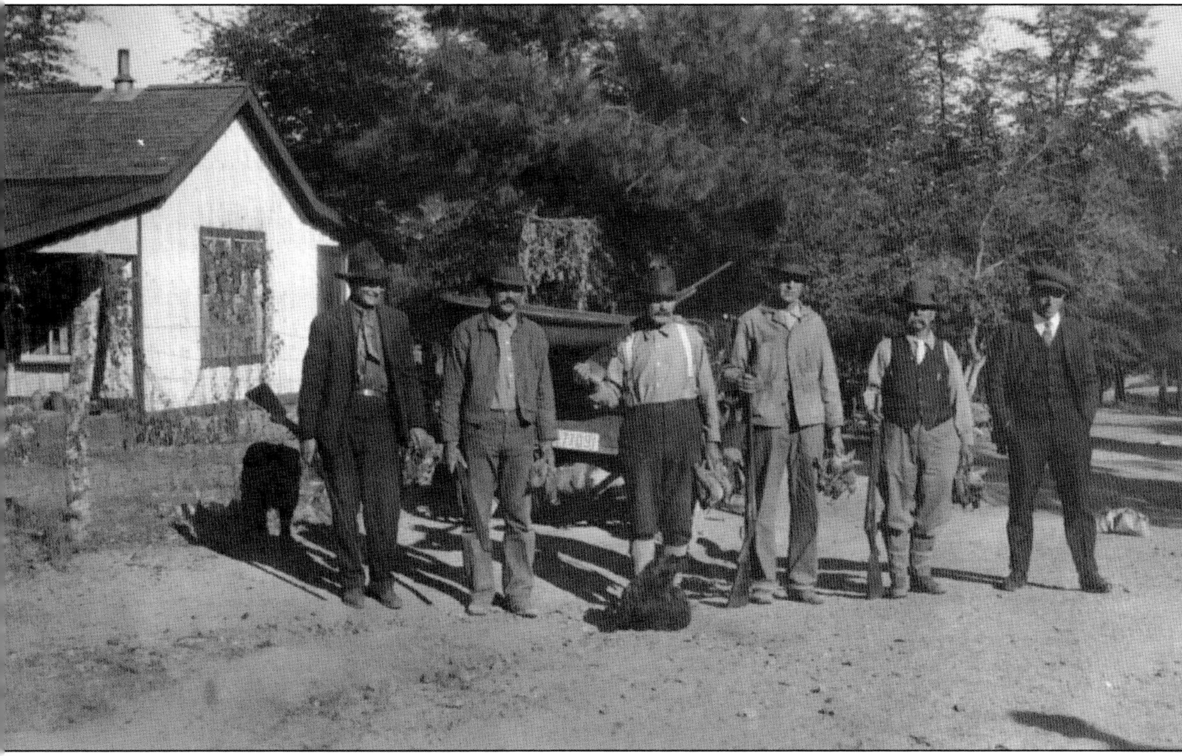

A hunting party sets out from the Goddard house in Cherry Creek, currently named Cherry.

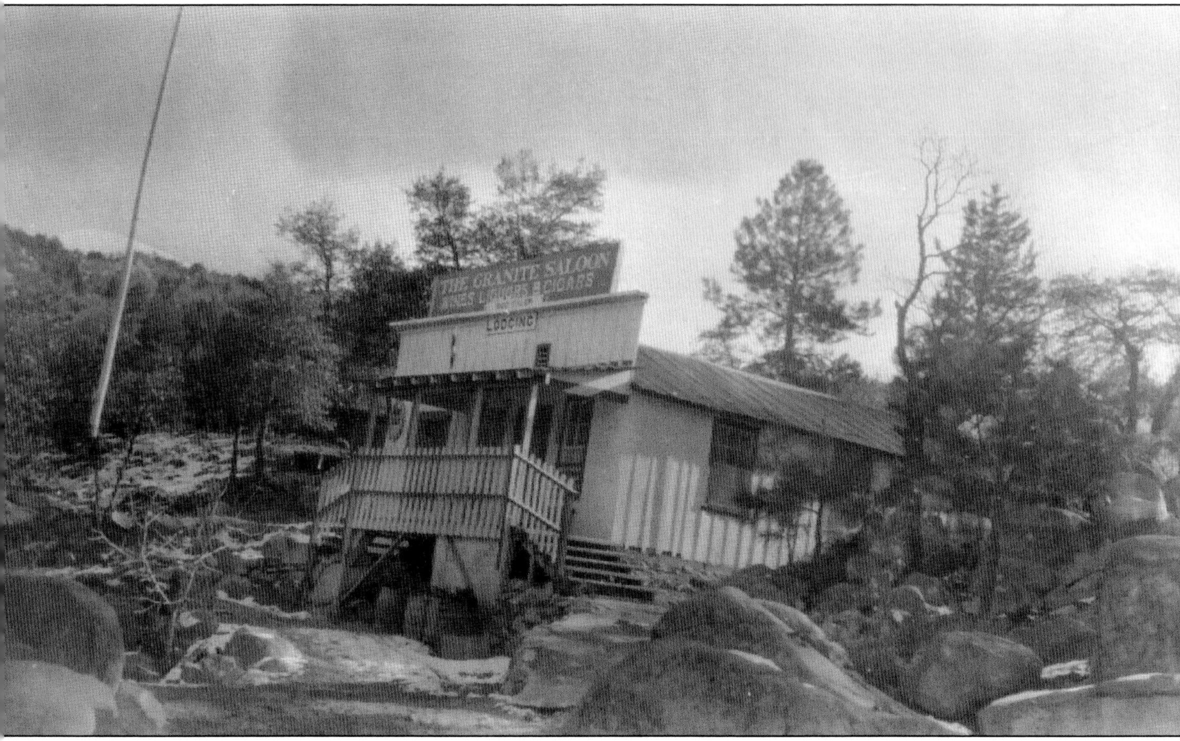

The Granite Saloon in Crown King is seen here in 1927. The saloon was a popular meeting place and had an adjacent small hotel.

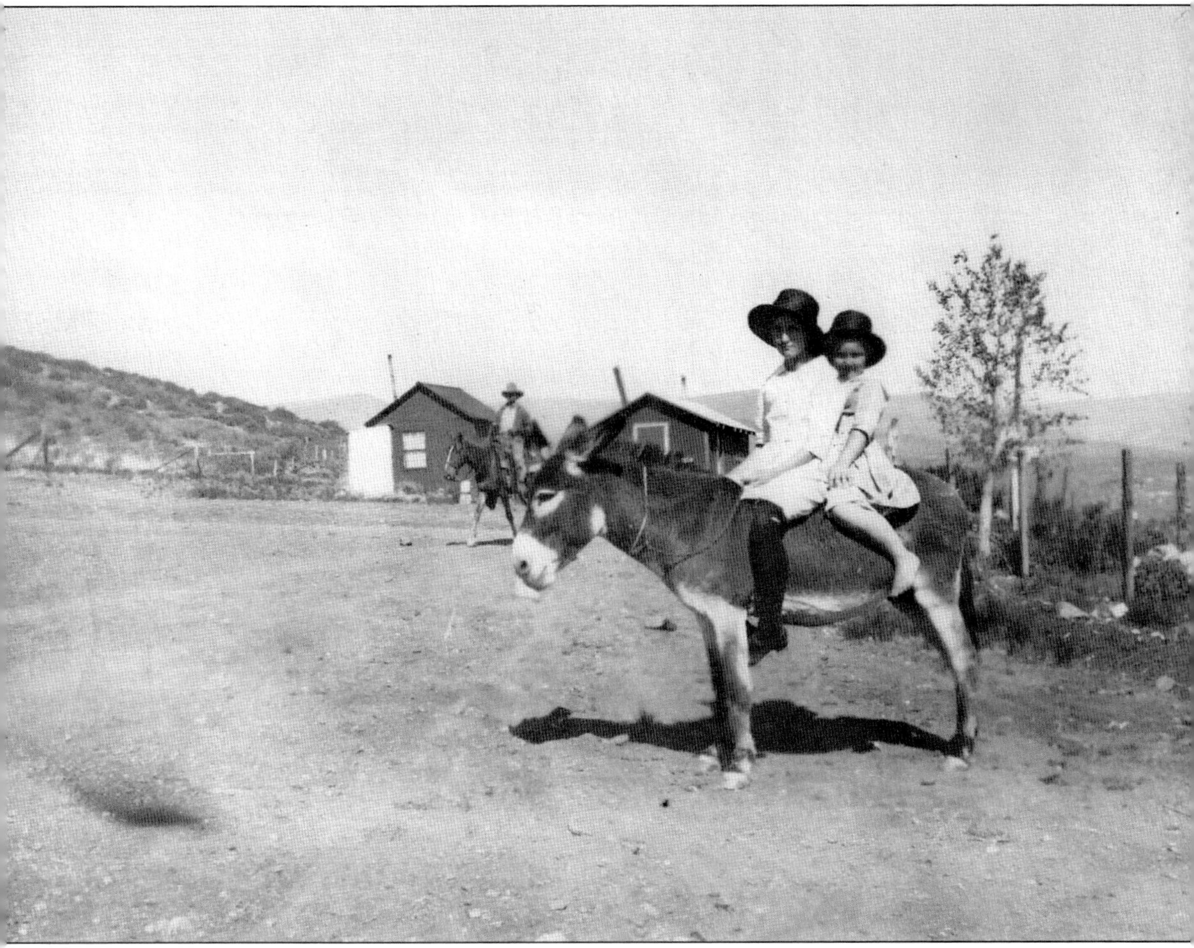

Seen here are Esther Cherry Henderson (left) and Agnes Cherry in 1919 in Bumble Bee on their way to school. Many children in Dewey and Humboldt traveled this way to school in surrounding areas until the big Humboldt School opened.

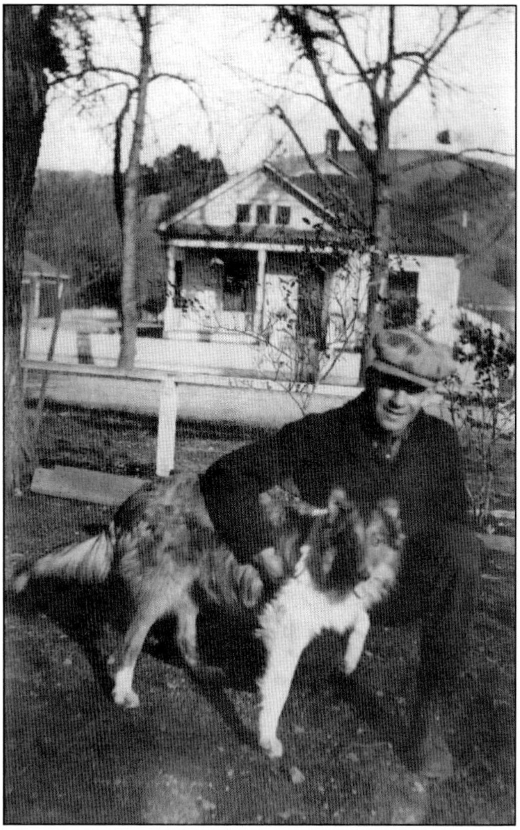

Doc Tyler poses with one of his prized collies at his home in Crown King. Tyler was an important part of the community for many years.

It appears a cattle drive is under way at Government Springs (currently Orme Ranch) in 1922. On cattle drives, cowboys attempted to move and herd cattle while sitting atop their horses.

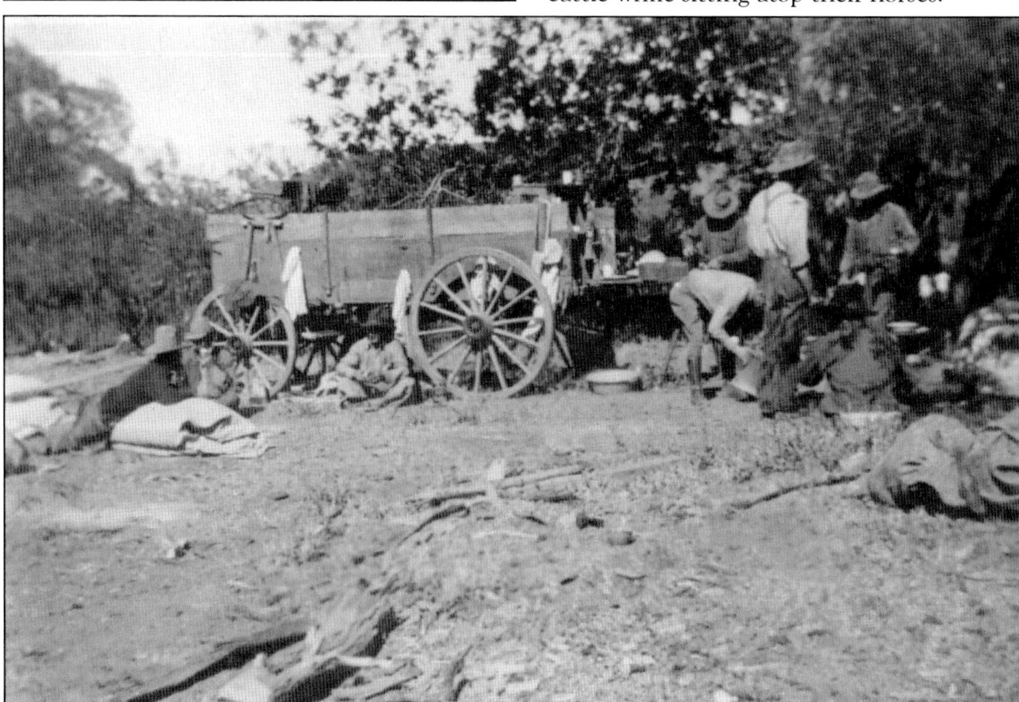

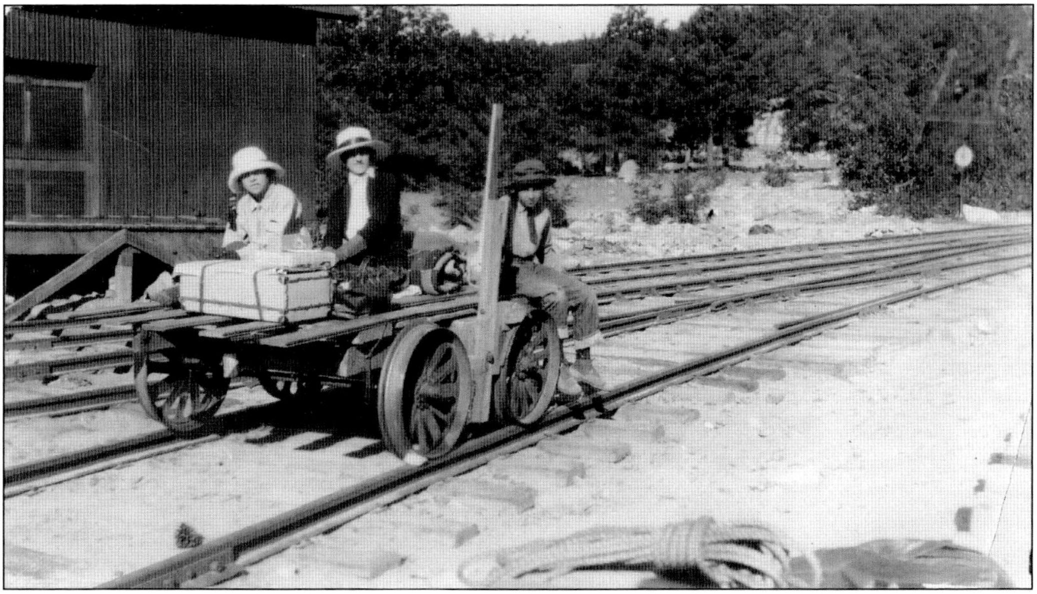

Several Crown King kids are out for an adventure on a railway handcart. There are many stories of residents using these carts to go on excursions, and a few tales tell of narrow misses with oncoming trains.

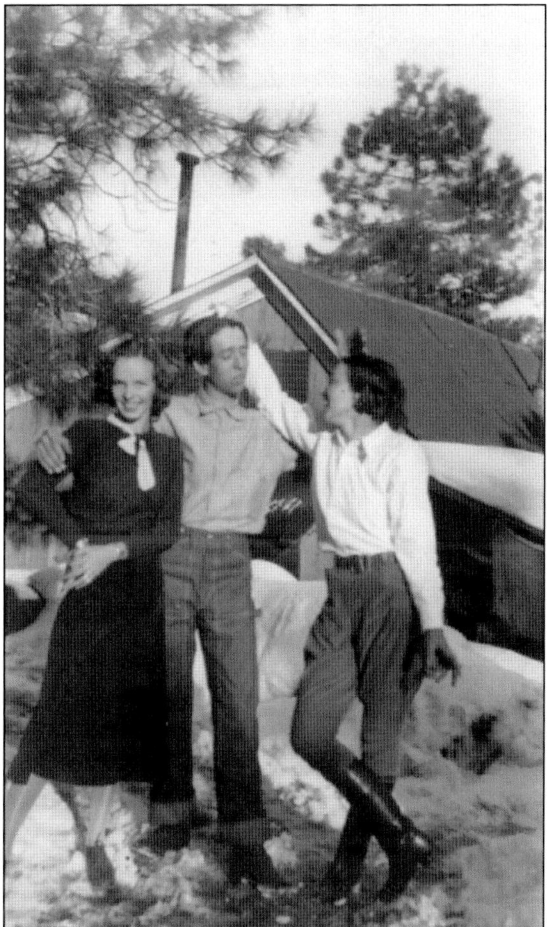

A lively group of young adults goof around in Crown King.

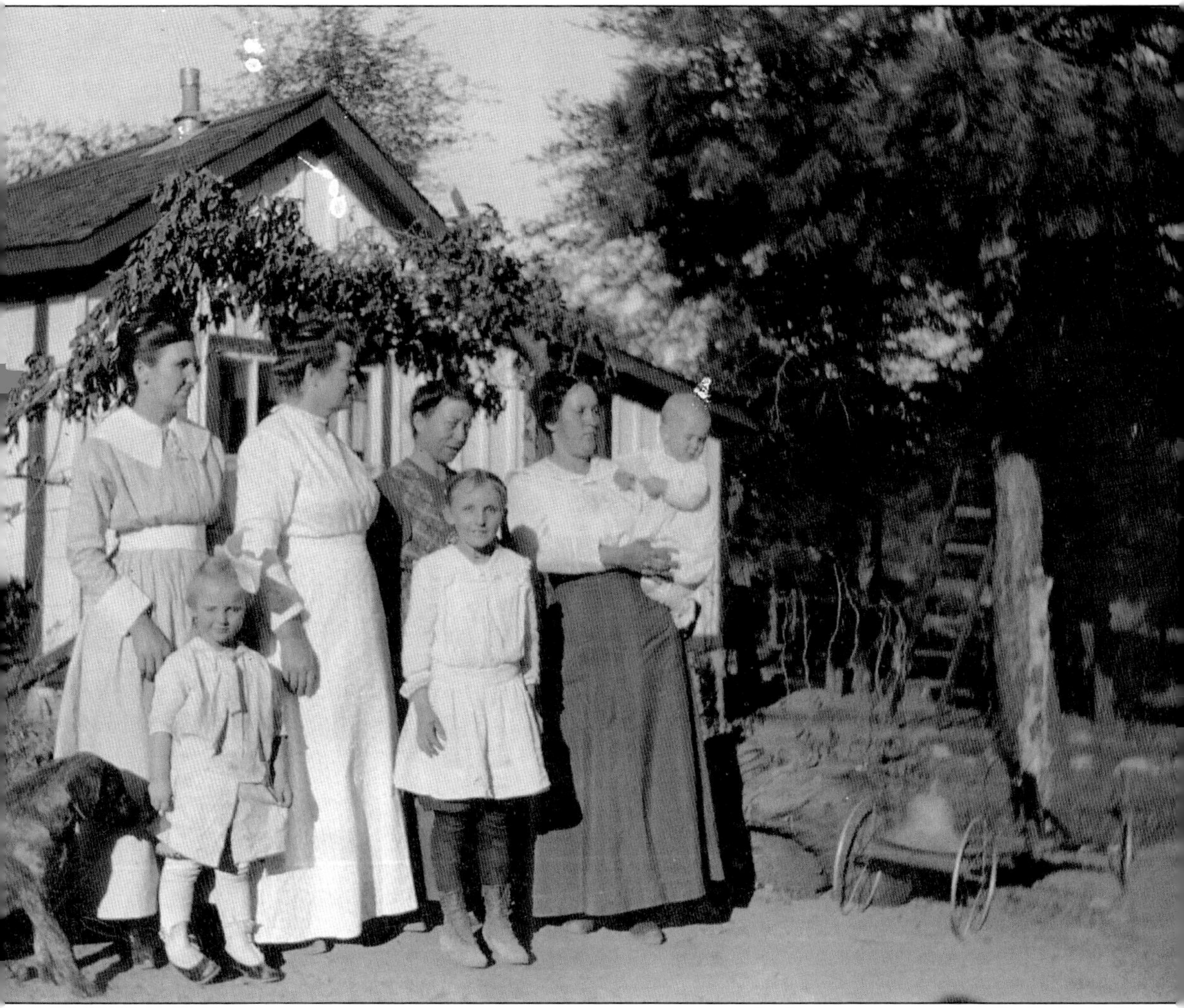

The Cherry family poses at their home in Cherry Creek (now Cherry). Shown are, from left to right, (first row) Agnes Cherry and Ester Cherry Henderson; (second row) Grandma Cherry, Mrs. George Miller, Mrs. Jack Guttry, and Jane Cherry (holding Cliff Cherry).

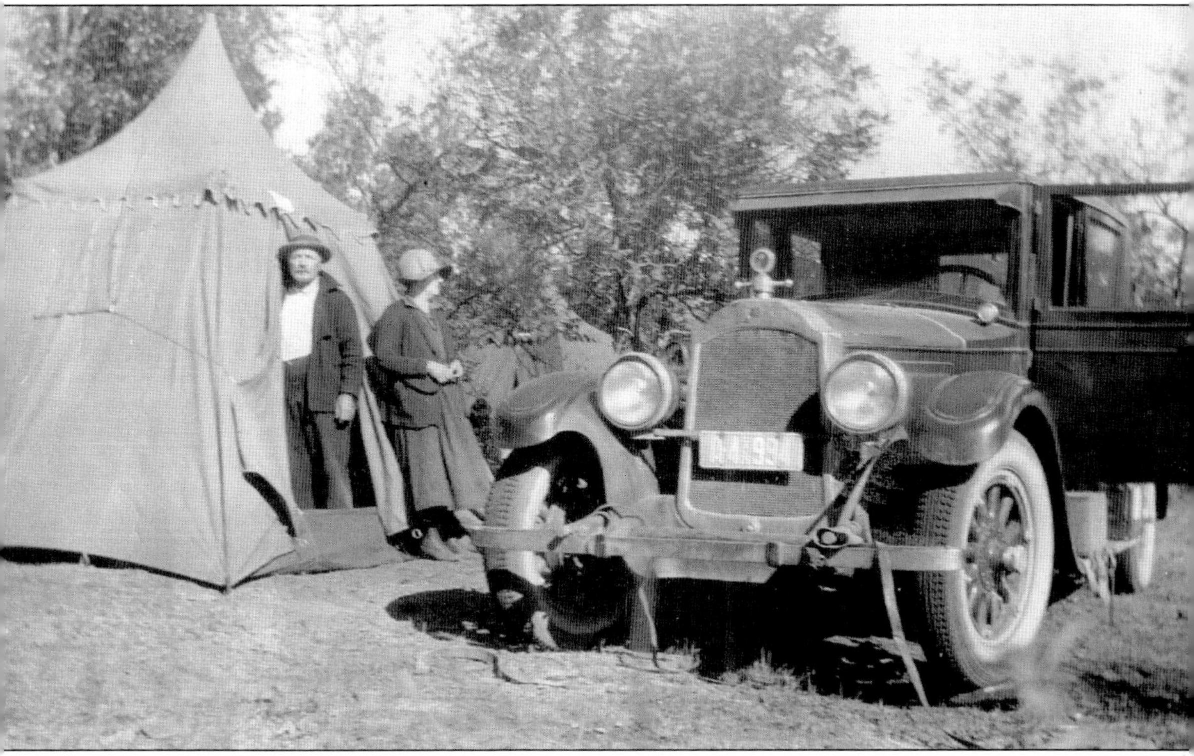

Grandma and Grandpa Cherry are pictured on Reeve's Ranch at Seneca.

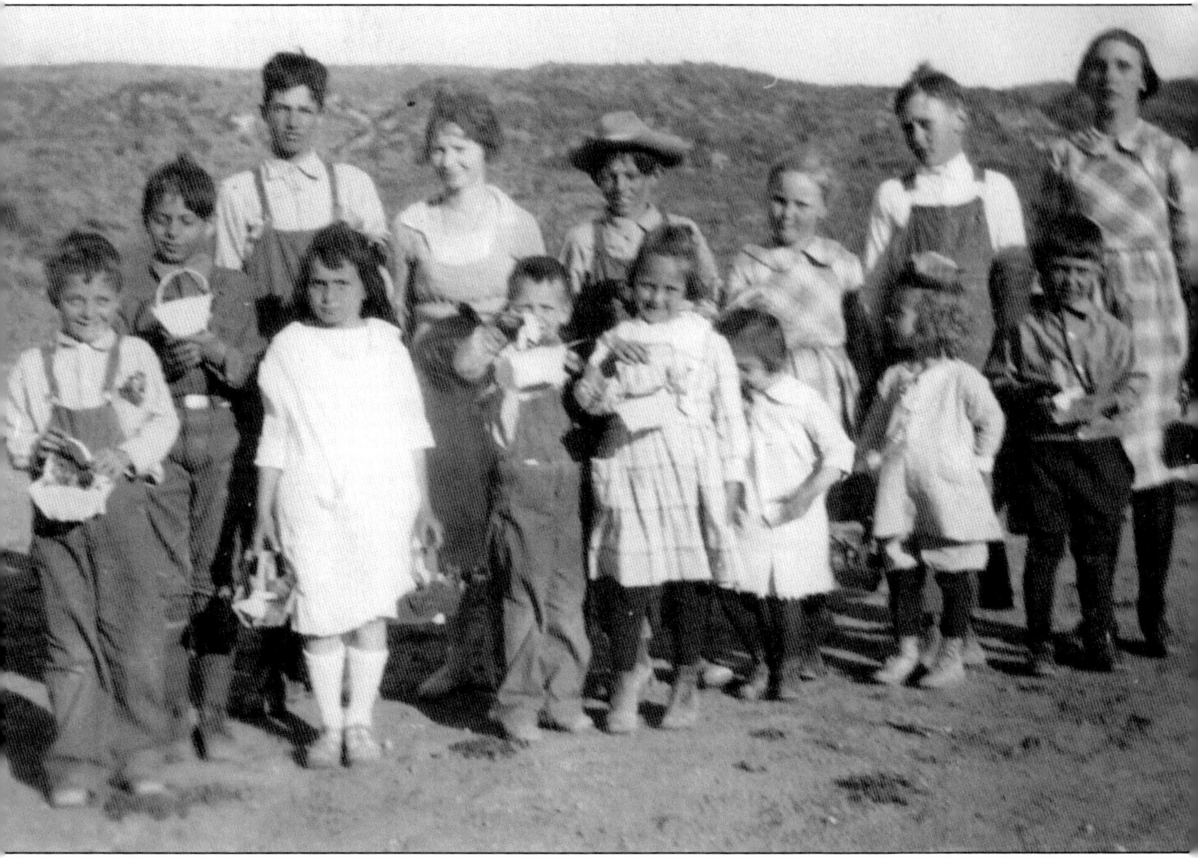

The Bumble Bee School class of 1921 is seen here. Esther Cherry Henderson is on the far right.

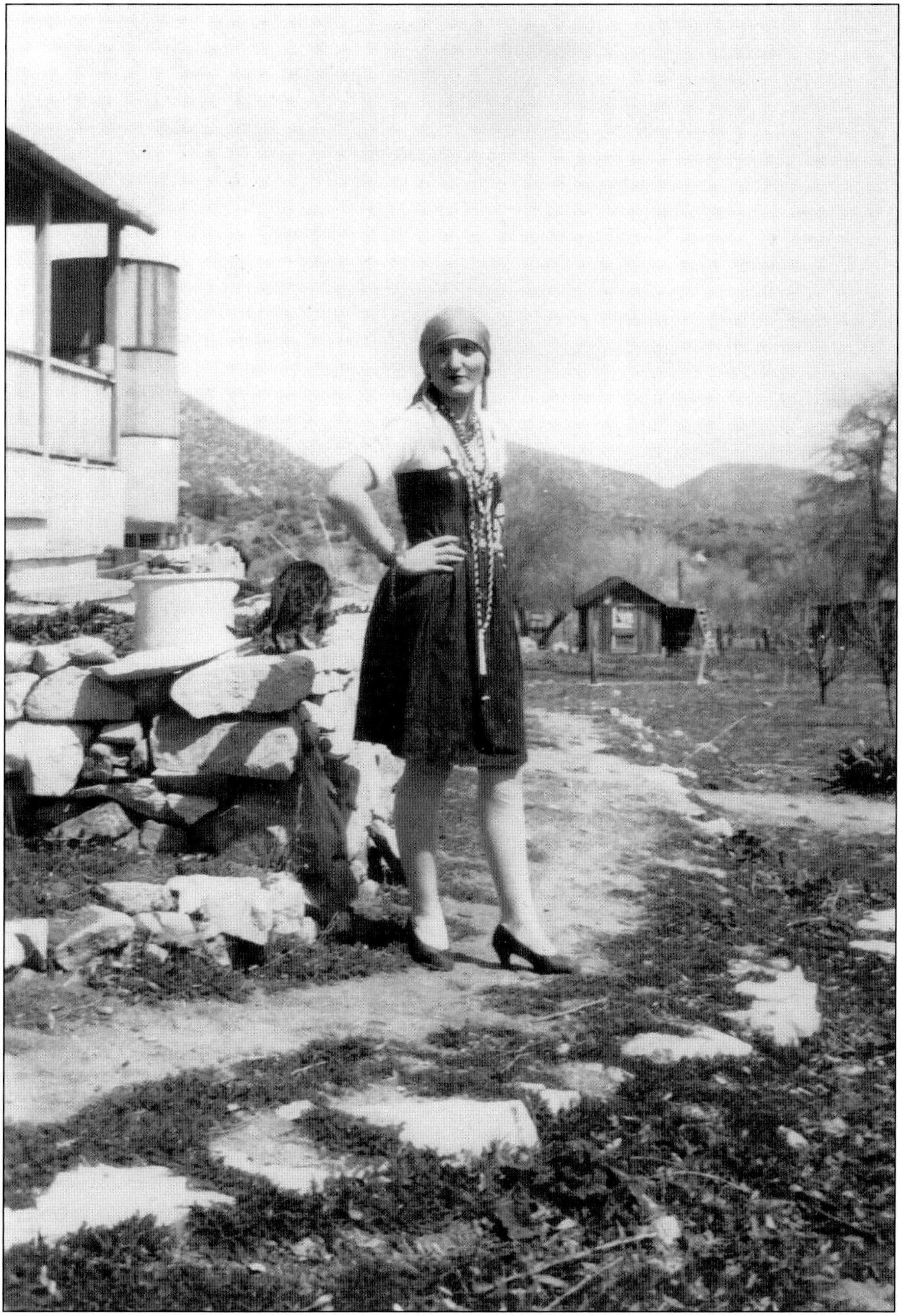

Esther Henderson appears to be having fun at her family's home in the early 1920s.

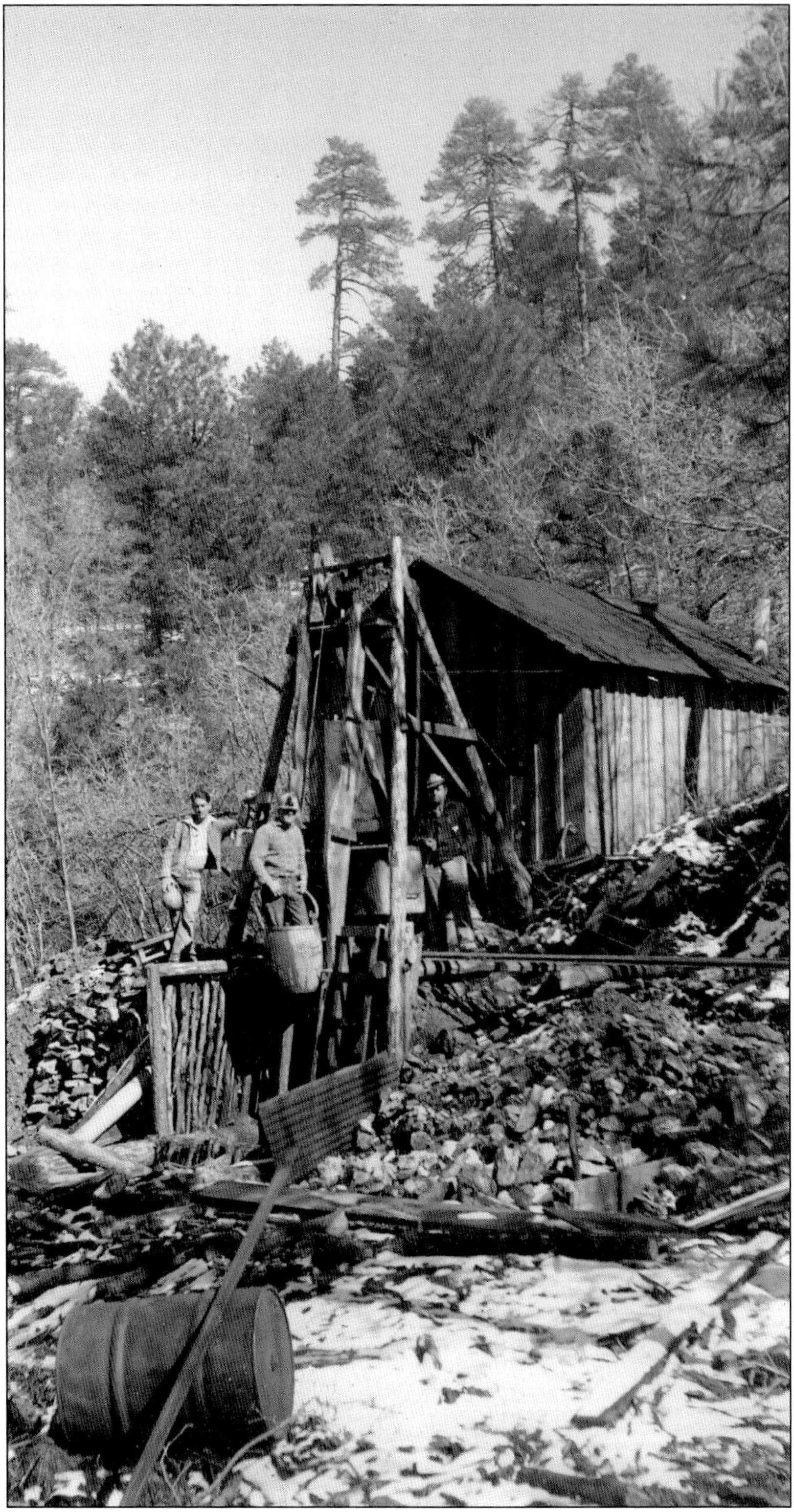

Mine workers in Crown King are shown in the early 1930s. An estimated $2 million was taken from the Crown King Mine in gold alone before it closed in the 1950s. Since then, tourism has been the only reliable source of income.

A Clarkdale teacher lends a hand during a cattle drive at Government Springs in 1922. The teachers were invited to help with the gathering and branding of livestock, and they enthusiastically got involved.

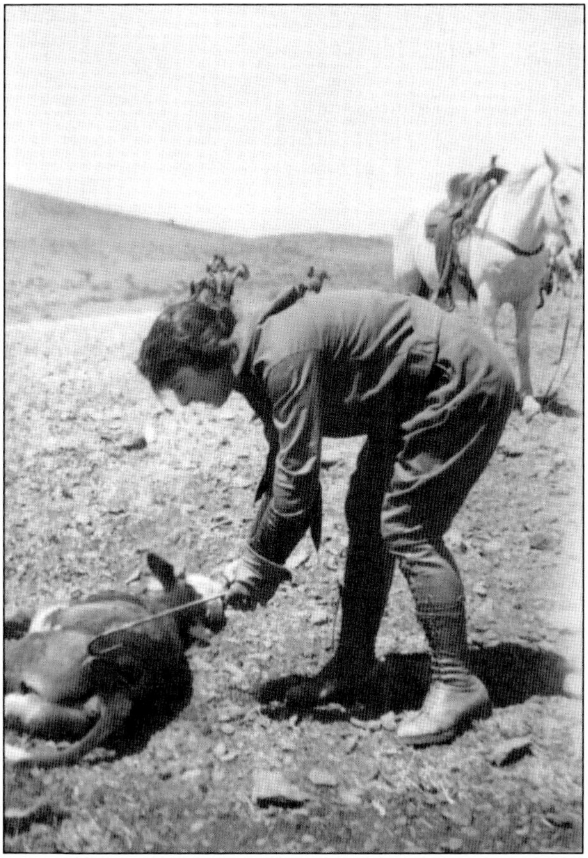

A cowboy herds cattle at Government Springs in 1922.

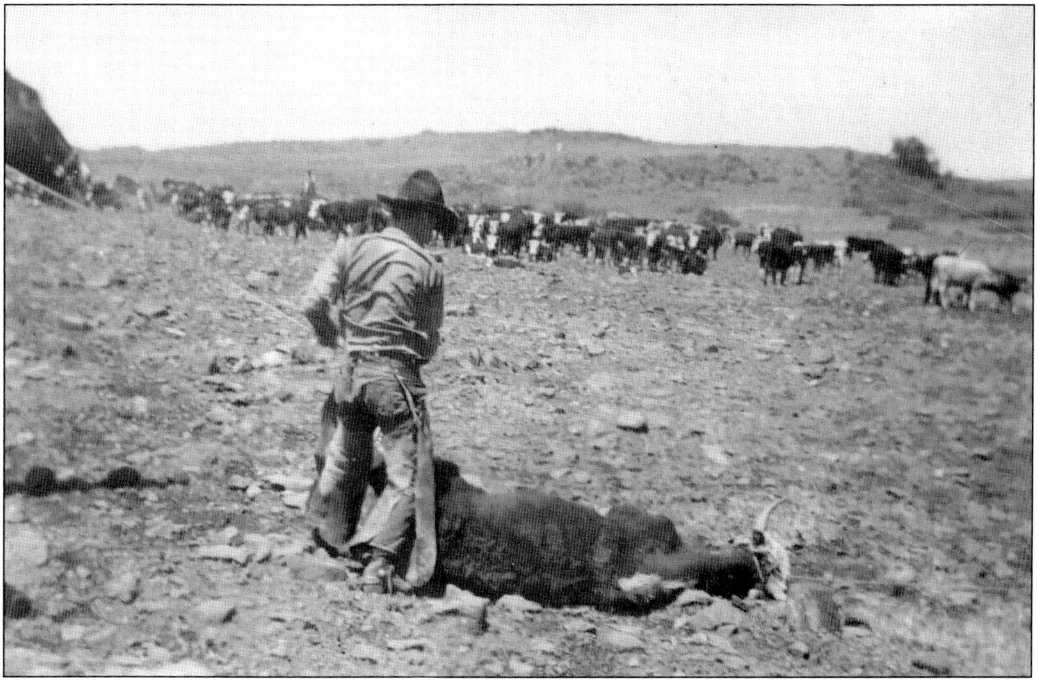

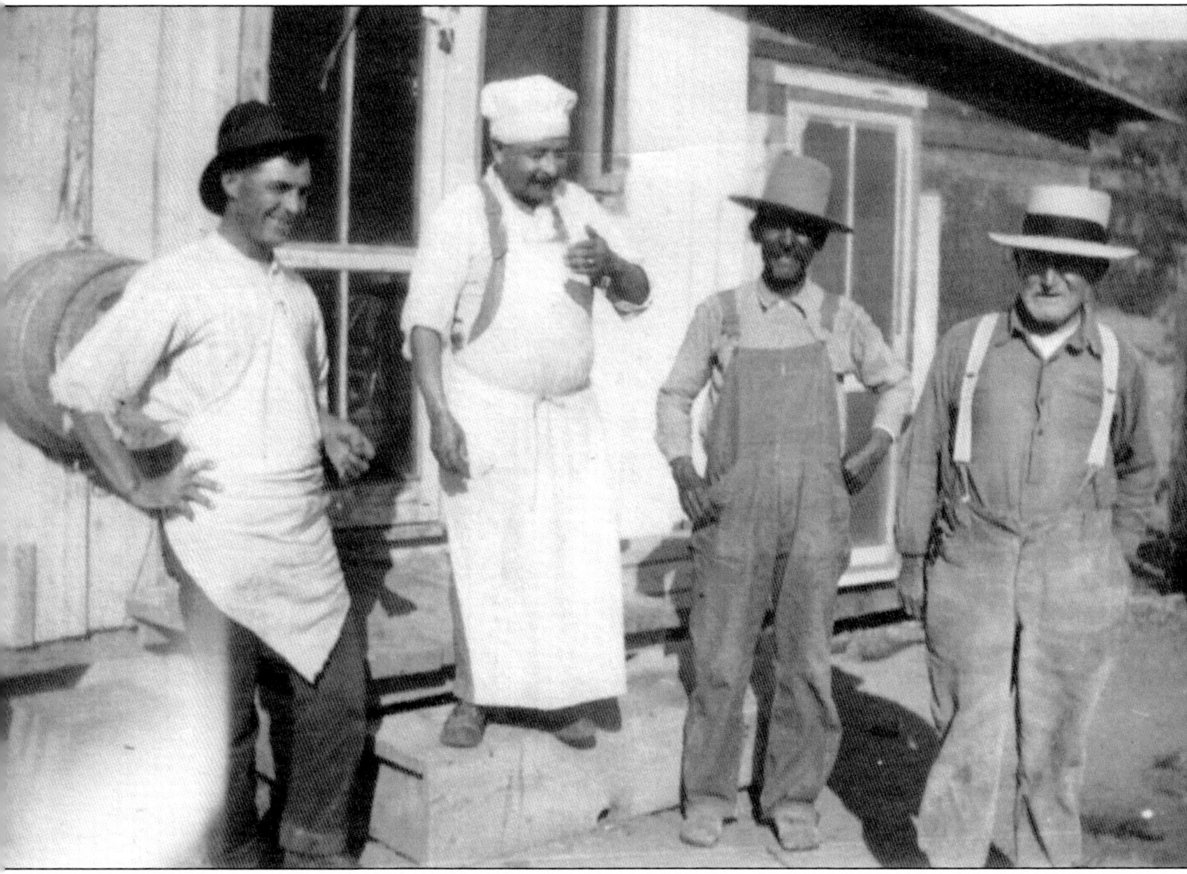

Pictured here is the 1921 Bumble Bee cooking staff.

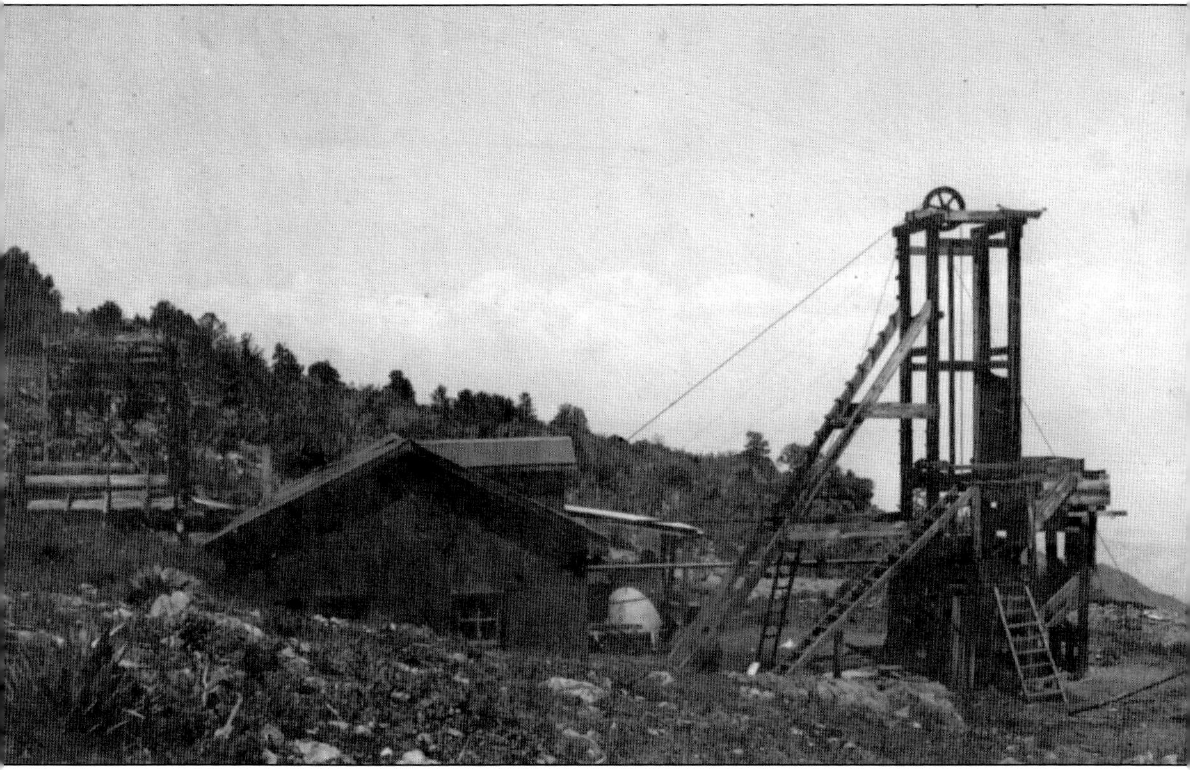

More than 15 mines or claims were made by the Crown King Mining Corporation in the area. At its peak, the town had 500 buildings. The town was electrified in 1897, and it had one telephone at the time.

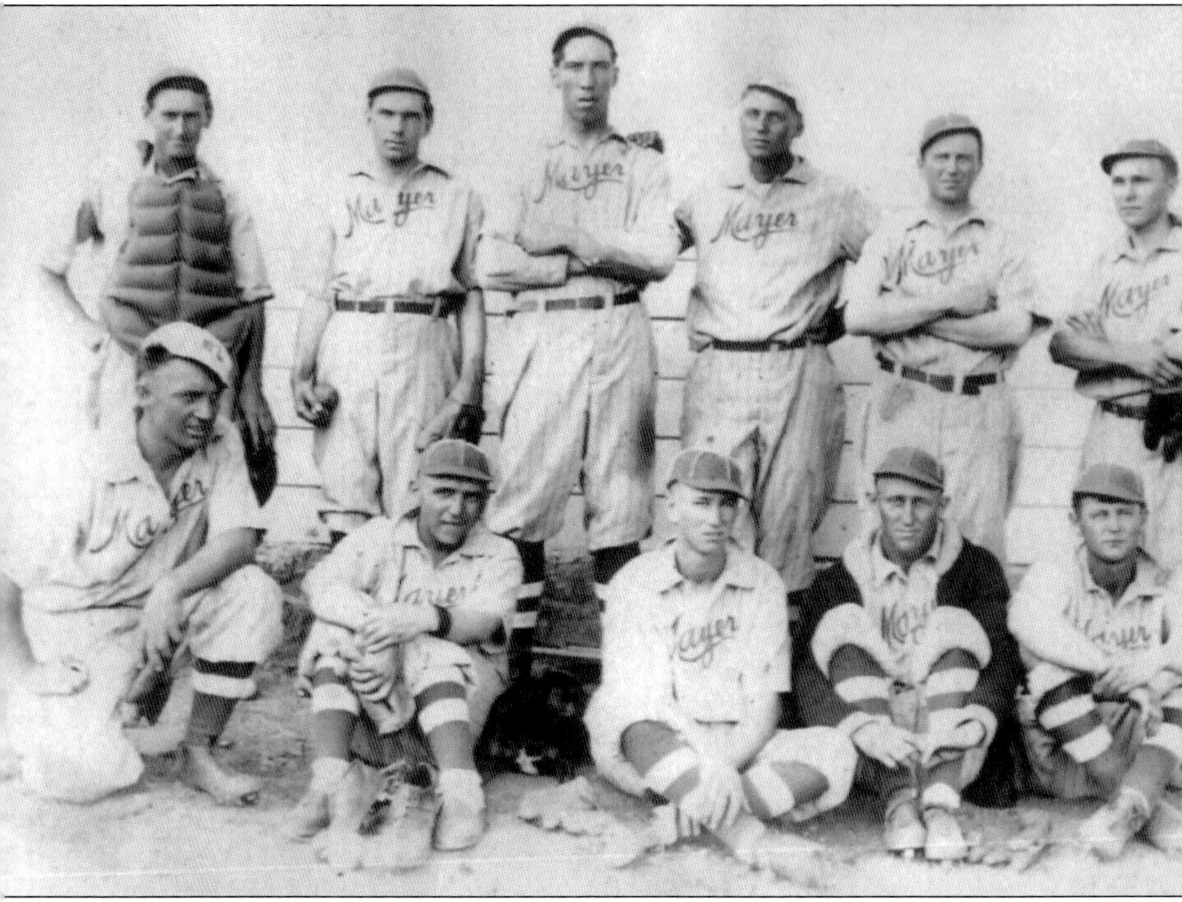

Members of the Mayer baseball team are pictured here, including Bill Larrimore, Frank Wilson, Bill O'Brien, and Jonnie Peel.

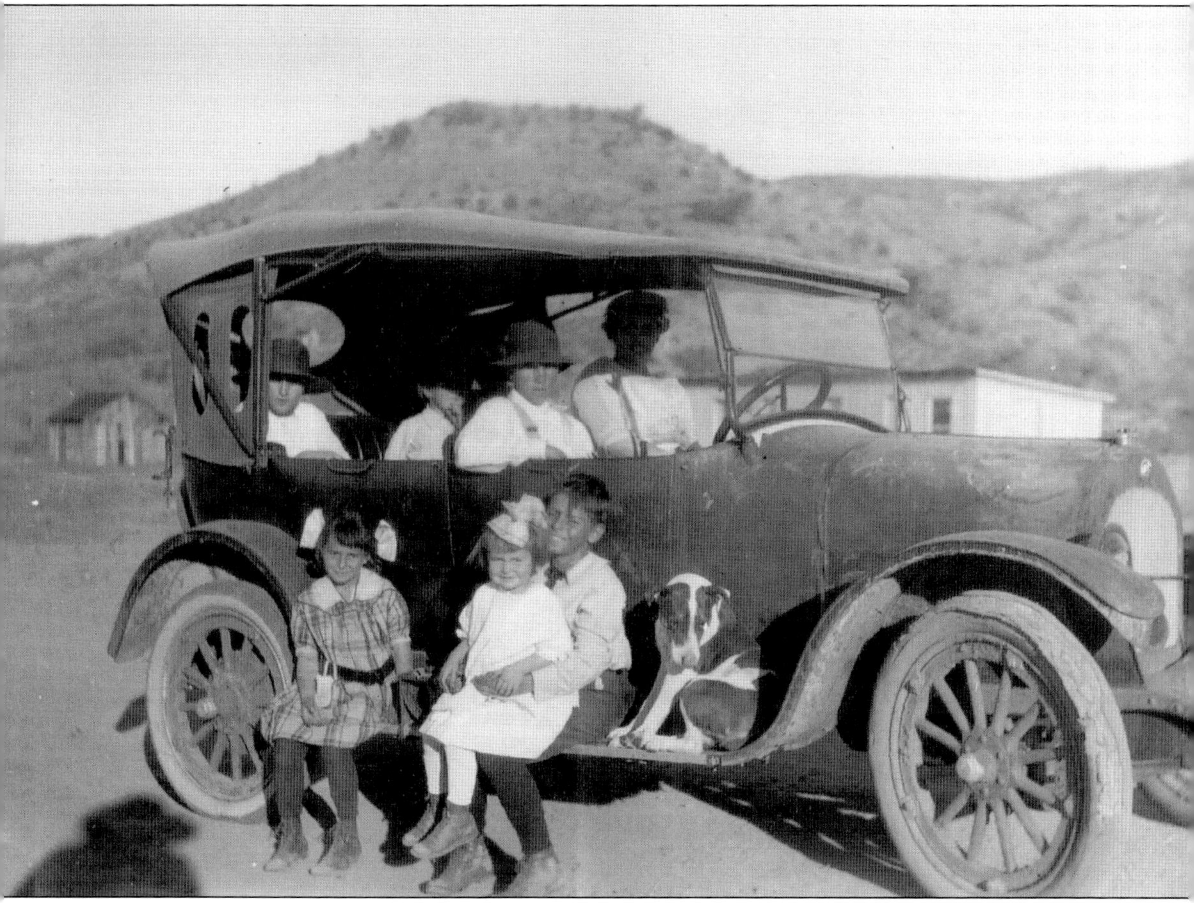

Esther Cherry Henderson is pictured in the back seat of a car in 1924. It must have been a thrill to ride in a car after making the trip so many times on a donkey.

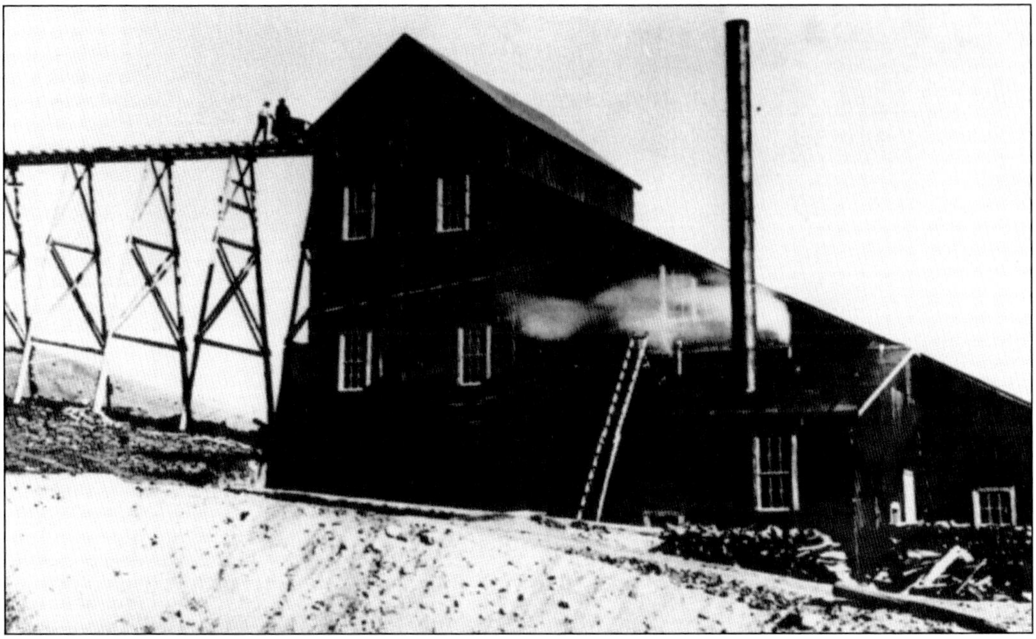

While an active mining town, Crown King was served by the Bradshaw Mountain Railroad beginning in 1904. "Murphy's impossible railroad" was a series of switchbacks and trestles that ascended the mountain terrain between Cleator and Crown King.

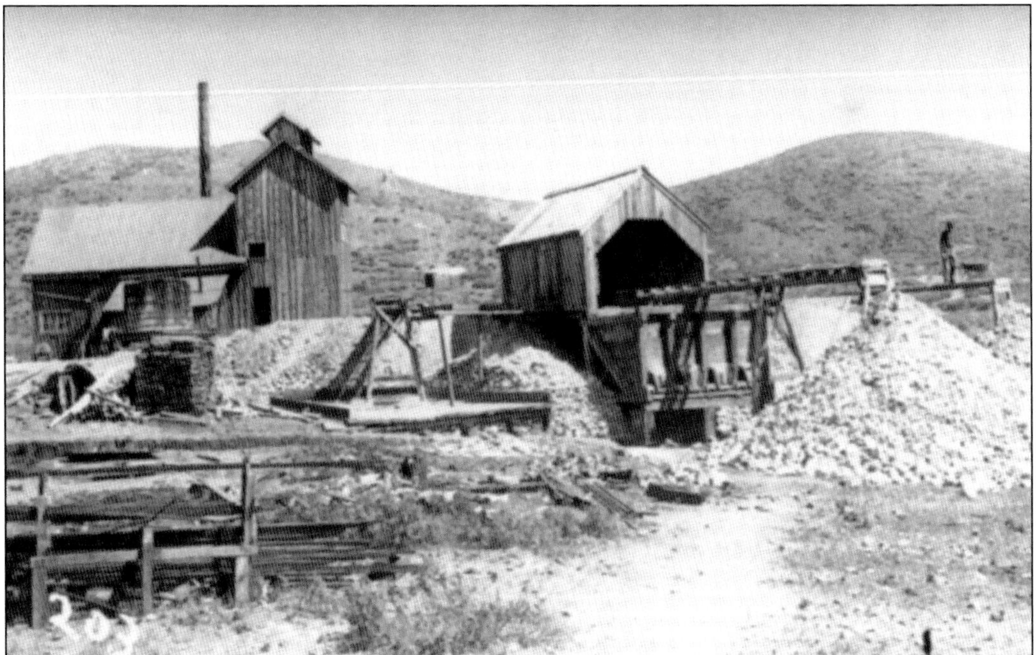

Local legend maintains that the first claim in the Crown King group was discovered by schoolteacher John L. Taylor. He reportedly traded the land claim in exchange for a saddle (or a saddle horse, depending on the version of the tale).

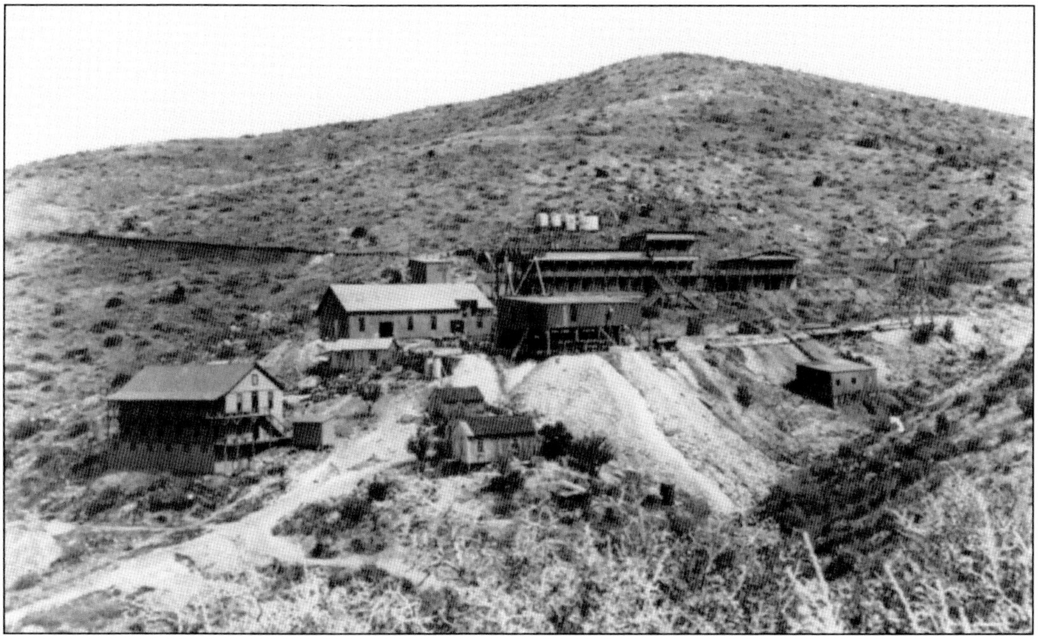

O.F. Place, who traded the rights to the claim with Taylor, then gave Bradshaw City storekeeper Noah Shekels a half-interest in the claim in payment for a debt at Shekels's store.

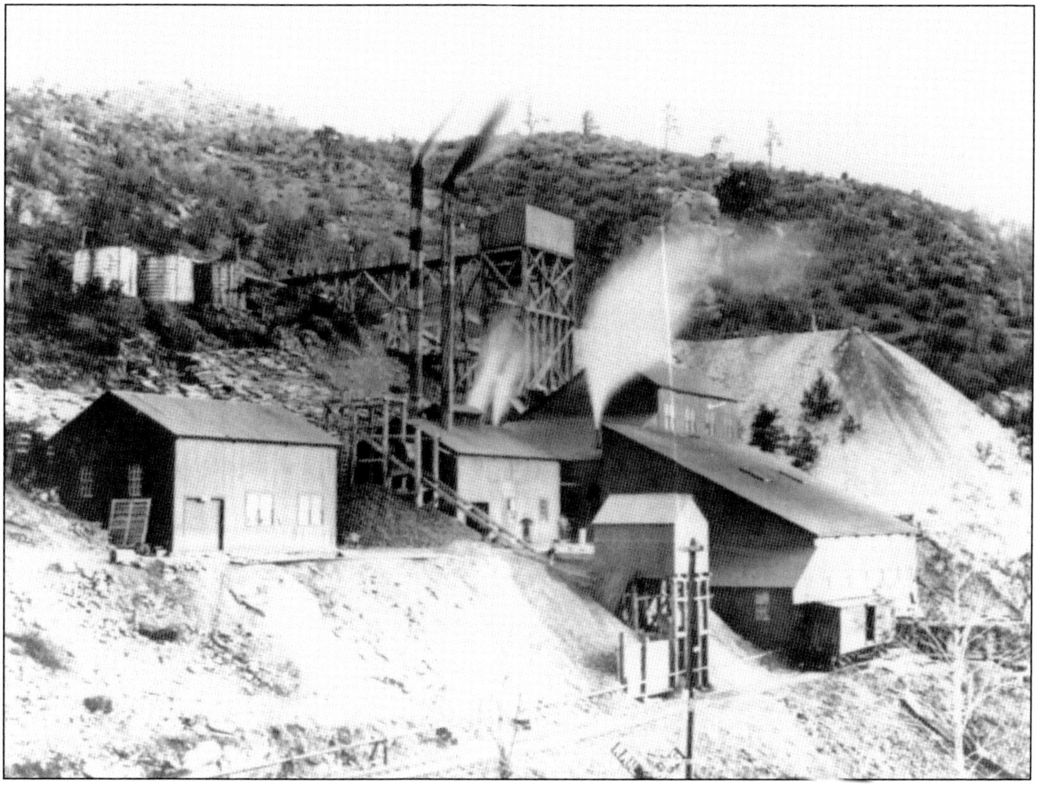

George Harrington, an eastern capitalist, joined forces with O.F. Place and Noah Shekels to form the Crown King Mining Company, filing in 1887.

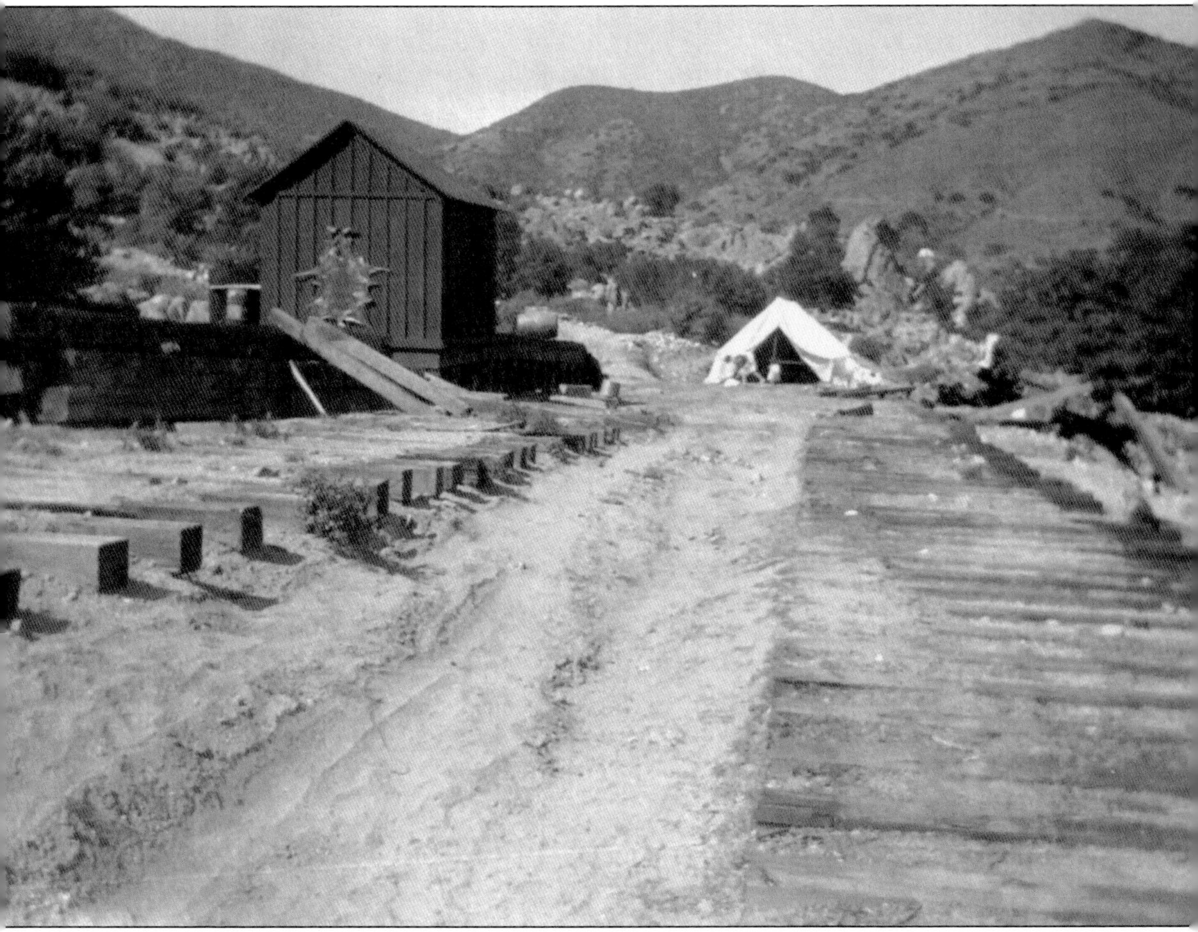

Shown here under construction are the railroad tracks into Crown King that drastically changed the production ability of the mines. Crown King was the terminus of the railroad, which operated from 1904 to 1926. The railroad was built by Frank M. Murphy to serve the Southern Bradshaw Mountains, but it was never very successful, and was abandoned in 1926. The current road to Crown King uses much of the old railroad bed.

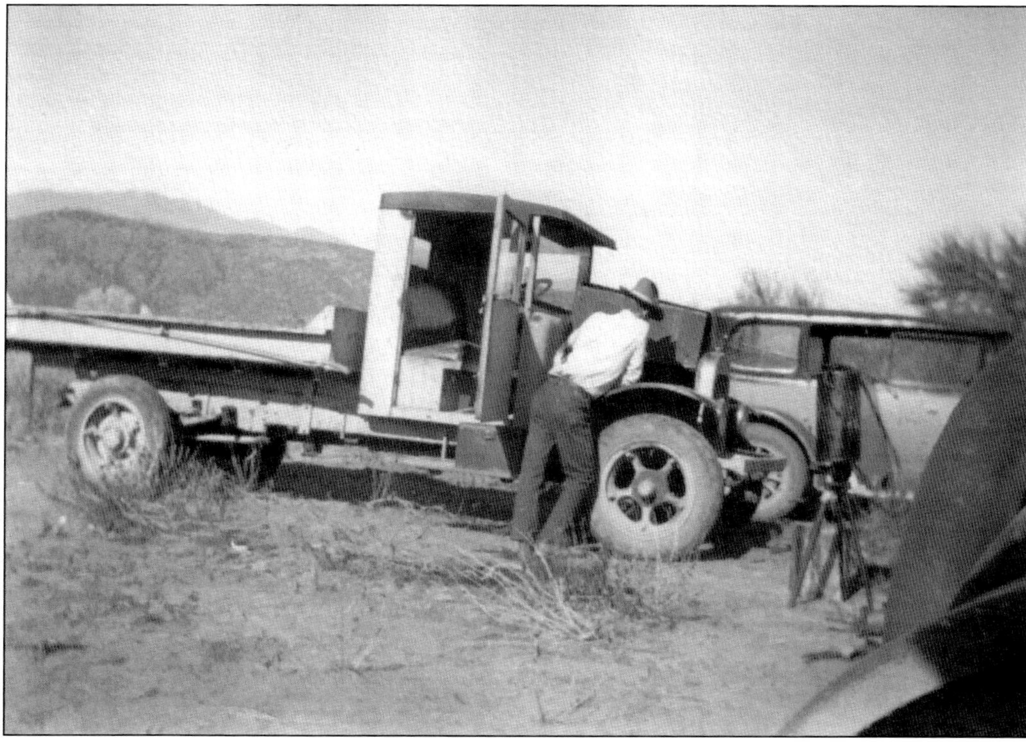

Building the road to Crown King was considered an engineering marvel of its time. The road changed the whole landscape of the area. Crown King had thousands of residents at its peak, but has a little over 100 today.

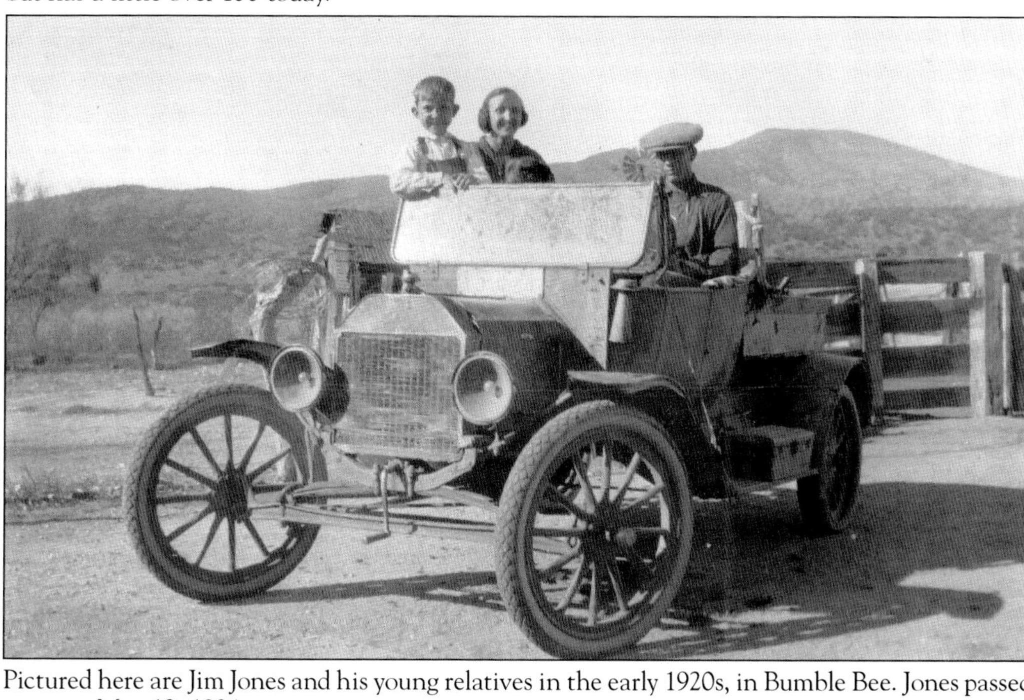

Pictured here are Jim Jones and his young relatives in the early 1920s, in Bumble Bee. Jones passed away on May 12, 1924.